At 28, **Saransh** TV show host, author, food co... columnist. He set a record in the *Limca Book of Records*, 2014, for 'the longest road journey by a chef,' when he hosted India's biggest food travelogue show, *Roti, Rasta aur India* on FoodFood Channel.

Saransh became a food enthusiast at an early age. He made his first *jalebi*, for his family, when he was only 12. This interest in food made him pursue his Bachelor's in Culinary Arts from the Institute of Hotel Management, Aurangabad.

His first taste of television success was when he won the FoodFood *Maha Challenge* in the year 2011, hosted by celebrity chef, Sanjeev Kapoor, and film actress, Madhuri Dixit. He is also popular for his online food and travel show, *The Spice Traveller*, and *Health Challenge*, where he makes favourite Indian dishes healthier.

He is a passionate traveller and has dedicated himself to promote regional Indian food across the globe.

INDIA ON MY PLATTER
The 20,000-km food journey

By Saransh Goila

Om Books International

Reprinted in 2015 by

Om Books International

Corporate & Editorial Office
A-12, Sector 64, Noida 201 301
Uttar Pradesh, India
Phone: +91 120 477 4100
Email: editorial@ombooks.com
Website: www.ombooksinternational.com

Sales Office
107, Darya Ganj
New Delhi 110 002, India
Phone: +91 11 2326 3363, 2326 5303, 4000 9000
Fax: +91 11 2327 8091
Email: sales@ombooks.com
Website: www.ombooks.com

Text copyright © Saransh Goila, 2015
Cover picture by Pallavi Gupta

ISBN: 978-93-83202-04-1

Printed in India

10 9 8 7 6 5 4 3 2

For butter chicken…my soulmate

For Grandpa's special *dum aloo*…I still miss
both every Sunday

For my forever hungry family

For India…because we have *chaat*

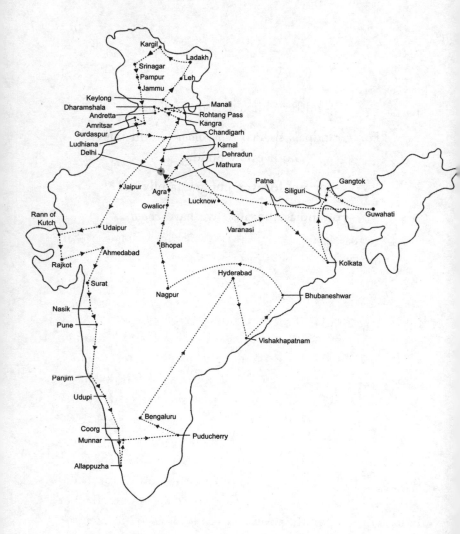

Foreword

I first met Saransh Goila as a contestant on my channel FoodFood's reality show, *Maha Challenge*. He emerged as a winner in that show and I wasn't surprised. I was impressed with his age (at 24, he was the youngest of all the contestants), his enthusiasm, his attention to detail, but most of all, his ability to perform beautifully under pressure, the hallmark of a good chef. Another notable point was his passion for chocolate-based desserts; he was a magician with chocolate. For one of the rounds, he made a chocolate brownie; the lovely taste of which still lingers on in my mind! It impressed fellow judge, Madhuri Dixit Nene, so much that she placed an order for it at the end of the show.

Soon after winning the show, he joined the channel as a Chef cum Food Editor. Through him I realised a dream and this book is all about that dream. Saransh did the show *Roti, Rasta aur India*, where he went all over India, chronicling the food and the recipes of that region. Needless to say, he did a brilliant job of it. It changed the way he looked at food and the world in general; I could see that change in him at the end of the show. He has age on his side, is dedicated and has a passion for Indian food—qualities that will take him far.

This book is not merely about food and recipes. He gives us a rare glimpse into the psyche of the people, the region and the story behind a dish. His experiences are scattered like glittering gems across the pages; it shows us how vast a country we live in and how varied a culinary treasure we possess. It is a fitting tribute to the unsung and undiscovered culinary geniuses.

Roti, Rasta aur India was just a stepping stone. It was indeed a pleasant surprise to see that he based a book on the show. I wish him many more journeys through which he can learn more. I also wish he achieves all that he has set out to do. This book, a kaleidoscope of the richness of Indian cuisine, is but a tip of the iceberg!

Chef Sanjeev Kapoor

The Inception

Life is not about reaching your destiny but about the journey travelled.

—*Anonymous*

Hello everyone! I am Saransh Goila. I really got lucky and learnt the lesson mentioned above early on in my life. How often does one get a chance to travel all across India to explore its vast culinary traditions and cultures and their symbiotic relationship? Very rare... So, I got an opportunity to try the most authentic dishes Indian cuisine had to offer by visiting local homes. In the process, I also got to meet new people who shared my love for food. It was like my ticket to the chocolate factory!

The statistics of this journey were epic. The mission was to travel 20,000 km within India, covering 25 states in 100 days, non-stop, and not to forget, all this had to be done by road! When the programming head at FoodFood channel (a 24-hour TV channel about food), narrated this concept, I couldn't fathom the scale of the project. My jaws dropped and what came out was, 'Woah! Really? Are you serious? You're willing to take a chance of shooting for so long with an inexperienced host for a TV show?' And he said, 'Yes.' He had this unshakeable faith in my passion to learn about food, perhaps, more than I did. The producer wanted a person without any 'baggage' to travel and express what he really felt.

So, I'll be frank. This is not only a recipe book; it is a lot more than that. There are about 50 recipes from 25 states, but then, it is a book written by a chef, hence, recipes are important. But, it is about India—the beautiful landscapes, the deserted roads, the changing colour of the skies and the food memories that I built while sitting on the corner of the road, on the highway, in an old age home, in the middle of the Ganges and more unique places. It is also the story of a shy and an introvert 12-year-old boy, who later went on to living his dream at the age of 25. This is the story of that chef who is independent now, travels like there is no tomorrow and hopes that he can bring the best of Indian cuisine to the world.

If you are a person who loves food—whether it is a hobby to cook, a love for eating or tasteful appetite—being a chef today has a lot of glamour. I was a chubby kid for whom food was the meaning of life. I cooked and I ate, and that's about all I did. My father wanted me to be an engineer; my mother wanted me to be a biotechnologist. My grandfather was the only one who wanted me to join the hospitality industry. And I wanted to be an actor. I come from a household where being a chef is not really on the cards, that is, if you really want to achieve something in life. And here I am today, writing a book about my love for food, travelling through India to eat and experience the culture and history around cooking.

Has my dream come true? Yes… More than that! Life has brought me to a point where I live and breathe food and I couldn't be happier. I started cooking when I was 12, not to be boastful, but it came to me very naturally. While other kids played football, or boys his age then chased after girls and spent hours trying to look good, I would be in the kitchen, following my mother around, asking her about spices, temperatures, dough and sweets.

I spent my college years getting a degree in Culinary Arts, pursued the career of a hotel chef, and learnt how to be part of the industry. By then, I had a lot of support from my family. They were the only ones who believed I was strong enough to endure the long routine hours of banquet kitchens. I quit because I had had enough of being part of only one dimension of food.

I didn't have a job for two years. Everything I tried— catering, food companies, publishing—they all failed me. And then, I found my way into the world of television. FoodFood channel, one fine evening in 2011, auditioned me for a reality show about chefs. I went on to win the show, and as a prize, I got the opportunity to make my own television show. I did a show called *Roti, Rasta aur India*, which was what the concept, mentioned earlier, materialised into. I was appointed the chef traveller. I was going to learn and travel and share my experiences with India through television. I would like to pause here and thank FoodFood and Chef Sanjeev Kapoor for giving me this opportunity. Just when food channels became a craze, I found the courage to combine my love for food and my dream to be an actor. I love being on screen, talking, laughing, sharing and learning. I have finally reached a place in life where my skills as a cook and my personality can be educational and entertaining.

I am not going to pretend that I know everything about food. I am just 28, and the idea is to learn every day. Allow me to finish by saying that I love movies, entertainment and drama. If at any point in the book I get emotional, please bear with me. I get carried away with stories and deeply involved in the minute details. On a side note, I must confess that I come from a vegetarian family and I prefer being a vegetarian. Having said that, I discovered such great meat dishes in different parts of the country that now, I stand converted. I have a special corner in my heart and undying love for butter chicken. This dish was cooked and fed to many people across India and it sort of went viral on Twitter as *#GoilaButterChicken*.

Without taking much time and endorsing myself… Here goes… Lights. Camera. Action.

DAY 1
6 August, 2012 / 5 a.m. / Delhi

It was still pitch dark outside; so silent in the Goila household that it felt strange. I barely slept, or let's just say I had too many butterflies in my stomach to get any sleep.

It was the day I started my 100-day journey. Mom had made sure, thrice, that everything was packed. Dad had ensured I had enough cash on me. Grandma had made me promise her several times that I won't, at any point, compromise on my health. My sister seemed to be the only sane person and was being totally casual about me leaving, although, I knew she was just trying to be cool because she felt sad. I had been staring at an empty wall, with the lights still out, for 15 minutes now and that was the moment. This was it! I had gone through a sea of emotions and skipped multiple heartbeats and everything was going to change for good from that day on. I clenched my fists, zipped through my past and got ready *à la* Anthony Bourdain to discover parts unknown!

The first leg of the journey was to cover the entire northern India in 22 days. Thereafter, we would make way towards the west. I bid farewell to my family, and as clichéd as it may sound, they fed me *dahi chinni* (yoghurt with sugar) for good luck. The car that I was travelling in was pretty jazzy. It was completely covered with stickers of tomatoes, hence, we decided to call it Tamatar—tomato in English—for the same reason. I say 'we' because I was not the only one travelling, there were another eight people travelling with me, including two drivers who played the biggest part in this journey, I guess. So, the first destination on Day 1 was Karnal. I learnt that it had earned an epithet for itself: the Land of Cows. Before we reached Karnal, we stopped at Murthal, about 50 km from Delhi, for a *desi* (local) brunch.

Murthal is a big village in the Sonipat district of Haryana. It is really popular for various kind of stuffed *paranthas* (flatbread made of wholewheat or flour dough): *aloo* (potato), *mooli* (radish), *gobhi* (cauliflower) and other varieties. That was our prime reason for stopping here. These *paranthas* are thick, filled with generous amount of stuffing, crisp on the outside, hot and soft on the inside. They're mostly wheat based and taste divine with dollops of freshly made white butter. The other favourite accompaniments are *dal makhni* (popular dish made with whole black lentils and kidney beans), yoghurt, pickle and raw onions. We decided to stop at my favourite *dhaba* (roadside food stall) there, Ahuja No. 1. I was feeling quite a hero today with my camera crew next to me. So I proudly went up to the owner and explained to him what I did, took permission to enter his kitchen and the action began. The kitchen was spacious but slightly dark. What distracted me was the number of tandoors or clay ovens! I met Santosh who was their tandoor specialist. First thing that Santosh said, even before I could shake his hand, was, 'I can make 120 *paranthas* in one hour; no one here can beat my record.'

These guys really don't need to spend any money on marketing; word-of-mouth praise from customers suffices, to say the least. Almost unbelievable if you ask me, we're looking at making one *parantha* in 30 seconds flat! I patted Santosh on his back and after his permission, tried and made one or two myself. Trust me, operating a tandoor isn't as easy as they make it look. The temperature is almost 350-400°C. There is no light inside the tandoor to actually spot a corner to stick the *paranthas* on its surface. It is purely a skill-based job and requires a lot of practice.

Being in the kitchen I got a few of my own ideas and wanted to experiment with those yummy *paranthas*. I also wanted Santosh to try something new as he'd been in the same kitchen for the past eight years. I churned out a very basic and simple **Satpura** *Parantha*.

SATPURA *PARANTHA*
(Traditional potato-stuffed flatbread with a twist.)

Ingredients *(For the* **parantha***)*

3 cups wheat flour *(atta)*
1¼ cup water
⅔ tsp clarified butter *(ghee)*, per *parantha*
½ tsp dry fenugreek leaves *(kasoori methi)*, per *parantha*
1 tsp salt

Method *(For the* **parantha***)*

1. Make dough by kneading the wheat flour—to which salt is added—with the help of water. Make soft dough; so be careful with the quantity of water you add. Less water is manageable, more will spoil the dough.

2. After kneading the dough, divide it equally to obtain golf ball-size dough balls.

3. Flatten it into a circular disc. Lightly brush the whole surface with *ghee* and spread dry fenugreek leaves on it. Cut this circle into seven equal strips. They will be equal only in width not in length.

4. Sprinkle some flour on the rolling surface or chopping board. Place the tallest strip on the floured surface with *ghee* side facing up.

5. Stack all layers on top of one another with tallest at the bottom and shortest at the top. Press lightly so they stick together.

6. Roll this stack like a pinwheel. Close the loose ends by tucking them in the centre. Lay it flat on the surface and then flatten it out again into a circular disc.

7. Cook it on a hot *tawa* (griddle) and as you see layers getting crisp and more visible, add *ghee*. *Parantha* is ready.

Ingredients (for railway aloo)

2 big or 3 small boiled potatoes
1½ tbsp clarified butter *(ghee)*
1½ tsp whole cumin *(jeera)*
⅓ tsp turmeric *(haldi)* powder
2 tsp coriander *(dhania)* powder
1 tsp red chilli powder
Salt as per taste
1 cup yoghurt
Coriander leaves *(dhania patti)* for garnishing

Method (for railway aloo)

1. Peel the potatoes and cut them into small cubes.
2. Heat the *ghee* in a pan. Once hot, add cumin and let it splutter.
3. Add turmeric, coriander and chilli powder to a small bowl and then add one tablespoon water; mix it nicely.
4. Add this wet spice mix to the *ghee*. Let the spices cook on medium heat for a minute.
5. Now add the potatoes to this mixture and toss gently. Add salt. Sauté potatoes for two to three minutes on medium heat.

Final Dish

1. Cut the *parantha* into pizza-like quarters. Top each of them with potatoes and a spoonful of yoghurt. Garnish it with coriander.

~

Well, it definitely looked new and very different from anything that was being served at the *dhaba*. Santosh couldn't get enough of it and made one for himself, whereas the owner didn't seem very convinced, more confused about why I had done that to his *parantha*! But he did end up saying, 'Swaad toh hai' meaning it was tasty nonetheless.

After having a soul-satisfying meal at Ahuja No. 1, it was time to move on. The next destination was a bit unusual. I wasn't told that we were going there, because my producer thought I'd refuse. The place in question—an 'akhada'—for professional fighters, or rather wrestlers, it is a religious place where they train in front of the God that they believe in. The motive was to find out what do these wrestlers eat to stay fit and in what quantities. I won't lie but after reaching there I was impressed to see how naturally these wrestlers are trained, so different from the confines of a gym. The men here had perfect bodies by doing exercises like rope climbing and *kushti* (wrestling) and lifting clubs. Pretty soon I was out in the field, a ring made out of moist mud, which felt like a surface of a semi-kneaded dough. I was given some lessons in wrestling and also thrown around three or four times like some action figure!

The general diet these people follow is pretty interesting. They have four to six bananas everyday with at least 10 *paranthas*. They prepare a special almond milk called *badam ras*. They grind almonds in a mortar and pestle with a little water until the almonds release their goodness into the water. Once they're ground to a very fine paste, a litre of water is mixed with 250 gm of almond paste and then passed through a muslin cloth to get the purest extract from these almonds. By the way, all this is for just one wrestler! As these people made *badam ras* for me, I too prepared a very traditional *chaat* (an Indian savoury snack made of boiled vegetables or raw fruit with spices) for them. It was super healthy and had all the elements of a Delhi-based *chaat*. It was sweet, tangy, sour, spicy and savoury.

DAY 2
7 August / Karnal

The fact that the journey had begun was still sinking in and I was doing all these crazy things just because I felt like doing them! No questions asked. Our car, named Tamatar, started again and our next destination was a *gaushala* (cowshed where handicapped or disowned cows are taken care of) in Karnal. The whole day was spent there learning how it functioned. The most beautiful thing about this organisation, that ran the cowshed, was that they ran the sheds purely because they wished to take care of the cows. For a city dweller like me, to think of such a place is a little amusing with a tinge of nonchalance. But then when you visit them and see the real scenario you realise how tough it is. All this was part of my learning at the Radha Krishna Gaushala in Karnal. After speaking to Ajit, the concerned head there, for about 30 minutes I realised that they take care of 470 cows. They didn't make any profit and most of the cows didn't give milk anymore. Since I had come a long way, Ajit made sure I learnt how to milk a cow. Just imagine trying to milk a cow for the first time in your life; it is a little awkward and a lot terrifying. There is a specific technique about it and if you go wrong, sometimes the cow might try to kick you too. So one has to be careful.

Soon, the whole village near that *gaushala* knew that there was a 'shooting' happening. At least 100 people gathered by sunset. Ajit introduced me to a very popular *ghazal* (soulful ballad) singer of that village. He came in with his harmonium and told me, 'I'll sing for you if you cook for us.' I graciously accepted the deal and soon I could see wooden cots all over with about 100 people sitting on them, just like traditional old Indian village set-ups that I'd seen in Bollywood movies. Cows in the backdrop...carefree people ready to sing merry songs...

I decided to cook **Dark Chocolate** *Kheer*, from fresh milk, for 100 people. (I had collected the milk, yes!) As the *kheer* (rice pudding made by boiling rice, broken wheat, tapioca, or vermicelli with milk and sugar; it is flavoured with cardamom, raisins, saffron, and nuts) preparation started, the *bhajans* (religious songs) got sweeter. I felt like a 12-year-old child who had cooked his first dish purely out of love. Soon the *kheer* was served; it was over and I could see kids licking their plastic bowls and spoons clean. I had never felt this happy feeding a customer inside a restaurant or any hotel I'd ever worked at. To see that satisfaction on their faces made me overjoyed and I wanted to stay for a while longer but it was time to say goodbye, take a selfie with the cows and move on.

DARK CHOCOLATE *KHEER*
(Sweet Indian rice pudding cooked with chocolate.)

Ingredients

1 cup rice
500 ml milk
7-8 strands saffron *(kesar)*
50 gm dark chocolate

2 tbsp malt powder

2 tbsp cocoa powder

⅓ cup brown sugar

¼ tsp cardamom *(elaichi)* powder

Method

1. Soak the rice in water for 30 minutes.
2. Pressure cook the rice with milk for one whistle. Instantly release the steam and put in a deep pan.
3. Keep it simmering for 20 minutes.
4. Now add the saffron and mix it nicely. Melt dark chocolate on the side on a double boiler or a microwave.
5. Add the melted chocolate, malt powder and cocoa to the almost ready *kheer*.
6. As the *kheer* thickens, add sugar. Cook for another three to four minutes.
7. Finally, add the cardamom powder at the end. Give it a final mix and serve it either hot or cold. I usually prefer to chill it and have it cold.

Day 3
8 August / National Highway 1

It had been two days since I left home… After an overnight halt in Karnal and wandering around the town, we headed to Punjab. The land was visibly becoming more fertile as we moved on. The agenda and challenge for this day was to eat somewhere on the road, but not in a *dhaba*, because we would be travelling the whole day. After much contemplation I decided to go on a bike ride for four or five kilometres with a stranger. The aim was to try and look out for unique highway eating experiences; we were running out of options and it was well past lunchtime. Finally, my luck worked and I saw a dozen trucks parked in a row on one side of the highway with only one *dhaba* in sight. I got off the car and spoke to one of the truck drivers named Kartar Singh. He was wearing an old blue T-shirt and a *lungi* (sarong-like garment wrapped around the waist and extending to the ankles, usually worn by the males), and with his curly hair and messy beard looked every bit like a regular truck driver. I asked him where he ate, what his routine was like and there I found a solution to our hunt for eating options. He said, 'Sir, we cook our food ourselves inside the truck… My helper, Ramu, cooks *dal* (lentils), rice and *sabzi* (vegetable curry) in these small utensils on a gas stove that we carry with us.' This whole concept of cooking inside a moving vehicle was quite fascinating.

Kartar Singh explained that he was usually away from home for 11 months. Because of his job, he considered the roads his real home. After I had a word with him, Kartar immediately and very generously, offered to cook *dal* and rice for me. The thing about Indians is that no matter how rich or poor they are, they believe in hospitality and have big hearts. Now, how could I say no to that? He quickly tossed a simple **Highway Style** *Dal*, with extra *ghee*, for me.

Highway Style Dal

(North Indian lentils tempered with cumin and chillies.)

Ingredients

1 cup yellow pigeon peas *(arhar dal)*, soaked for 15 minutes and drained
¼ tsp turmeric *(haldi)* powder
Salt to taste
1½ cup water
1 tbsp clarified butter *(ghee)*
1 tsp cumin *(jeera)* seeds
2 slit green chillies
2 tsp chopped garlic *(lasun)*
A pinch of asafoetida *(hing)*
¼ cup finely chopped onions

Method

1. Place the lentils in a pressure cooker, add turmeric powder, salt and one and a half cups of water and pressure cook till two whistles. Put the gas on low flame after the first whistle.

2.   Open the lid when the pressure reduces and let it cool down.

3.   Heat the *ghee* in a deep non-stick pan, add cumin seeds and let them roast and give out a nutty aroma.

4.   Add deseeded green chillies, garlic, asafoetida and onions and sauté till the onions are lightly browned.

5.   Now add the cooked lentils, mix and bring the mixture to a boil and then reduce the flame to low and cook for another three minutes. If you like the *dal* to be of thin consistency, add a cup of water and cook it for seven to eight minutes. Have it hot with homemade *rotis* (unleavened flat bread made of wholewheat flour).

~

We cooked all this food sitting on the road right next to his truck; this had to be the wildest kitchen I'd ever cooked in. The simplicity of the *dal-roti* is what made it so special. I learnt a small tip from Kartar about using green chillies in *dal*. Always deseed them to control the hotness and then let them splutter with the cumin seeds for extra flavour. When I asked him, 'Where did you learn to cook such delicious food? From your mother? Did your wife teach you?' He replied humbly, 'Sir, I told you I live on the road for 11 months. My hunger for simple home food taught me how to cook.' Being a trained chef, from heavily equipped kitchens, we tend to take many things for granted. I never realised that a single need, food to quell hunger, could make you cook. My question was simple but his answer was simpler; it overwhelmed me. While I savoured that *dal*, Kartar gave me a thought that I would carry with me throughout the day. Though it was just the beginning, I could already see a glimpse of what this country had in store for me.

DAY 4

The entire day was spent travelling to Anandpur Sahib, Punjab. I arrived late evening and slept early as there was to be an early start the next day.

DAY 5
10 August / Kangra

It had been four days already on the road and we had covered almost 400 km. We made our way through Punjab as we headed to Dharamshala. I was up at 3 a.m. and the reason was to get ready to reach Gurudwara Anandpur Sahib, located in the Roop Nagar Zilla. The idea was to be there before 5 a.m. to be a part of the early morning prayers that are offered to Guru Sahib. So after the usual grooming formalities, we were on our way to the gurudwara. It was still dark outside, so quiet that it made you feel sleepy.

As we were nearing the gurudwara, I saw a huge pole around 80 feet high; an indicator that the gurudwara was nearby. This huge flag pole is actually called 'Nishaan Sahib.' There is a reason why all the gurudwaras have a Nishaan Sahib; sometimes people might miss the structure but when they see their sacred flag on this huge pole from a distance they know that a gurudwara is nearby.

The first reaction after reaching there was of pure joy. It was huge, serene, pure, covered in angelic kind of white and divided in two parts, one being the place where prayers are offered and the second where you take the holy bath. I quickly washed my feet in the holy water and tied an orange handkerchief on my head, as one's head should always be covered when they enter a gurudwara. I headed to the *takhat*: the place were the *granth* (religious text of Sikhism) is read and prayers are offered. It is called a *takhat* because it was from here that

Guru Sahib, in his own time (1690), recited and passed religious and political orders for his followers.

After offering my prayers, I sat there staring at the orange sky, waiting for the sun to rise. I have never really been a religious soul, but at that moment, I felt calm, peaceful and could actually count the number of breaths I took in those 15 minutes. It was time to take the Holy Dip, to relieve myself from any sins that I might have committed. Though the only one that I know I am guilty of is gluttony! Also, taking the bath was a norm before I could visit the *langar* (common kitchen where food is served in a gurudwara to all the visitors, without distinction of background, for free) kitchens there. The first kitchen that I visited was purely dedicated to making the *kadah prasad* (devotional offering made to God, typically consisting of food, which is later shared among devotees). I won't lie, but a lot of times I've visited a gurudwara only to eat that *prasad*. There is something heavenly about it. It is grainy, extremely sweet, earthy and laden with *ghee*.

As I entered the kitchen, I saw a bearded man in simple off-white *kurta pajama* (loose collarless shirt worn by people from south Asia, usually with a pair of loose trousers tied by a drawstring around the waist), a turban, with a *kirpan* (short sword or knife with a curved blade, worn as one of the five distinguishing signs of the Sikh Khalsa) hanging from his left shoulder to his waist. He was making 45 kg of *halwa* (Indian sweet dish consisting of carrots or semolina boiled with milk, almonds, sugar, butter, and cardamom) as the *kadah prasad* in one go! Anyone can make *halwa*, but to make it as the main *prasad*, one must be an Amrit Dhari Sikh (a Sikh who has tasted the holy water). This procedure is to convert a Sikh into a Singh and only then can the person make *kadah prasad* in the temple. So for this reason I wasn't even allowed to interfere with the cooking process of the *prasad*, but they did give me the recipe. It is very simple, for one kilogram of *halwa*, you need a kilogram each of *ghee*, sugar and wheat flour (*atta*). When I was told about this one is to one ratio, I almost had a heart attack; no wonder it is so tasty! But then, there is also another mystery ingredient...the love and blessings with which they make it; all the time that they take to make that *halwa* the cook is reciting '*Satnaam Wahe Guru*.'

After learning and tasting the *kadah prasad*, I headed to the main kitchen and what I saw left me amazed. There was a *kadhai* (wok) big enough for eight people my size to fit in and the cook who was making the *dal* inside it was shorter and slimmer than me! He was tiny! This kitchen was like a big open banquet hall with huge boilers, pots, and a gigantic *roti*-making machine, which I was told, churned out around 30,000 *roti*s a day. There was a lot of steam and humidity in the air as food was being cooked in bulk all around. Wood was being used as the fuel to generate fire to cook pulses, vegetables, and tea; no gas was used for this purpose. A boiler and steamer were used to cook the rice. There were three or four women sitting next to the *roti*-machine, only to apply *ghee* on hot *roti*s so they could be quickly served to people while still hot and soft. Now, I'll let you in on a small secret here, people love eating at the gurudwara because they associate the food served here with a certain smoked taste that the fire from the wood imparts. So, for the *langar* effect try cooking *dal* on wood-fire back home!

The statistics here were enormous; in one go almost 300 kg of pulses, or any vegetable for that matter, are cooked. Almost six kilograms of salt and one kilogram of chilli powder are added in almost every dish. Despite the tough stats handled in the kitchen by the chefs, if I may call them so, they have never served food that is not tasty or is too salty or spicy or burnt. As a chef myself, it seemed an impossible feat to achieve; how could one not go wrong ever? When I asked one of the volunteer cooks there to explain this strange fact, he said, 'This food is devoted to our guru and the people we serve; it can never go wrong as the main ingredient is pure selfless love.'

After the tour of the biggest kitchen I had ever visited, it was time to go to the *langar* hall and do *seva* (selfless service). It was a big rectangular hall with at least 20 rows of people sitting back-to-back in straight lines and waiting for food to be served. The rules were simple; you've to feed as many people as you can till the time your heart, soul and body allow you to. Being a chef, and from the service industry, this bit was fairly easy for me. I have served many people with a huge smile. After an hour of service, I couldn't resist anymore and it was time for me to sit down and finally taste the dishes I'd observed being made in the kitchen. The menu was *urad chana dal* (black and split Bengal gram lentil dish), *kala chana* (staple black chickpeas curry) and *roti*. The smoky feel in the *dal* was evident, the *rotis* were thick and topped with hot *ghee* to fill you up. My biggest lesson from this meal was that even as a chef, or a cook, your conscience while cooking has to be clear. It may be a profession, but it is a noble act to feed people, so love, respect and selflessness have to be there whenever you cook.

After a brilliant morning and afternoon in the gurudwara, it was time to head towards Dharamshala. There was no scope for a nap. We were some 100 km away from our destination when the weather took a sudden turn. It turned cloudy, the skies were unclear with the onset of thunder and lightning. About 20 km before Dharamshala, Kangra begins. It has a beautiful fort. Some of the crew members insisted that we take a small tour of the fort as it had started raining and they would be able to get beautiful shots. The breeze smelled fresh with rain, the fort was picturesque and the whole plantation surrounding the fort was a happy dark green in colour.

The fort was beautiful, almost 5000 years old, and had been ruled by 490 royal families to date. It is a must-visit whenever you're planning a travel to Dharamshala. My dear producer fixed a meal with one of the maharajas who had once ruled this fort; the perks of my job are just awesome! It was time to drive the Tamatar to Maharaja Bhupinder Singh's house in Dharamshala. Unlike all the royal palaces that I had been to, this one was like a royal house built in the hills. It had huge ceilings with a lot of greenery around, and twisted pathways that led to small guest cottages and open gardens.

Maharaja Bhupinder Singh was dressed simply. He was wearing a long off-white *kurta* with a traditional Himachali, or rather a mountain herder hat. He explained how, with a lot of effort, they had tried to save the fort after a major earthquake in 1905. The effort continues, also, to save their culture, language and food that are disappearing with time. The cuisine they refer to is called Kangra, and has major influences from Himachal, Kashmir, Punjab and Chamba. Not many people are aware of this cuisine today. The dishes that are popular and were served to me were *lugdu* (fern that's mainly pickled), *patoday-arbi ke patte* (dish made from colocasia leaves), *dham* (*chana dal* with dry coconut), *khatta chana* (tangy horse gram), brown rice, different sautéed varieties of wild mushrooms, pickled flower buds, mango curry served with saffron and dry fruit sweet *pulao* (dish of rice cooked in stock with spices, typically having added meat or vegetables). Jealous? Well, there were more than 12 dishes on the menu and each and every dish had a new surprise for my palate. I couldn't have left the palace without presenting with, and dedicating one royal dish to the humble, graceful and down-to-earth Maharaja Bhupinder Singh. I quickly stirred up a **Moti Pulao** (*moti* literally means pearl. Here, it means the small cottage cheese ball added in the pilaf) in his kitchen to add to this feast. After the royal feast and a long day, I thanked the maharaja profusely for the hospitality we received. I hurriedly searched for a bed in the small cottage in Kangra and passed out.

MOTI PULAO

(Also known as pearl pilaf, cottage cheese balls coated in silver make it a royal treat.)

Ingredients

1 cup basmati rice
200 gm cottage cheese *(paneer)*
3 tbsp cashew nut powder, grind the cashew nuts
1 tbsp cornflour
Salt to taste
10 silver sheets *(varq)*
2 tbsp clarified butter *(ghee)*
4 cloves *(laung)*
1 bay leaf *(tejpatta)*
2 one-inch stick cinnamon *(dalchini)*
6 green cardamoms *(elaichi)*
10 strands saffron *(kesar)*
2 tbsp milk
¼ cup dry fruits for garnishing (assorted and lightly sautéed in *ghee*)
Oil to deep fry

Method

1. Wash and soak rice in water for about half an hour. Drain water and keep aside.
2. Finely mash the *paneer* and add cashew nut powder, cornflour and salt to it. Knead it nicely and then roll out balls that look similar to big pearls.

3. Heat oil in a wok and deep-fry these *paneer* pearls on medium heat till light golden brown. Drain onto an absorbent paper and keep aside.

4. Cover these balls with silver *varq* (beaten gold or silver edible leaf adorning many desserts). They will almost look like pearls now.

5. Heat *ghee* in a *kadai*. Add cloves, bay leaf, cinnamon sticks and green cardamoms. Once they start to crackle, add the rice. Gently sauté for two minutes.

6. Add two cups of hot water and salt to taste. Cover and cook till rice is done. Cook it on low heat.

7. Crush saffron in warm milk. Add this to the rice to give it a beautiful flavour and colour.

8. After rice is done. Let it cool down for 15 minutes; if you open and mix it when hot, the grains tend to break and rice becomes mushy.

9. Now, toss half the *paneer moti*s with saffron rice. Serve this rice garnished with more silver pearls and dry fruits on the top.

DAY 6
11 August / Dharamshala

Covered with dense forest, filled with pine trees, Dharamshala has to be one of the most beautiful and unexplored hills in the northern part of India. Until the IPL (Indian Premier League) cricket happened, not many people even knew about it. Actually, the scenic cricket stadium of Dharamshala, which has hosted many international and 20-20 matches, has attracted large crowds from different states and cities resulting in an influx of tourism here. After taking a morning stroll in the hills, with rains following me wherever I stepped, it was time to visit Norbulingka. The Norbulingka Institute was established in 1988 to teach and preserve the traditional Tibetan art forms, including woodcarving, statue making, *thangka* painting and embroidery. It is a part of upper Dharamshala, known more commonly as McLeod Ganj, which is the seat of the Tibetan spiritual leader, the Dalai Lama. The artwork depicting their culture, a beautiful spiritual garden, and excellent souvenirs are what you'll like about this place. But, what I loved the most was visiting the Norling Café that served traditional Tibetan food. I don't know if my words can do justice, or these pages can give you a whiff of the aroma, but the *thenthuk* here is a must-try. It is basically a cold-weather soup made with noodles and various vegetables. The spices were controlled, herbs were balanced, a bittersweet symphony was playing in my head with the pretty rain outside. Perfect lunch I would say!

Next mission of the day was to visit a momo place in Dharamshala. It would have been a sin had we not tried some Tibetan cuisine while in McLeod Ganj. Numerous Tibetan street vendors sell momos here and they sell it pretty cheap; Rs. 20 for four pieces. One of my dear friends, who had visited Dharamshala earlier, suggested I go to Mama's Kitchen, run by a middle-aged lady Neema. It is a cute little café overlooking the valley, orange in colour, with posters of her sons who perform as a popular rock band called J.J. Exile Brothers. As I entered the kitchen there, it ended... It was perhaps the smallest kitchen I'd ever visited, so much so that it was difficult for two people to fit in at the same time. But, because it overlooked the valley, it had a breathtaking view which any chef would gladly accept.

Now came the moment that I had long been waiting for; it was time to eat the famous *aloo* (potato) momos. Yes, you read it right! The only tip I could gather from Neema*ji* was not to make the dough very soft else it would be difficult to handle and shape the momos. The potatoes were yellow because there was turmeric in them. Apart from that not many spices went into the stuffing, as it was rather bland. The chilli sauce served was super hot. So, that balanced the subtle potato flavour extremely well. They were delicate and had a wheaty taste to them. Potatoes though weren't doing much for me. Regardless, I had a great after-meal snack, thanked Neema*ji* for being a great host and quickly got myself a bottle of some fizzy drink as I stepped out because my tongue was burning like hell. That sauce was fiery!

Day 7
12 August / Dharamshala

'You tend to appreciate and value a lot more when the absence is felt…be it for a person, a place or an entity,' is what my dear friend Anamika Singh truly believes in. She mostly speaks so for her hometown, which is Dharamshala, and now I understand her love for this place. She has played a major role in promoting teas from this region. Dharamshala has beautiful tea estates. Anamika is the founder of Anandini Himalaya Tea and the marketing director of Manjhee Valley Tea Estate. I had promised her that I would visit the tea estate whenever I get a chance to travel to this part of the country, and here I was, standing in her tea estate early morning, learning how to pick the best tea leaf—the *dhai patta* or two leaves and a bud—which makes the perfect tea.

There were a lot of ladies in this gorgeous tea plantation carrying baskets strapped to their heads. They were all extremely sweet and a bit camera shy while they taught me how to pick the best leaves; they made it look so simple while I couldn't even figure my way into the plantation as there were no set paths here. If you have a bucket list for travels, make sure you add a 'tea plantation visit' to it. Anamika is one of the most vibrant people I've met in my life and as camera savvy as her tea estate was. She hated the fact that many people, including the vendors, over brewed their tea. Anamika's tip for a perfect cup of tea was to time the brewing of tea with precision, which is four minutes. It was a delight to see her personally brew some tea right there at the plantation. The procedure was fairly easy as this was a no sugar, no milk tea. This would not dilute the essence and flavours of her special handcrafted blend of one of the varieties of green tea with Himalayan *tulsi* (basil) and pomegranate flowers. You had to infuse the tea in hot water for four minutes and then fill all the cups halfway through first and then top them up. This was because the tea in the top half of the kettle was lighter than the bottom half. So to balance the flavour and depth of the tea in all the cups this procedure needed to be followed. After some Delhi-style gossip, overlooking the tea estate and sipping one of the lightest and most aromatic teas I've ever had, I gave Anamika a big hearty hug and left with some fond tea-time memories.

DAY 8

From Dharamshala, I now moved towards Andretta in Himachal Pradesh.

DAY 9
14 August / Andretta

Waking up today was a bit tough. After spending eight days with no real rest, I could now see how tough pulling off 100 continuous days would be. It all sounded very romantic and adventurous while it was being planned; well, till now, it had been a super trip, so I wasn't complaining, though the bum did hurt a little bit. My journey had brought me from Punjab to the state of Himachal Pradesh, a land which people called Dev Bhoomi or the 'Abode of the Gods.' The art, beauty and taste of this place inspired me to explore its culture and tradition.

Andretta, a small village, is close to Palampur, whose serenity has inspired many artists from all over India, for generations. Everybody knows about Shimla, Mussoorie, and Nainital, but Andretta is the village where art is born and the valleys here take your breath away.

We were going to visit a very famous art studio here, and meet the manager of Andretta Pottery and Craft Society. People from all over the world came here to learn pottery and take short and long courses for the same. Being a chef, it excited me because it was something that needed similar kind of attention to detail that we gave to food; so it was a combination of great craftsmanship and creativity. Why shouldn't I also give it a try was the question, which was quickly answered by Jugal, a master potter and teacher at Andretta Pottery. He was a nice south Indian Brahmin with a hint of Tamilian accent in his speech, who had decided to become a potter many years back. They were very strict that I should wear an apron before I sat on a wheel where they shaped the pots. Jugal pointedly noted, 'Just as you wear an apron in the kitchen, you have to wear an apron here too.' I was sitting on the wheel where the pots were shaped. Jugal further explained, 'First, you will need to prepare the clay. I have already done this for you. Now you take the clay dough and place it in the middle of the potter's wheel by hitting it hard. Hold it with both your hands and smoothen it. You move first to the centre, then to the bottom, towards the wall and finally outside.' With the passion that Jugal explained his art to me, I felt I was back in the kitchen. Just like a knife, a pan and a pot are a chef's best friends, the same way the wheel is a potter's best friend. With very delicate hands I had to mould the clay.

The beauty was that even after giving the clay a shape, it took just one more turn of the wheel to change the mould into something new. After you have shaped the pot, you proceed to reach the harsh stage. Jugal further explained, 'After the harsh stage, you have to put the clay on the wheel upside down and then start trimming it. After the trimming, you have to dry it in the sun. Then, the pot will be put through the first firing, and later the brisk firing. After that, glaze will be applied to it and then it will be given the second firing. It is a 10-day process. If the sun is good and everything goes well, then the pots will get ready in a minimum of 10 days' time. It took a lot of patience and skill to make one pot and no two pots were similar. So after I'd learnt the magic that potters had in their fingers while they shaped a pot, it was my duty to work my magical fingers and make something tasty and serve it in those beautiful pots. I had picked up some nice green tea from Kangra and I thought it would be a great idea to prepare some green tea rice. The process was simple; all you had to do was soak green tea leaves in hot water for a few minutes, and then strain it. Thereafter, this was used to make rice. It turned out to be pretty aromatic and was served in a beautiful clay pot. Next time when you're cooking rice, just cook it in water flavoured with green tea. Jugal was a great teacher and a true motivator. 'It is really tasty. What you're doing is also an art, and I really appreciate the journey you've taken up to explore India and show it to the world,' he remarked. I had a huge smile on my face as I walked out on the street to explore the local Himachali culture.

I don't think there is any place in the world like India where, as you go from one place to another, there is a change in the way people speak, live and eat. In order to see these changing colours, one must travel in local buses. As we were on a journey across India, there was no better way other than travelling in local buses to discover the real India. And that's the mode of travel that we opted for Kullu. It cost me only Rs. 80. What I gained was a bunch of local people singing Pahadi songs and giving me guidelines on what to eat and what to do while in Himachal. We arrived in Kullu well before lunch time. Kullu is a broad and an open valley, between Manali and Largi. This valley is famous for its temples, beauty and its majestic hills covered with pine and deodar forests and sprawling apple orchards. So, a conscious call had been taken to mix with the locals here and eat like them too. The hype around this lunch had been massive and the whole crew was waiting for this experience. It was going to be my first meal with a typical Himachali family in a small village; the food was cooked in a traditional manner. To help us out with this arrangement we had Dheeraj, who was a local resident and our guide for the day. We had to trek four kilometres uphill to reach a certain village and en route, Dheeraj made me pluck apples straight from the trees and introduced me to the wild growing *gucchi* (morel) mushrooms that were present around us. He said we were plain lucky to find these mushrooms in this season. In Delhi it costs us Rs. 20,000 per kg to have these morels. For a second I wanted to steal a kilogram from here! Chefs, I tell you!

Tired, and exhausted,we finally found our way into a tiny little village and located the house of the Himachali family who were playing host to us. The rustic feel of that place, stone architecture paired with wooden ceilings acted like a rejuvenating tonic for my mind and body. As I entered, I was greeted by a large family who had been waiting for me. I touched the most senior person, Mr. Karam Singh's feet, and he quickly gave me a hug, and said, 'My name is Karam Singh and this is my entire family and from today you too are a part of our family.' There was a part of me that felt so accepted and at such peace that I wanted to cry.

What I quickly noticed was that the women of the house were missing. Any guesses? Yes, they were still in the kitchen. From what I gathered later, they had been inside for the past six hours preparing for the feast. Without wasting a single second, I took permission from the eldest lady of the house, touched her feet and entered the kitchen. For me, that kitchen was an era lost in time. It was made out of clay and mud, and had a lovely charcoal smell. Ah! I felt like Charlie who had found his chocolate factory in this kitchen.

I considered myself fortunate that instant. I saw women, dressed in traditional Pahadi dresses, cooking their regional cuisine with love and devotion. After finding a spot for myself on the floor, I crossed my legs and started helping them. There were six dishes on the menu. *Kodra* (type of local millet) *ki roti*, *jaatu* rice, *kaathu* (local spinach preparation), *bhalle* (yellow lentil dumplings), **Siddu** (local buns stuffed with lentils) and *rajma* (kidney beans). There were a few accompaniments like locally produced cow *ghee* and fern pickle. The food was slow-cooked over wood-fire. All the spices and vegetables used, were grown and produced locally. It was a village style sit-down dinner as everyone assembled on the porch and we sat down on carpets with beautiful copper plates in front of us. My mouth watered and I drooled at the fragrance of the food being served. Did you know that you can survive the entire day by just eating one *kodra ki roti*. It has an amazing amount of fibre and gives warmth to the body in winters. The local spinach was divine to taste and I packed some *ghee* for my onward journey.

SIDDU
(Stuffed steamed bread served with clarified butter.)

Ingredients

1 tsp baking powder
Salt to taste
4 cups wheat flour *(atta)*
½ cup white poppy seeds *(safed khus khus)*
½ cup split bengal gram *(chana dal)*, soaked and ground
¼ cup coriander leaves *(dhania patti)*, chopped
2 onions, chopped
3 green chillies, chopped

Method

1. Add the baking powder and a bit of salt to the wheat flour.
2. Knead the wheat flour in water (1¼ cup approximately) to make a soft dough. Leave the dough overnight (covered with wet muslin cloth or in an air-tight container in the fridge). In the morning it would turn light and fluffy.
3. Dry roast the poppy seeds in a non-stick pan for three to four minutes. Keep stirring so the seeds cook evenly, else a few might burn. Let it cool and then grind them finely in a mixer.
4. Mix the ground poppy seeds and *chana dal* together. Add coriander, onions, green chillies and salt to this mixture.
5. Divide the dough equally to obtain golf ball-size roundels. Flatten them out slightly on your palm and

then stuff them with the poppy seed mix. Pinch all the ends together to make it into a roundel again. They should look like fat dim sums or buns.

6. Steam these buns for 15 minutes in a steamer or make a temporary steaming arrangement by preparing a double boiler; placing these buns on a sieve or a similar plate and shutting it with a lid.

7. Remove from the steamer and then slightly brown it from all the sides on a heated *tawa*. Serve it warm with hot *ghee* on the side.

~

Alas! Every perfect meal comes to an end, so it was time for me to leave. This family had treated me not like a guest, but like one of their own. This is the speciality of Indians. In our houses, and our hearts, we have a place for everybody. With a heavy heart, I tried offering them some money for their hospitality. Not only did they refuse, but in return they handed us a huge box of apples. I did not want to leave, but India's various other flavours were waiting for me. My next destination: Manali.

DAY 10
15 August / Manali

After a long journey from Kullu to Manali, we were all very tired and just wished to quickly eat and sleep. But we just had 100 days and so did not want to miss out on anything that was particular to the hill station. Kullu and Manali are two sides of a coin, but I could smell some Italian herbs in Manali. That's because it is extremely popular for its Italian cuisine. For the past 10 years the culture of Italian food has really developed here because of the number of expats who visit Manali. We went to one such spot famous for their pizzas called Casa Bella Pizza. The restaurant was very quiet and was totally painted in white; it seemed like a place where couples would come for a romantic wine and dine experience. They had a huge outdoor seating, a small indoor seating allowing people to enjoy the weather outside and perhaps enjoy the warmth from the wood-fired oven for times when it was cold.

Italy also has many options in vegetarian food just like India. People are mistaken if they think they have to eat a lot of meat when they go to Italy. Basil is one ingredient that I can live by for a lifetime. The chef there on request quickly tossed a thin crust wood-fired oven pizza with lots of fresh vegetables and basil on it for all of us. The pizzas were delicious and were far better than any I've had in Mumbai or Delhi. So this whole 'Italian food in Manali' hype actually lived up to its reputation. After this, it was time to relax, get a good night's sleep and wait for the morning to begin my exploration.

Day 11
16 August / Manali

The Mall Road is the liveliest and the most throbbing street of Manali and is lined with plenty of hotels, eateries and shopping options. The street, being a popular hang-out, was teeming with people everywhere. After doing the regular touristy window-shopping and buying small tokens for family, it was time for something new. Our journey brought us a new adventure every day. Today's adventure was to explore a hidden food gem in the city: Dylan's Toasted and Roasted Coffee House, whose logo said, 'We are here to serve you with love and care.' It reminded me of my mom and that family in Kullu we met the day before.

I asked the owner of the café, Raj, 'What is Dylan's café about?' Raj's response was prompt, 'The name is inspired by Bob Dylan, the great music legend. I think that food is the most important thing in our lives. We want to love it and people are passionate about the food they eat, and that's why they want to cook it as well. The most beautiful thing that we miss is food cooked by our mother. So, we thought why not cover the gap to provide what backpackers are really missing. So, we are here to provide the taste of home with a bit of a wow factor through the music.'

The story of how this café began was interesting; it revealed a great cross-cultural connect. In 2005, Raj started this project with two Californian hippy guys. A guy called Eric taught Raj how to make the world-famous cookies the café is known for. Basically, these cookies are American chocolate cookies. After hearing so much about the cookies, I was shameless enough to ask Raj to share the recipe with me, and he said it was all about our love for food. There were a few secrets though that Raj did share with me. First was, that there should be at least two big chunks of chocolate in every cookie. Second was, you have to make small balls like we make for *rotis*, that shouldn't be too hard and there was no need to flatten them totally. Also, most of the times the tray went directly to the customers, fresh from the oven and it was sold out within minutes.

As the cookies were being baked and the aromas were sifting through my soul, I got a chance to join a table with a small group of foreigners who were backpacking through India. There were three guys, Alexter and Amir from Israel, Alex from England and Natasha from Spain. They had been regularly visiting this café for the past three days and were totally in love with Manali. On being asked what he loved the most about India, Alex answered, 'It is very different from what we thought. People are extremely hospitable, it is not as crowded as we imagined it to be, at least not so in the hills, and it is given me a lot of peace and love.' It made me feel very proud and it was encouraging to hear such great words about my country. In a short while, the cookies were with me; I shared the whole batch with my new friends, bid Raj goodbye and sat inside the Tamatar for our next destination, where we would be catching a fresh Himalayan trout and then cook it.

It was 3 p.m. and I was sitting on the banks of a mountain stream, the city rush, long forgotten. There was a cool breeze and the sounds of waves rushing by, which transported me to a different realm. When I had left home for this journey, I had promised myself that I would overcome all my fears. I wouldn't get scared of anything. Fish was one of those things that I never fancied, catching it, definitely not! But a promise is a promise! It was time to face that fear and I was told by my director that till the time I wouldn't catch a fish we wouldn't leave the place. Hence, catching a fish was of paramount importance for me.

The trouts of this region are very popular. January to March are the best months to catch trout, but unfortunately, we were here in the wrong month. So, it would be a miracle if I happened to catch one. Thirty minutes had already elapsed since I put the hook in and nothing happened. After an hour of staring at the empty hook, disappointment sunk in and it was one of the first defeats I faced on this trip. To not dampen the spirits, I still decided to cook a fresh trout bought from the market and made it as tasty and simple as possible. I dedicated this recipe to the region and called it **Kullu Manali Trout**. One important thing to remember while cooking this trout is that you don't remove the skin because the taste lies in the skin of this fish. Within 10 minutes, the fish was ready with a lot of help from the crew.

Kullu Manali Trout
(Pan-fried trout marinated with local herbs.)

Ingredients

2 trouts
2 tsp curry leaf *(kari patta)* paste
2 tsp crushed coriander *(dhania)* seeds
1 tsp red chilli flakes
1 tsp orange rind
1 tbsp lemon juice
1 tbsp mustard *(sarson)* oil
Salt to taste

Method

1. Clean and wash the trout. Do a fillet and do not remove the skin. Trout is best cooked with its skin on.
2. Make a marinade by mixing curry leaf paste, crushed coriander seeds, red chilli flakes, orange rind, lemon juice, salt and mustard oil in a bowl.
3. Rub this marinade all over the fish and let it rest in the fridge for about 10 minutes.
4. Heat two teaspoon olive or mustard oil in a pan and add the marinated fish and cook on both sides on medium flame for five to seven minutes or until the fish curls up.
5. Have this hot fish like a starter or with a bowl of rice.

~

Despite not having caught a trout together, the whole exercise of cooking the fish for my team definitely established a great bond between all of us. This journey of Kullu and Manali was very different and it challenged my thought process as a chef; having trained in professional kitchens, a chef's outlook is very different from someone who cooks in home kitchens. Kullu made me realise the importance of instinct and a constant thirst for knowledge for a chef. After having seen people cook at a wood-fired stove and pickling a fern, it opened my eyes to a completely new dimension of food. I started questioning myself, what all could be created if this knowledge was transferred into a professional kitchen and then developed further? I started realising that food is bigger than I ever thought, it doesn't stop at serving a good meal to a guest. To go beyond I'll have to unlearn a lot and then accept all these new learnings. Also, someday I'll catch a fish! Kullu and Manali are usually mentioned together. But during my visit, I saw two very different flavours; while the Kullu cuisine has very localised flavours of the mountains, Manali's eating joints are cosmopolitan with a lot of Mediterranean influence.

DAY 12
18 August / Rohtang Pass

If one is willing to let go of all food inhibitions while travelling, that is when the right kind of food will find you. There are many ways to find the right place to dine at in an unknown city, from guides to websites to blogs. The real deal, though, lies with the people of that city. It is always a much more interesting way of discovering local eateries, talking to the people of the city or friends who have visited that city before and you'll be amazed at the in-depth information people are willing to share when it comes to food. If you're planning a road trip to the serene and enchanting Leh in Ladakh, these guidelines will definitely come in handy.

So, I was expecting this leg of the trip to be definitely the most scenic and adventurous one. And I couldn't believe my luck, I was actually going to Leh!

If someone in Ladakh smiles and says 'Julle!' don't get confused. Because that would mean he or she is saying hello in the local language. That was also my first word to Ratan, who ran a small *dhaba* called Maggi Point, which was the only place to eat before Rohtang Pass. Also, it was raining, so the possibility of getting stuck in a four hour-long jam at Rohtang Pass was certain. The journey to reach Leh, about 473 km away, was a two day-long trip. It was amazing to see that Maggi was a lifesaver even in this part of the world. As it was 4:30 a.m. in the morning, that was the only thing Ratan had to offer. He served a hot bowl of Maggi to each one of us, and

I must appreciate the fact that he had a lot of courage to have opened a shop just 10 km below Rohtang Pass. Ratan explained his business model by saying, 'During season time around 1000 vehicles go to Rohtang per day, out of which 100-200 are sure to stop here.' It was a tough bet as he lived in Manali but it was necessary for him to run this shop to support his family.

As presumed, I knew what was going to come next. After driving uphill for another three kilometres, we got stuck in a seven kilometre-long traffic jam at Rohtang Pass. To top it all, our poor Tamatar got stuck in a mud pile. After remaining stuck there for two hours and running low on patience, I finally decided to trek on foot for at least two or three kilometres. The beauty of Indian roads is that you can be sure to find food somewhere near them. To my surprise, I met this incredible entrepreneur with a mobile kitchen who would wait every day for passers-by to get stuck in a similar jam at Rohtang. His mobile kitchen comprised Indian *chaat* items like *matra kulcha* (a popular street food consisting of round Indian bread made from flour, milk, and butter, typically stuffed with meat or vegetables and a chickpea curry) and *bhel puri* (an Indian dish of puffed rice, onions, spices, and hot chutney). He would sell 100 plates in a day just because of the traffic jam. It does need some business acumen and guts to do this! He has served food to people from at least 50 countries. He said of his venture, '*Sahab*, I've served everyone, from Amreeka to Dilli and I feel blessed and thank God every day for this opportunity.' He quickly dished out three kinds of *chaat* and I tasted all of them. They were not only finger-licking good, but it was astonishing to see him serve another seven Australians that same *chaat* with a dozen chillies in them!

Talking about epic kitchens and cooks, this man certainly had a certain kind of magic in him to run his mobile kitchen. At the moment, I felt small, thinking of times and of challenges I would cry about in a fully functional kitchen in a five-star hotel. After being stuck in the jam for almost the entire day, everybody was numb with frustration and had a backache to accompany the fatigue. So we decided to take a stopover after a mere 100 km and called it a day.

Day 13
19 August / Keylong

After a rather difficult start to the Leh trip, we decided to start this day with some good luck. It is believed that travellers who visit Leh make *stupas* (piles of stones) en route at a popular spot meant for good luck and to receive blessings and prayers for a safe journey. Believe me, things actually changed after the *stupa* ritual; the day turned sunny and the landscapes became breathtaking. Have you ever seen five different colours in one go from the sky above to the ground below? The scenes were so unreal as if God had painted his own canvas. My eyes won't tire staring out of the window as the sky was so perfectly blue. After a long day and one of the best scenic and picturesque journeys of my life, we finally made it to Leh. All thanks to the good-luck *stupa*.

DAY 14
20 August / Leh

After a very long journey we did finally reach Leh; it was a very tiring trip and the oxygen levels here were not the greatest, so it took a while to adapt. Leh being a spiritual land, I needed some peace and calm after being 15 days on the road without any break. So the first place we decided to visit was Thiksey Monastery. The monks in the monastery had a certain sparkle in their eyes that seeped in the beholder's gaze and was attractive. The air here was different, with a peaceful wind blowing, there was always a smile on people's faces, bright eyes sparkled and there was melody in their voice. I wondered why? I reasoned that it could have a lot to do with what they ate. So, I decided to explore their food culture?

Upon taking a general tour of the streets, Leh as a town seemed very similar to Manali, perhaps a bit more untouched. I found a lot of dried yak cheese, red chillies, sun-dried tomatoes (yes, you have them in India too) and even apricots being sold on the streets in bulk. Then there was the fresh vegetable and fruit market that had some weird and interesting vegetables that I'd never encountered before, like pink radish, baby carrots and a certain branch of turnips. It made me realise that the local organic food culture was very strong here. After some scouting we chanced upon a bistro called the Open Hand Bistro and Espresso Bar. It had its own organic farm and the interesting bit was that the head chef Jack was an American. His six feet one-inch frame was a bit lanky and he wore a bandana all the time and loved living in Leh.

On being asked about the menu in the café, Chef Jack explained, 'I designed it to cater to a lot of Indian tourists who come here so we have things like *thali* (a set meal at an Indian restaurant) and *khichdi* (primarily made of rice and lentils) on the menu. We also offer *dal* every now and then. Leh also has a huge influx of Western tourist now so I have got to keep European salads as well, so we have varieties of Greek and Spanish salads. My absolute favourite on the menu is the healthy salad as everything in it is fresh from our own farms.'

Later, Jack was happy enough to give me a walk through his farms, taught me how to pick vegetables of choice and then we cooked for each other. It was an absolute delight to be cooking with vegetables that were smiling back at you. Tomatoes were so juicy that I felt like biting into them while they were still uncooked. As Chef Jack made the healthy salad for me, I made **Lettuce Wraps** for him. My dish was wholeheartedly approved by Chef Jack; it was a happy moment, trust me, so I unapologetically dug in to that soulful spiritual salad that Chef Jack had prepared. Well, I sort of understood the new world food culture here but traditional food was still a big question mark to me. Coming back to lettuce wraps, here's the recipe:

LETTUCE WRAPS
(Freshly tossed salad served in lettuce cups.)

Ingredients

12 large lettuce leaves
2 tsp olive oil

200 gm mushrooms
1 large onion, chopped
100 gm water chestnut
2 tbsp minced ginger-garlic *(adrak-lasun)*
1 tbsp thick reduced soya sauce
¼ cup Hoisin sauce
1 tbsp red wine vinegar
2 tsp chilli sauce
100 gm tofu or cottage cheese *(paneer)*
100 gm radish
¼ cup pine nuts or walnuts, chopped
1 tbsp sesame oil
Salt and pepper to taste

Method

1. Rinse the lettuce and then soak it in ice water.
2. Cook mushrooms, onions, and water chestnuts in a large pan over high heat for two minutes in olive oil.
3. Then add ginger-garlic, soya sauce, Hoisin sauce, red wine vinegar and chilli sauce. Cook until the mushroom just starts to sweat. Add the tofu or cottage cheese, radish and pine nuts or walnuts. Cook for about one minute more.
4. Stir in salt, pepper and sesame oil. Arrange lettuce leaves with their hollow side facing up (trim the leaf to make it look like a neat cup). Spoon the mushroom mixture in the centre, chill for five minutes and then eat it like a taco.

~

There are different types of confluences, be it people coming together, of food, music and others. An interesting one in Leh is the confluence of the Indus and Zanskar rivers. The confluence point is located on the National Highway 1 from Leh to Srinagar. Watching the muddy Zanskar water mix with the blue-green Indus is breathtaking. Sitting at this junction you're living in the moment, there is no past or future.

I was patiently waiting here for my friend Neema whom I'd never met but known for a long while. He ran a water sport training company and used to train a very close friend of mine in kayaking; I had heard great stories of Neema being a kayaking champion several times. After 10 minutes Neema shouted from afar, 'Julle!' It was a crazy moment to finally meet a person you'd known for so long but never met. He is a gem of a guy and does adventure sports for a living. Neema insisted that now that we were in Leh we had to visit his home for a traditional and special Ladakhi feast. Who could say no to that?

As we reached his house, which was a beautiful cottage in the hills, the aromas emanating from the kitchen made me head straight to it. It was quite a sight to visit a traditional Ladakhi kitchen. My first reaction was, 'Wow! It is flamboyant and very ethnic.' Most of it was made with brass and copper. Even the equipment being used was traditional. Neema's grandmother, who was cooking in the kitchen, was an octogenarian and looked extremely cute in her traditional Ladakhi dress. She was generous in giving her 50-year-old *Thukpa* recipe to us.

While I helped her blend and crush spices in a mortar and pestle (not in a mixer), she explained, 'You must be getting a different aroma from this vessel that we are cooking in; this *handi* (an earthenware or metal pot) is made of brass. You will not only get a different taste but when we cook in this, the food doesn't get spoilt easily.' She was very active for her age and deftly made very thin and fine *paape*, which were like torn lasagna sheets made from wheat flour. She almost made 100 *paapes* in a minute! The *thukpa*, by now, was cooked and I had the company of Neema, his family and other friends who had joined us to make that dinner memorable. In Ladakh, before eating, they always remember the Lord. So, we thanked God for this lovely meal, played some music, and made some great memories.

THUKPA
(Spicy soup with hand-rolled noodles.)

Ingredients

2 tbsp mustard *(sarson)* oil
3 spring onions, chopped
8-10 garlic *(lasun)* cloves, crushed
3 tomatoes, chopped
1½ tsp cumin *(jeera)* powder
1 tsp garam masala
1 tsp freshly cracked black pepper *(kali mirch)*
1 cup spinach, chopped
3 radishes, chopped
4½ cups water
3 cups wheat flour *(atta)*
1 egg for making *paape* (kind of wheat pasta)

¼ cup spring onion greens, chopped
¼ cup coriander *(dhania patta)*
1 tsp lemon juice
Salt to taste

Method

1. In a heavy pan, or preferably a copper pot, heat lots of mustard oil until hot and smoky.
2. Add the onions and garlic and sauté until onions are translucent. Then add the chopped tomatoes and cook for three to four minutes or until the tomatoes are soft and mushy. Now add cumin powder, garam masala and pepper.
3. Add the chopped spinach and radish and sauté for two minutes. Top it up with four cups of water and bring to boil. Immediately lower the heat and let it simmer. Meanwhile, prepare the pasta-like *paape*.
4. Mix flour with egg and half cup water. Add water in parts while kneading to ensure there isn't too much of it. When it is nicely kneaded, roll out the dough like a *roti* and then, just like Neema's grandmother, try to make 100 *paapes* in a minute (and fail miserably like I did). Keep adding these irregular bite-sized dough strips into the simmering broth, as you tear them. Add about 30 pieces. Cook for another 10 minutes.
5. Neema's grandmother mentioned how they add less salt in food so they can taste the ingredient as it is supposed to be. So finally, add a little salt, garnish with coriander and spring onion leaves and have it hot.

Day 15
21 August / Ladakh

If you're a food traveller, you must always try figuring out the basic foundation of a cuisine, like what kind of spices and herbs are used, what's the vegetation like, what kind of meats or seafoods are popular. A lot of the food that people eat also depends on the climate, soil and water of the region. Ladakhi cuisine, as we tasted, is not high on spices; it relies more on the fresh herbs and produce available to them. A few traditional Ladakhi dishes like *thukpa*, *gud-gud chai* (butter tea) and *thenthuk* (soup made with handmade noodles) are found easily in the city and people are willing to share their *thukpa* stories and family recipes if you ask, like Neema's grandmother did.

The Leh journey was almost coming to an end and there was one life lesson yet to be learnt. I came to Leh in search of good food but this city had given me more than that. Apart from people there was this deep sense of spirituality that was omnipresent here. There was one such example of spirituality in Leh, which was recognised as 'Mahabodhi.' This was a school/institution where students were taught spirituality and even special courses were designed for common people interested in it as a subject. So today was all about spending time with the students in the kitchen, learning a thing or two from them and teaching them a thing or two about cooking. It was a fun exercise to see 12-year-olds cook as well, it made me nostalgic and reminded me of my cooking days when I was a kid.

Guru Bhikkhu Sanhasena, who founded Mahabodhi, was present there when we visited, so I did not want to leave without his blessings. The spot he chose to meet me at was so spectacular that time stood still. I was sitting next to the prayer flags on a small plateau above Mahabodhi which was overlooking the sun. People travel all over the world for beautiful sunsets and I've had my fair share of travel too, but I can tell you this, I had never seen a sunset like this before.

As Guruji arrived he sat down right next to me with his legs folded. Before I could say anything, Guruji spoke, 'Saransh, we are very happy to know that you are headed on this journey, discovering different parts of our country and we are also very happy to have you in Ladakh, on top of the world. You know Ladakh is also called the Land of Three Ms: mountains, monasteries and monks. We as human beings need spirituality; we need meditation, prayer to keep our mind, heart and soul healthy. So, I believe it is the spiritual values, which bring beauty, fragrance and colour to life.' These words were still sinking in when I touched his feet and asked for his blessings to complete this dream journey and he prompted, 'Your whole life is a journey. I wish and pray to the Lord, and give blessings to all of you. May you have all the strength and skills needed to continue the journey and overcome the difficulties you face. There will be ups and downs but it makes you stronger. So I think all parts of your journey will be successful.'

I am not sure if this trip to Leh made me spiritual, but yes, I could sense some calmness within me. It was now time to head to Kargil.

Day 16
22 August / Kargil

The first episode of our journey, documented for TV, got telecast all across India today. Five years back, no one would have thought, not even my family, that one day I would be on national TV talking about food. Three years of struggle, perseverance, and endless jibes from various people finally paid off. But this was not going to be easy. It was just the beginning and I had already started getting calls from the channel and creative head that I hadn't delivered up to their expectations. They said that my connect with the audience was low, I seemed under-confident and definitely camera conscious. Trying to imagine the camera as a friend was perhaps one of the biggest hurdles that any good TV presenter, or actor, had to cross. Living and learning through an experience was a much easier thing to do in comparison to sharing it with people through videos and words. As these thoughts weighed heavy on my head, we started our day in Kargil after a late night drive to this district.

The road from Leh to Kargil is indeed one of the most fascinating drives as it is a series of high passes and fragile mountainsides. Not only is there a dramatic scenic change but also a cultural one; there's a shift from a Buddhist region to a Muslim dominated one. Kargil, at 2740 metres above sea level, had been an important trading post many years back and a subject of debate and war between India and Pakistan. So, to pay homage to our soldiers, I had set out for my first destination, Kargil.

The most recent and significant chapter in terms of war in Indian history was the Kargil War. I was only about 12 when this war took place. As a patriot, reading about it in the newspapers and in magazines everyday, watching it being talked about on television was hard but standing at the border and realising the sacrifices that the Indian Army has made, so that Indian families could sleep every night in peace was a different thing altogether. I had, and always will, salute the courage of our soldiers. While crossing Kargil, one should visit the Tiger Hill and pay homage to the soldiers who have sacrificed their today for our tomorrow.

After meeting the *jawan*s, it was time to meet the *kisaan*s. We travelled to a small town called Drass. Despite being the second coldest place in India, it was incredibly hot and I was sweating. A lot of barley is harvested in this part of the country and this was the first time I was seeing a crop being harvested. It was very interesting; we helped the farmers and got the barley cleaned and packed. In the ground form, there is a husk or chaff around it, which is removed by the process of threshing, which happens after harvesting but before winnowing. It separates the grain from anything inedible though the bran still remains. All this talk of barley was reminding me of a chilled glass of beer in this hot weather. I wish I had a pint while I was helping the farmers here to pick the right grains. Trust me, it is a lot of hard work, very laborious to be on your feet and keep cutting grains from a sickle.

I decided to do a small experiment by making *khichdi*, the regular Indian one, but with the freshly harvested barley. I decided to name the dish **Fresh Barley *Khichdi***. It was a fun moment to cook and share this lunch with these hardworking farmers, especially because Eid was around the corner and it seemed like a mini celebration.

FRESH BARLEY *KHICHDI*
(Popular rice dish made with fresh barley in this case.)

Ingredients

1½ tsp cumin *(jeera)* seeds
1 whole cinnamon *(dalchini)* stick
4 cloves *(laung)*
A pinch of asafoetida *(hing)*
1 medium-size onion
1 cup barley *(jaun)*, soaked in water for a minimum of two to three hours
½ cup split Bengal gram *(chana dal)*, soaked in water for 30 minutes
¼ tsp turmeric *(haldi)* powder
1 tsp red chilli powder
1 tsp black peppercorns *(sabut kali mirch)*, crushed
Salt to taste
8-10 fresh coriander leaves *(dhania patti)* for garnish

Method

1. Heat the *ghee* in a pressure cooker. When heated, add cumin seeds, cinnamon, cloves and asafoetida.

2.   Once the cumin seeds release a nutty aroma, add the onion, barley and *chana dal*. Sauté this for two to three minutes.
3.   Add the turmeric powder, chilli powder, crushed peppercorns and salt. Mix well.
4.   Now add three cups water and give it a mix and let it come to a boil.
5.   Put the lid on, and cook for three whistles. (Reduce the flame to low after the first whistle.)
6.   Switch the gas off. Open the lid when the pressure reduces completely and serve hot, garnished with coriander.

~

After the *khichdi*, I got a chance to join in a special celebration with a local Kashmiri family that does threshing for such crops. As I entered their beautiful house garden I was first greeted by the eldest man in the house, whom I acknowledged as Chacha Jaan. He wished me Eid Mubarak and as per the culture, gave me their traditional hug, right-left-right. It was a heart-warming gesture. Soon the whole family was out, greeting everybody. Chacha Jaan offered me the traditional *kahwah* (tea). I asked him about the drink and its ingredients, and his instant answer was, 'After putting 12 different ingredients in a green tea it becomes *kahwah*. Things like almond, cinnamon, cardamom and other such ingredients go into it. The saffron in it is responsible for its rich colour.'

They served it in a traditional brass kettle called *samovar*. It consists of a 'fire-container,' running as a central cavity, in which live coals are placed to keep the tea perpetually hot. Around it, there is a space for water to boil and the tea leaves and other ingredients are mixed with the water. This kettle is used mainly for celebrations; it was indeed a celebration of great humility shown by this family for welcoming me and celebrating Eid with me. As I deeply inhaled the *kahwah*, I was lost in its aroma; the spiciness of cardamom, bittersweet taste of cinnamon, and the nuttiness of the almond. In short, it lived up to its reputation and the hype. After the tea and post-tea discussions I touched Chacha Jaan's feet, promised to come back someday and bid adieu with a '*Salaam Alaikum.*'

The car was now headed to Srinagar. It was a long six-hour journey. While passing through some rough, almost barren hills, we saw a small community that was living in tents in the middle of nowhere. It was surprising and made all of us very curious. We stopped and decided to have a word with them to gratify our curiosities. They turned out to be from the Gujjar community. In Kashmir, this community mostly rears sheep. Their head chose to come and speak with me; it was a bit scary and unsettling, to be honest. I was surrounded by at least 60 to 70 people now and I was like a well-dressed alien for them. He explained, 'We rear goats and sheep. We sell them too. There are goats, sheep, horses, and we take them to Punjab, sell them and come back. We mostly walk within these hills; we have our hidden and internal secret routes. We also use the milk from these animals and we make *ghee*, butter and Kalari cheese.'

I was quite fascinated to hear that name and also their secret internal passage story. It was a rare cheese to come by for anyone not living in Kashmir. Kalari is a traditionally ripened cheese product indigenous to Jammu and Kashmir; it is a very dense cheese and usually fried in its own fat and salted prior to being eaten. Now I was sure that random moments of joy only come to you when you choose to do random things, which in this case was stopping the car to meet a Gujjar community and being introduced to Kalari cheese!

DAY 17
23 August / Srinagar

Welcome to Srinagar, the capital of Jammu and Kashmir, the city known for Dal Lake, Lal Chowk, the Old City, and the houseboats. Dal Lake is like a self-contained city in itself and one of the most popular attractions of Srinagar. One of the most exciting things about this lake is that thousands of families are a part of this lake ecosystem where they have their own markets, schools, houses and temples. The most fascinating aspect for me was the floating *sabzi bazaar* (vegetable market), that takes place two kilometres inside the lake, between 4 a.m. and 6 a.m. everyday. The day started very early for me, at 3:45 a.m. to be precise. By now I had given up on looking like a good clean shaven boy for the camera; it wasn't that easy anymore! At 4:30 a.m. it was still dark and the lake was faintly lit by the dark bluish sky; I had no idea how the person rowing the boat was figuring his way out.

Soon the dawn broke through the dark blue sky. It was 5 a.m. and the market was flooded with hundreds of boats around it. It looked like a wholesale vegetable and flower market but it was all floating. This market is primarily where farmers bring their produce and vegetable sellers buy them to be sold in the market. If you are wondering where do the vegetables come from, don't be surprised when I tell you that the lake is fertile enough to produce vegetables. As I was looking around, I noticed that all the vegetables looked very fresh, as it was all organic. While exploring the floating market we also discovered little routes and alleys inside the lake. There was a whole world hidden within the lake, a lot of shops selling wooden artefacts and houses and gardens that you'd not notice from the outside. What an amazing start to the Srinagar trip!

If the vegetable market is on one side of the Dal Lake, houseboats take up the other side. To enjoy the houseboat experience, I met Javed Bhai. Once we reached the houseboat area on the lake, we noticed hundreds of houseboats in a line. Most of them looked old and weathered from outside, though I was told that a lot of owners had reworked on them and had updated the interiors. Javed Bhai's houseboat was similar. As I entered, it seemed I had come to a different world; there were exquisite walnut-wood carvings and Kashmiri rugs lining the interior. There was not a single spot that didn't have carvings. He explained, 'All this is handmade, the whole inner panel of the boat is made by small pieces that are joined together and it is made of deodar wood. Houseboats are made with a lot of passion; it is a novelty, is supposed to give a unique experience to the guest that includes sampling Kashmir's traditional food. The best bit was to be able to sit on the porch of the boat and gaze at the floating *shikaras* (light flat-bottomed boat); all peaceful and serene. Given a choice, I would always stay on a houseboat if I visit Srinagar again; no hotel compares to this experience. Javed Bhai had been an excellent host so it was time to repay him back by cooking in his houseboat kitchen. To remember the sweet memories of Srinagar, I made a sweet dish, **Saffron Fruit Cream.**

SAFFRON FRUIT CREAM
(Fresh fruits served in a smooth saffron flavoured cream.)

Ingredients

1 cup or 200 gm vanilla ice cream
2½ cups or 500 gm heavy cream
¼ cup or 50 gm powdered sugar *(bhura)*
8-10 strands Kashmiri saffron *(laccha kesar)*
1 tbsp warm milk
1 mango, cubed
1 banana, cubed
1 apple, cubed
15 grapes, slit in half
2 tbsp almond flakes
2 tbsp raisins

Method

1. Leave the ice cream out in a bowl for it to soften. Start beating chilled cream (very important for it to be chilled, or it might split) with a hand blender or an egg beater. Gradually add sugar in three parts and keep beating till sugar dissolves with the cream. When the cream is just light and fluffy and not totally whipped, set it aside. If you overdo the whipping, it might just curdle.

2. Soak the Kashmiri saffron strands in warm milk for five minutes. Once saffron gives out its brilliant colour and flavour to the milk, mix it with the softened ice cream.

3.   Gently mix this saffron ice cream with the sugar and cream mix.

4.   Add all the chopped fruits and nuts to this saffron cream mixture. Chill it for 30 minutes.

5.   Enjoy as many cups as you like. Also these are some fruits that I like, you can skip any or add more of your choice.

~

After this wonderful houseboat journey, it was time to meet a local family who was treating me to the king of all *thali* meals or the *wazwan*. This family, that I was supposed to meet, was related to Javed Bhai (from the houseboat) and the head of this family, coincidentally, was also named Javed. As I reached the latter's house, I noticed that though the house was huge, it was very minimalistic in design and white in colour. He took me straight to his huge kitchen made up of a combination of marble and stone. The whole family was waiting for me so they could start their dinner. It was amazing how in only 20 days of travelling I had been loved by the entire group of families wherever I had visited. As I sat down on the floor in a group of four men facing each other, Javed explained, 'Wazwan is a unique concept in which "waz" means the chef who has rare culinary skills passed on to him through generations. He is an artist who is passionately involved with his art and carries the great Kashmiri tradition within him, and "wan" is a shop with the abundant supplies of meats and delicacies.'

These meats are then used for detailed preparation of delicacies and presented traditionally to showcase the charm of the nobility of Kashmiri cuisine. This meal is served on a big copper plate called *trami* containing the steamed rice on which the varieties of meat, that include *methi korma*, *seekh* kebab, *tabakh maaz*, *zafrani murgh* and *daniphul*, are beautifully placed dividing the *trami* into four, so that four people can eat from one plate itself to enhance the bond of brotherhood. Traditionally, a *wazwan* has 36 courses out of which 15-16 courses are made from meat, but I was just getting a glimpse of it. What got me worried was the thought of eating so much meat in one go; I doubt I had ever seen so much meat on one plate ever. Now it was time to begin the meal, but, first the lady of the house took me through a ritual washing of hands at a basin called the *tash-t-nari*. As one *trami* was finished, a new one was brought in, and then removed, and again a new one brought in, until the dinner was over. Five dishes that I was served on this occasion were *rista*, *rogan josh*, *tabak maaz*, *aab gosht* and *gushtaba*. The meal ended with *kahwah*. My favourite was the *gushtaba*, also called the king of *wazwan*. The size itself is so overwhelming on the plate that it does remind you of the king pawn on a chessboard. The meal, though too heavy on the meats for me, was delicious and super filling. The curries and gravies had a different texture and flavour to each of them. A lot of green cardamom was used in various dishes.

Eating *Wazwan* in Kashmir was a big check on my bucket list, but the experience of eating from the same plate with three different men changed a lot of notions regarding eating for me, as we have been taught to eat from our own bowls and plates and seldom have the shared plates. At first, I was shy and felt odd but as I shared that *trami* with them I realised the importance of a family eating together. It gives you more satisfaction and peace. I couldn't thank the ladies and Javed enough, so I promised to make them look good on TV and headed to my next destination, which was my bed. Imagine having eaten a kilo of meat all by yourself? A bed is all that you need after that.

Day 18
24 August / Pampur

It was a hot sunny day and before we started for Jammu there was one thing that was yet to be experienced, and that was the saffron culture in Kashmir. There are very few, only about two or three, places in the whole world where saffron grows and Kashmir has the privilege of being one of these places. We visited one of the plantations on the city outskirts—Pampur, 13 km from Srinagar—for information on saffron, a spice used for its beautiful colour, medicinal properties and fragrance. I met Kedar there who took me through the process of producing saffron. Kedar explained, 'The saffron plant is very small and its flower is the only part which is seen above the ground. The blooming time of this flower is autumn. There are only three stigmas in it when the flower blooms. This is painstakingly harvested manually.'

The aroma I got while sorting saffron was enchanting. These strands were also incredibly fat, as big as *aloo lacha*s (potato finger fries) and a deep purple in colour. I just couldn't miss this opportunity to make something with saffron. So I chose to make a chilled saffron-flavoured milk with it. Meanwhile, the weather turned beautiful, it started raining heavily, both of us raised a toast with our saffron milk and I wrapped up my Kashmir visit with beautiful memories. I will agree with the saying, if there is heaven on earth, it is right here in Kashmir.

Day 19
It took us the entire day to reach Jammu.

DAY 20
25 August / Jammu

Jammu is famous for *rajma*, or kidney beans. I spoke to one of my friends and he told me there was a certain sardar*ji* in the Nandini locality, who owned a small *dhaba* at some hidden corner there and served the tastiest *rajma chawal*. So after an hour of making 'U' turns and trying to locate the shop, we entered the quaint little *dhaba*. Sardar*ji* greeted me and I replied, '*Sasriyakal paaji*, do you serve *rajma chawal* here?' He smiled, asked me to have a seat, and explained, 'Not just any *rajma chawal*, we serve it with lots of *desi ghee*.' They get the beans from a region called Bhaderwah, in the foothills of the Himalayas, which is said to produce the best *rajma* in India. People from different parts of the country ask for *rajma* as a gift whenever somebody is travelling to Jammu. So it was a great idea to pick some for my grandmother.

Sardar*ji* further explained, 'Usually, people who go to Vaishno Devi come here to eat *rajma chawal* made in *desi ghee*. This is a famous dish here.' Though I wasn't very enthusiastic about having it there, since I get to eat it almost every Sunday back at home, I was curious why it was so popular? Soon a steel plate arrived in front of me, and I was overwhelmed by the aroma of *ghee*. It was a very traditional way of serving *rajma chawal*; there was rice on the bottom topped with *rajma*, a bit of sliced onions and dollops of *ghee* on top. The beauty of this *rajma* was that it was buttery and melted in your mouth, so soft, unlike the ones served in Mumbai or Delhi that takes hours to cook. Using the Jammu *rajma* I decided to make a Mexican bean salad for sardar*ji* and his co-workers as a token of appreciation for cooking such fabulous food for the past 40 years. Mexican bean salad was pretty *desi* in nature. It had fried nachos-shaped *papad* (thin, crisp disc-shaped food typically based on seasoned dough made from black gram, fried or cooked with dry heat), topped with thick *rajma* plus curry, finely chopped mixed salad tossed with *chaat masala* and lemon juice and lastly garnished with grated cottage cheese.

After it was ready and sardar*ji* had had the salad, he and his working family gave a verdict, 'The mixture you made, the salad with *papad*, is something I am eating for the first time. It is very tasty but needs *ghee*.' Everyone burst out laughing. We took a group photo, which sardar*ji* promised would be stuck on the entrance wall as a fond memory.

DAY 21
26 August / Jammu

Jammu has a sizeable Dogri population and they are known for their cuisine, which has a distinct taste with local flavours. The idea today was to explore a cuisine that most of us hadn't heard of. Mr. Mangotra, who has lived in Jammu all his life, had invited me to taste and learn the basics of Dogri cuisine. We found him through an agency that had been preserving Dogri culture, art, craft, music and food for years.

After doing the usual greetings and a bit of chit-chat, I realised that we were in Dr. Raina's house, who was a big fan of FoodFood channel and the real Dogri cook that Mr. Mangotra highly recommended. Mr. Mangotra came across as a good conversationalist, who was well-versed with the Dogri culture. He explained, 'The Dogris inhabit the hilly tract bounding the mountains of the Kashmir Valley on the south and extends to the plains of Punjab. They are descendants of the Aryan race and speak the Dogri language, a mixture of Sanskrit, Punjabi and Persian, whose origin goes back to the Indo-Aryan branch of Sanskrit.' He also mentioned that Dogri people are fond of singing folk songs and are passionate about their art, culture and food.

From here, Dr. Raina took the lead and explained, 'For Dogri people life is a struggle because of the weather and the topography but food is a means of celebration. Dogri cuisine is a perfect blend of *satvik* (class of foods that are fresh, juicy, nourishing and gives necessary energy to the body to achieve balance) and *rajsic* (class of foods that are bitter, sour, salty, pungent, hot, or dry, and are thought to promote sensuality, greed, jealousy, anger, delusion, and irreligious feelings) qualities as mentioned in ancient scriptures. It purifies, nourishes and is beneficial to the body and helps in the evolution of higher senses.' The beauty of the cuisine is in the preparation, combination and the sauté procedures that are followed. The food is not extravagant and is perfect for digestion because of certain spices and the ingredients used.

Dr. Raina had already prepared a lot of food and made me taste six different dishes. First was the popular *madra* (pulses cooked with yoghurt and garnished with dried milk and dry fruits). **Maa Ka Madra** is a delicacy relished by the Dogri community on festive occasions. With that there was *anardana* chutney (raw pomegranate seed relish). *Anardana* is a speciality of Jammu, as they grow only in hilly areas, in the wild. The seeds are dried and sold in the market. As a community, the Dogris are also fond of relishing sweet, sour and tangy tastes all in one go, which is present in their *auriya*, a dish of yoghurt and potatoes, spiced and fermented with rye. Another dish, called *ambal*, was made of pumpkin, jaggery and tamarind. This sounded super yum and I thought would perfectly complement a *puri* (unleavened deep-fried Indian bread). The fifth dish was *khatta meat*, a preparation of goat meat curry cooked with sour pomegranate seeds and lime juice. Lastly, there were the breads and rice, which included *mitha path* (sweet anise-flavoured rice cooked in *ghee*) and *thothrus* (lightweight fried balloon-shaped breads).

MAA KA MADRA
(Pulses cooked in a yoghurt gravy.)

Ingredients

2 cups black gram *(urad dal)*, soaked overnight and half
   boiled
1 black cardamom *(badi elaichi)*
4-5 cloves *(laung)*
8-10 black peppercorns *(sabut kali mirch)*
1 inch cinnamon *(dalchini)* + 1 inch for tempering
1 tbsp rice flour
2 tbsp mustard *(sarson)* oil
1 tsp cumin *(jeera)* seeds
A pinch of asafoetida *(hing)*
1 tbsp coriander *(dhania)* powder
¼ tsp turmeric *(haldi)* powder
1 tsp chilli powder
Salt to taste
1 cup water
1 cup yoghurt
2 tbsp clarified butter *(ghee)*
¼ cup dry fruits
Coriander leaves *(dhania patti)*, chopped

Method

1. Soak black gram overnight and pressure cook it
    with little salt and one and half cups of water until
    almost cooked.
2. Remove the seeds from the cardamom and discard
    the shell.

3. Grind together cardamom seeds, cloves, black peppercorns and one cinnamon stick. Break the other cinnamon stick into small pieces.
4. Mix rice flour with one cup of water and keep aside.
5. Heat mustard oil in a saucepan and add cumin. When the cumin seeds turn light brown, add asafoetida and fry it for few seconds.
6. Add the fresh masala powder we made, cinnamon pieces, coriander powder, turmeric powder and fry for few seconds.
7. Add cooked black gram, chilli powder, and salt. Mix properly and fry for two to three minutes until spices coat the gram.
8. Turn the heat to low, gradually add beaten yoghurt while stirring and continue doing so until the yoghurt mixes well. Keep stirring and cooking the mixture to save it from curdling.
9. Add rice flour mixture with *ghee* when the yoghurt thickens and starts leaving oil. Once it comes to a boil, cook for three to four minutes on low flame, until the gram is fully cooked and reaches the right consistency. Add roasted or fried dry fruits.
10. Garnish with coriander and serve hot with *roti* or rice.

~

So many dishes were on the agenda that day that there was no way that I wasn't helping them. Also, it was a massive learning experience for any chef. While preparing the *ambal*, I saw that they used a very interesting technique called *dhuni*, in which mustard oil is poured on a hot burning charcoal and put into the utensil containing the freshly prepared dish, which lends the dish a smoky aroma. Dr. Raina further explained that the Dogris were fond of community feasts known as *dhams* which were organised on various ceremonies. They were mostly vegetarian dishes made in a *dham* and then served on plates made from broad leaves of a tree, most commonly, Banyan tree leaves. Also, all these meals are incomplete without the tasty pickles that they locally make. After two hours of hard work, I had earned my meal and it was time to eat. For lunch, Dr. Raina's mother and wife joined us as well. It was a fabulous sight to see the whole family eat together with me and I was asked to eat with my hands.

It was a colourful meal; all dishes had a distinct colour, texture, aroma and presentation. The *ambal* was one of the best pumpkin dishes I had ever had. It was packed with flavours; the tanginess of tamarind blended well with the pumpkin and the smoky taste took it to another level. The *thothrus* were so light that one person could have 10 of them and still eat a couple more.

The meal was finger-licking good. A cuisine I'd never even heard of blew me away, it proved that no amount of learning is enough; there is always room to explore and learn more as you travel. It also made me think that there had to be someone responsible to make such near-extinct cuisines popular all across India. It was time to move on to my next destination, which was a sweet shop. For the same reason, we had requested Dr. Raina to not prepare any desserts. We thanked him for sharing all his passion and knowledge of Dogri cuisine with us, and we drove off to Pahalwan Di Hatti.

Pahalwan Di Hatti is located in the Old Heritage city and was opened in 1934 by Nanto Shah. It is one of the iconic landmarks for visiting famous politicians and celebrities. Most people believe it is the quality of milk used in making desserts that stands out. It is also a shop which is visited by a lot of youngsters and they love the chocolate *burfi* (an Indian sweet made from milk solids and sugar and typically flavoured with cardamom or nuts) here, which sells like hot cakes. The other popular dessert is the *sund panjeeri*, loaded with good quality and quantity of dry fruits. I ended up eating four pieces of the chocolate *burfi* despite it being a bit high on the sweetness quotient; the taste of chocolate was coming through. The next day's journey would be a long one, from Jammu to Punjab, and hence, after the sweets, we called it a day.

Day 22
27 August / Gurdaspur

I hadn't shaved for 23 days at a stretch. I was now getting used to the thick stubble, though it made my face look a bit untidy and frankly, I looked a lot older too. We were about to reach IHM Gurdaspur, Punjab, after a long journey to meet the new generation chefs and inspire them to do crazy things in life. A dear chef friend, Aarti Thapa, a senior faculty at the college, welcomed us to share our travel stories and experiences with the students. It was a great interactive session, which was followed by an internal cooking competition organised by the college. Amidst all this, having been an IHM student in the past myself, it reminded me of how strict we were with grooming standards, so I chose to shave my beard off and it felt like shaving off memories. Those 15 minutes I spent in front of the mirror were great to reflect back on what all I'd learnt in the past three weeks. After this small breather and an inspirational trip to IHM, I felt rejuvenated and I was ready to move further into Punjab and experience some authentic drool-worthy food.

DAY 23
28 August / Amritsar

The land of five rivers, lush green fields and people with big hearts, is how I would sum up Punjab. I was back to my schedule of rising early morning; this day was going to be exciting as we were headed somewhere unusual. The destination was Attari village in the Amritsar district of Punjab, three kilometres away from the Indo-Pakistan border at Wagah. It is situated 25 km west of Amritsar and is the last Indian station on the rail route connecting Lahore, Pakistan, with Delhi.

Punjab has one of the most fertile lands in India and same is the case with Attari. The speciality of this village is that a lot of rice is grown here. The merit of being a traveller who loves to talk and socialise is that you find good people who not only feed you good food but they also make you a part of their family. To be my kind of a traveller you have to be a bit shameless and greedy, that's the only way you get the real deal. So my objectives were very clear; I had to climb on the tractor, visit the fields, eat yummy earthy food. My producer had found a family of farmers who were ready to host us for the day and also happy to educate me about their life.

Farmers who were well off had simple but well spread out houses next to their farms. They generally lived in big joint families and milked their own cows in their backyard. So I was going to spend the whole day with Harpreet Singh and his family. Harpreet was an educated farmer and belonged to the new generation and believed in making a change in the way they cultivated rice. As I entered their house there was that earthy, rustic fragrance in the air. The porch was spacious, as big as a two BHK in Mumbai; here I was greeted by more than half a dozen men sitting on a wire cot, called *charpai*. One of them was his father who was wearing a blue coloured turban and was the head of the village. He was a highly respected man known for keeping his word and giving valuable suggestions for the development of their community. They all gave me a hearty hug and welcomed me in traditional Punjabi style with a glass of *lassi* (yoghurt-based drink) and *kheer*. They immediately asked Harpreet to give me a tour of the fields to make me understand how they irrigated their fields through a tube well.

As I went through these huge rice growing farms, or more commonly known as paddy fields, the idea of living in boxed cities suddenly felt claustrophobic to me. There was a huge tube well right in the centre, which was used to send water to the entire field. There were ways paved out for the water to flow in a certain direction. Harpreet, without hesitation, asked 'Do you want to take a bath from this tube well? We do it all the time and the water is chilled and clean.' Now, that was the best shower that I have ever had! Trust me, the force of water was fit for an elephant to take a bath in, and yes, the water was crystal clear. After the bath, I changed out of my city clothes and opted for a simple village style vest and *dhoti* (garment worn by an Indian male, akin to a skirt, consisting of a piece of material tied around the waist and extending to cover most of the legs) with an orange turban. It was time now to climb a tractor and ride back to the house for the real deal: food. The tractor ride was as fun as it could be; I felt like Sunny Deol from one of his movies! It was already late afternoon, so I decided to take an afternoon siesta on the *charpai* outside in the porch before the big party in the evening.

In the evening, the porch was full of hearty laughs as we discussed food, life, religion and India. Harpreet had promised that the dinner would not be any ordinary one; it was a local feast prepared by the ladies of the house. Every single dish was cooked on slow flame, lit by wood and dry dung. What was on the menu? *Sarson ka saag*, *matar paneer*, chicken curry, *boondi raita*, *dal jeera*, *meethe chawal*, *parantha*s and *makai roti*. As they had done so much, the least I could do was teach Harpreet how to make a *parantha*, as his mother complained that he did not know how to cook at all. I taught him how to make a *chana dal parantha*, as he wanted to learn something healthier. To top it all, Harpreet had planned a surprise Bhangra party. Around 50 villagers came together and there was a huge bonfire that was lit. We sat around it with our plates filled with food and hearts filled with happiness. No hotel food would ever come close to this meal. Every bite I ate, I wanted to shake my head and look at the camera and give a 'Nigella' kind of expression. This was real Indian food, no fuss, filled with pure spices, *ghee*, vegetables and love.

I learnt my lesson that slow-cooking is a technique that makes a world of difference to any dish you cook, it helps the dish retain its nutrients and makes it tastier. With a full-hearted meal, drinks and dance, the day came to an end and I bid goodbye to everyone with a heavy heart. I had earned a friend for life: Harpreet. One tip: the next time you travel, look for people in the interiors of the city, and they'll give you a day to cherish for the rest of your life!

Day 24
29 August / Ludhiana

'*Sat sri akal. Ki haal chal?*' is the way you greet in Punjab and ask, 'Hi, how're you?' with respect. Now that I was in Punjab I had picked up a few Punjabi words. Besides the lush fields of Punjab, the state is unanimous with its big road-side *dhabas*.

I was in Ludhiana, one of the richest cities in Punjab. A year back someone had given away 50 BMWs as wedding return gifts to his closest friend and relatives. The real objective for me was to try a *dhaba* or two for their famous *rara* chicken; it would have been unfair had I not tried good chicken dishes after coming all the way to Punjab, wouldn't it? Apparently, the best *dhaba* serving excellent *rara* chicken in Ludhiana was Aman Chicken. Manpreet, the owner's son, explained, 'Aman Chicken is about 30-years-old now; it was established in 1985. Our speciality is *rara* chicken. There's an endless list of chicken dishes. If you'll read about our restaurant on the internet, it'll tell you that our butter *naan* (a type of leavened bread, typically of teardrop shape and traditionally cooked in a clay oven) is very famous. We wrap it with a special white butter and cream.'

I could already envision myself gaining at least three to four kilograms from today's meal. Soon, I was in the kitchen and I met the tandoor specialist who revealed the secret behind the butter *naan*, 'Make the *naan*. Spread dollops of butter, and then fold it like a handkerchief and put more butter from the top.' They were very hush-hush about the *rara* chicken recipe and I was sure they wouldn't give it away. Nonetheless, they were doing so much for me that it would have been unfair to not showcase some of my own culinary skills to them. With help from their tandoor specialist I invented a new dish called **Balle Balle Chicken**. It used chicken *tikka* (Indian dish of small pieces of meat or vegetables marinated in a spice mixture and grilled) as a base, which was wrapped with a thin *roti* and the corners were pinched so that the chicken stayed inside the roll. Then, it was covered with a tandoori marinade and grilled in the tandoor. It came out perfectly cooked in a beautiful colour. 'Trust me, you'll do a *balle balle* dance step once you try it!' owner Manpreet said as he took a big bite.

BALLE BALLE CHICKEN
(Charcoaled chicken stuffed inside a bread roll.)

Ingredients

½-inch pieces or 500 gm boneless chicken breasts, *tikka* cut
¾ cup or 6 tbsp thick yoghurt
1½ tsp red chilli paste
2 tbsp ginger-garlic *(adrak-lasun)* paste
¼ tsp turmeric *(haldi)* powder
½ tsp garam masala powder
1 tsp coriander *(dhania)* powder
1 whole lemon, juiced
½ tsp sugar
1 tbsp mustard *(sarson)* oil

Salt to taste
2½ cups refined flour *(maida)*
¾ cup water, to knead
1 tbsp butter

Method

1. Marinate the chicken pieces with a marinade prepared by mixing thick yoghurt, red chilli paste, ginger-garlic paste, turmeric, garam masala powder, coriander powder, lemon juice, sugar, mustard oil, and salt together.

2. Keep only two tablespoons of the marinade aside for later use.

3. Keep the marinated chicken *tikka* in the fridge for at least two hours.

4. Meanwhile, prepare the dough with *maida*, butter, salt and water. Make soft dough just like you would make for *rotis*.

5. Preheat the oven/electric tandoor/BBQ. Mix one tablespoon *maida* to the chicken *tikka* marinade that had been kept aside. Now put only two chicken pieces in each skewer or shashlik sticks. Cook this for seven to eight minutes in the oven on high heat (220°C) until it is 80 per cent cooked and has a slightly charred appearance.

6. While the chicken is cooking, roll out small round *rotis* from the dough.

7. Now wrap this *roti* around both the chicken *tikkas* (that are 80 per cent cooked) on one skewer. Pinch

the ends (basically, you're enveloping the chicken with the dough). Brush little leftover marinade on this outer cover. Repeat this for all the *tikka*s.

8. Put these back in the oven for two to three minutes. Keep rotating to ensure that the outer layer is cooked evenly and gets a nice colour.

9. Gently pull these out from the skewers, in similar fashion in which you would take out *tikka*s.

10. *Balle Balle* Chicken is ready! Now you can dunk these in chutney and enjoy with your drinks. (This recipe may look tough but when you pull it off, you'll be glad!)

~

After the cooking was done, I moved on to explore the Chaura Bazaar of Ludhiana. One is sure to get something or the other to eat at every corner of this popular street; be it the famous Amritsari *dal ki wadiya* or the *dal chaat*. Panditji di Hatti is where you would get special *parantha*s. It was a small shop with 10-12 seats and all *parantha*s were being made only on the griddle, no tandoor at all. Pandit*ji* explained, 'We make it with butter. We have *parantha*s stuffed with potato, onion, cauliflower mixed with roasted carom seed masala (*ajwain* masala) and they are all cooked only on a griddle.' I ordered my favourite, the *aloo-pyaaz* (potato-onion) one. And as I took a bite, the flavour of onions and its crispiness satiated me. The combination of potato and onions was also superb. I must admit that the secret of Pandit*ji*'s *parantha*s was in his kitchen. As I had mentioned, there was no tandoor, all *paranthas* were made on the *tawa*, there were eight *tawas* in one line to help bring out the orders speedily, as a *tawa* makes the process slower because *paranthas* take time to cook on a *tawa* in comparison to a tandoor. Pandit*ji* shook my hand, charged me no money, and said, 'Son, there is no other secret to cooking; it is God's grace and your love to feed people.'

DAY 25
30 August / Ludhiana

After such excessive culinary binges for the last few days, it seemed like a good idea to start the day with some physical exercise. Today's agenda was to learn about Gatka, a traditional South Asian form of combat-training in which wooden sticks are used to simulate swords in sparring matches. The terms Gatka and Shastra Vidya are often used specifically in relation to Punjabi-Sikhs. However, the art is not unique to any particular ethno-cultural group or religion but has been the traditional form of combat throughout North India and Pakistan for centuries. Attacks and counter-attacks vary from one community to another, but the basic techniques are the same.

Harmandeep, the teacher of this particular Gatka group that we met, explained, 'We have been doing it since childhood. It is not a game and is usually meant to be done in the battleground. It is specially practiced in Punjab, because this is considered the land of the Gurus.' It was mesmerising to see young students perform; their movements were swift, they could use all sorts of defensive weapons and had an enviable amount of energy. Gatka involves the mind, body and soul; you have to be physically, emotionally and spiritually strong. Like most Asian martial arts, Gatka begins with footwork and tactical body positioning (*pentra*). To make it more rhythmic and to keep up the energy levels, a *dhol* (drum) is played continuously. The weapons used are called *shastra*. There were many, like swords, sticks, shields, polearms but the sharpest was the *kirpan*.

I loved the dedication these kids had and wanted to cook something sweet and special for them. So, I decided to cook **Mishri Halwa** (*mishri* means crystallised sugar lumps) for them. The kids loved it, I learnt a lot and now it was time for me to bid farewell and climb into the waiting Limousine. (Yes, a Limo! Someone in Ludhiana heard I was visiting and had generously offered a Limousine as my ride until I reached Chandigarh. WOW!)

MISHRI HALWA
(Sweet wheat flour pudding cooked with crystallised sugar lumps.)

Ingredients

¼ cup clarified butter *(ghee)*
½ cup wheat flour *(atta)*
½ cup water
Mishri, according to taste
A pinch of cardamom *(elaichi)* powder
1 tbsp almond flakes

Method

1. In a wok, heat the *ghee*.
2. Add the wheat flour and fry over medium flame till the flour gives out a nice aroma.
3. Add water and keep stirring to avoid lump formation. Cook for seven to eight minutes on low flame.

4.   Add *mishri*, almond flakes and stir well.
5.   After the flour is nicely cooked and the *ghee* starts leaving the sides, add the *elaichi* powder and switch off the gas.
6.   Top with some more almond flakes and serve hot. Ensure not all *mishri* has melted away as it adds to the texture of the dish when you bite into it.

~

After almost four weeks of bumpy rides, my entire back and body, head to toe, was sore and this Limousine ride was what I surely deserved. It was my first time in such a super luxury car and the first thought that crossed my mind on seeing it was that it was big enough for three people to comfortably sleep inside. The bar in the Limo was open for me but I preferred the good old Punjabi *lassi* to keep me company on my two-hour drive to Chandigarh. God bless Mr. Prabhjot for arranging that luxurious Limo for me!

The launch of
Roti Rasta aur India with
Chef Sanjeev Kapoor
and Himanshu Joshi,
band member of the group
Indian Ocean, in
New Delhi

One of the
pchalwans in a
Karnal *akhada*
revealing the
benefits of having
almond milk

A simple *arhar ki dal*
can be tasty when
made in a new setting;
cooking lunch
with truck drivers on
the Karnal Highway

Cooking 200 kgs of *dal*, at a go for the *langar* at Gurudwara Anandpur Sahib

Learning how to brew green tea with Himalayan tulsi and pomegranate flower, from tea aficionado Anamika, Dharamshala

Relaxing before I reach Andretta village

Ghee rajma, siddu, bhalle, kaathu, and *jaatu* rice: typical dishes of the Kullu region

With Karam Singh and his wife, who served me the above meal at their village home, Kullu

Making my version of Maggi at its namesake shop, Manali

Making my own good luck stupa after Rohtang Pass

Jumping with happiness on finally reaching Leh

This Ladakhi aunty liked the way I said *Julle'*, meaning 'hello', while I bought local spices from her; the dried yak cheese and sun-dried tomatoes caught my attention

A kayaking champion, Neema took me inside his grandmother's kitchen, where she made *thukpa* for us, Ladakh

Afternoon with the students at Mahabodhi after a cup of *gud-gud chai* or butter tea

Prayer flags at the Mahabodhi, Ladakh

My moment of truth: life lessons from Tibetan guru Bhikkhu Sanhasena, Ladakh

Taking it easy after a sumptuous *wazwan* experience; reading beside the Dal Lake, Srinagar

Vegetable shopping at 5 am in the floating market, Srinagar

Sorting kilos of saffron before using it to make fruit cream, Srinagar

Harpreet (to my right), taught me to ride a tractor, before taking me to his farm where his mom made delicious *sarson ka saag*, Amritsar

After the flaming hot *mirchi vada*, it was time I made chocolate-cashew *laddu*s, wearing a traditional *pagdi*, Udaipur

Posing against a salt mountain, little Rann of Kutch

Learning *moong wadi*s from Jasodha *behen* in Mahila Ashram, Ahmedabad

Sipping Chenin Blanc with Ajoy Shaw, Chief Winemaker, at Sula Vineyards, Nasik

Tired of cars! A new way to ride to Goa where I was waiting to have local delicacies like *xacuti*, *bebenca*, vindaloo and prawn balchao

Peace and prayers in Krishna Matha, Udupi

In the houseboat, waiting to have some authentic Kerala cuisine like *thoran* and *avial*, in the backwaters, Allappuzha

Making filter coffee in the street, Allappuzha

A day with Saji, the friendliest elephant in Munnar

Reddy House is part of
the French quarters, where
local cafés serve yummy
Meditterranean cuisine,
Puducherry

Offering blueberry *peda*s to
ISKCON pandits, Bengaluru

In a contemplative mood
atop Tamatar, our car,
waiting to be taken to the
local fish market at the
harbour, Vishakhapatnam

Decoding the secret of the tasty Nagpur oranges

A traditional *rizala* with Chandu Bhai (extreme right) and his family, Bhopal

Jai ho! Time for some Raas Lila, Mathura

Learning the art of making *sheermal*, Lucknow

In my Eid outfit, trying to impress the nawabs with my *dal sultani*, Lucknow

Mouth-watering *aloo bedmi*s of Varanasi

On my way for an evening *aarti*, I was thinking how to make *kuliya ki chaat* on the boat next morning and getting it filmed, Varanasi

My *halwai* avatar: shaping my own 'Maner *ka laddu*', Patna

Cholar dal, shukto, potol bhaja, luchi and rice: a true-blue Bengali meal, Kolkata

Eating *khapse, zhedro* and *thukpa* at a traditional Sikkimese wedding

My rugged look after 90 days of travel all over India, en route to Assam, where I would meet *outenga*

Cooking with a bamboo hollow, with Chef Lahakar, Guwahati

Hundred days on the road were rounded off by mom's Sindhi *kadhi* recipe, Delhi

Nothing to beat the famous *Dilli ki Chaat*

Celebrating Diwali at home after 100 days of Bharat *darshan*

Day 26
31 August / Chandigarh

Chandigarh was the dream city of India's first Prime Minister, Pandit Jawahar Lal Nehru, and was planned by the famous French architect Le Corbusier. Picturesquely located at the foothills of the Shivaliks, it is one of the best experiments in urban planning and modern architecture in twentieth century India. Chandigarh derives its name from the temple of Chandi Mandir, dedicated to the deity Chandi, which is located close to the city.

Apart from the love I have for the city for being extremely spacious and beautiful, I have another close connection with it; it is my best friend from college, Kanwardeep Singh Ahluwalia's home town. Unfortunately, when I was there, he was busy working in Bangalore. However, his father is famous in Chandigarh for his superb pickles and had graciously agreed to have me over and give me a lesson or two in making them. When we had had *parantha*s at Gulshan Dhaba in Murthal and at Pandit*ji*'s in Ludhiana, we realised that a *parantha* is incomplete without a pickle. So we were all eager to have a go at it at uncle's house.

Kanwardeep's father, Mr. Rupinder Jeet Singh, was a man of many passions. He loved cooking, travelling and flowers. He had already travelled most of India by car and his knowledge about the country was extensive. After having a long chat with him about India and his experiences on the road, it was time to enter the kitchen. He had already displayed 10 different types of pickles, in front of me, that he had prepared for the summer. It was fascinating to see pickles made out of chickpeas, mango, yam, chicken, bitter gourd *(karela)*, glue berry *(lasoda)*, turnips, radish, carrots, and drumsticks *(sehjan ki phali)*. In a good year, uncle would prepare at least 50 varieties of pickles.

When I asked him where he learnt this art from, he replied, 'No one has really taught me, I loved pickles and I followed my instinct to develop all these recipes.' To increase the longevity of most pickles, he sun-dried the vegetables with salt and lemon and then fried them before pickling, especially in the case of yams and bitter gourd. As promised, uncle was now ready to teach me one of his favourite recipes, the **Bitter Gourd *(Karela)* Pickle**. It was very interesting to observe how organically the ingredients were treated and pickled and also how the blend of spices varied for each pickle. After this visit, I surely had new secrets in my 'chef's arsenal' to pickle my food. I touched uncle's feet, asked for his blessings, and headed for the second leg of my journey to the western part of India.

BITTER GOURD *(KARELA)* PICKLE
(Pickled and spiced bitter gourd.)

Ingredients

500 gm small bitter gourd *(karela)*
A pinch of asafoetida *(hing)*
2 tsp cumin *(jeera)* seeds
3 tsp fenugreek *(methi)* seeds
3 tsp fennel *(saunf)* seeds
½ tsp dried mango powder *(amchoor)*
½ tsp turmeric *(haldi)* powder
1 tsp red chilli powder

1 tsp black salt *(kaala namak)*
3 tsp plain salt (approximately)
1 cup mustard oil

Method

1. Clean the bitter gourds. Remove stems and chop them in half.
2. Rub these pieces of bitter gourds with salt and keep aside for an hour in a utensil. They release the bitter water; strain these gourds. Now pat dry them or let them sun dry for two to three hours. Deep fry these bitter gourds for seven to eight minutes.
3. On the side, in another vessel, dry roast the asafoetida, cumin, fenugreek and fennel till they slightly change colour. Grind these spices to a coarse powder (do not make a fine powder).
4. Now add these coarsely ground spices, the dried mango powder, turmeric, chilli powder, and black salt to the fried bitter gourds. Mix well.
5. Add smoked mustard oil (not warm) to this mixture. Do a final stir. Check salt.
6. Fill a glass or plastic container with the bitter gourd and mustard oil mix. Stir the pickle every day for the next two to three days. It has a long shelf life if you add enough mustard oil to cover the pickle.

DAY 27

It was time to leave the well-planned urban setting of Chandigarh. I left for the Pink City, Jaipur.

DAY 28
2 September / Jaipur

Monsoon had struck and it was time for some rains in this dry part of the country. For some, rains were a thing of beauty, while for others, it just meant traffic and inconvenience. We experienced the rains in Rajasthan and Gujarat. It was an absolute pleasure to drive on the highways through these states. I requested the driver to park our car, Tamatar, beneath the orange sky, plugged in my iPod and watched the sunset. The pleasure of experiencing nature's bounty, sometimes, cannot be described in words.

It took us an entire day to cover the distance of 450 km between Chandigarh and Jaipur. It was in Jaipur that I had the good fortune of meeting Gulabo Sapera known worldwide for her snake-charming dance form called Kalbeliya. She made me realise that life is all about doing bigger and better things. She was born and brought up in a family of snake charmers in a small village in Rajasthan, but today, she had her own dance school where Kalbeliya was taught. She also had a primary school on the anvil that educated girls who never got the opportunity earlier to see the world outside their homes. And as if that wasn't enough, she was also one of the few people responsible for putting Kalbeliya dance on the world map. After having a long chat with her, it was my luck that I got to perform one dance sequence along with her team in their traditional black dress. Next time you visit Jaipur, make sure you attend one of her performances.

This meeting happened on a scenic setting in a temple that was located on a small hilltop overlooking a lush green valley. The temple had an open kitchen and Gulaboji had kept a *chullah* (wood-lit stove) ready for some food to be made. She surprised me by cooking *bajre ki roti* (flatbread made of pearl millet) and **Tomato Garlic Chutney** for me. To thank her, I requested her to allow me to cook for her as well. I quickly churned up a dish called *gulabo mirchi* (Rajasthani chillies stuffed with cottage cheese and garnished with rose petals).

Tomato Garlic Chutney
(A local spicy dip made from tomatoes.)

Ingredients

2 tbsp clarified butter *(desi ghee)*
1 tsp cumin *(jeera)* seeds
½ tsp mustard *(sarson)* seeds
A pinch of asafoetida *(hing)*
4 big and thick green chillies, deseeded and chopped
12-15 garlic *(lasun)* cloves
2 onions, finely chopped
¼ tsp turmeric *(haldi)* powder
2 tsp coriander *(dhania)* powder
½ tsp red chilli powder
½ tsp garam masala powder
5-6 medium-sized tomatoes, finely chopped
Salt to taste
2 tbsp fresh coriander leaves *(dhania patti)*, chopped

Method

1. Heat the *ghee* in a pan. Add cumin seeds and mustard seeds and when they begin to change colour, add asafoetida, green chillies and garlic and sauté for a minute.
2. Add onions and sauté till they are translucent.
3. Mix turmeric powder, coriander powder, red chilli powder and garam masala powder in one fourth cup of water and add. Sauté for two minutes.
4. Add the tomatoes and salt. Mix well. Reduce heat to low once the mixture comes to a boil and cook for 10-15 minutes.
5. Garnish with coriander leaves and serve hot.

~

Each bite into that *bajre ki roti* made me smell the flavours of Rajasthan. Technically, it is very difficult to make this *roti* as you cannot knead the dough too well because of the rough texture and the low gluten content that the grain has. It is almost impossible to roll out the dough into a round shape with the help of a rolling pin; you have to shape it with your own hands. It was very clear that Gulabo*ji* was an expert at making these *roti*s. The tomato garlic chutney, made strictly in *ghee*, was an icing on the cake. After this unforgettable meal, and the lovely inspiring story of Gulabo Sapera, it was time to move on, to be back on the road and experience different sunsets through different eyes.

DAY 29
3 September / Jaipur

Rajasthan has a unique relationship with its palaces. The Hawa Mahal or the Palace of Winds is made of pink sandstone. Built in 1799, the front elevation, as seen from the street, is like a honeycomb web of a beehive. The design takes the form of the crown of Lord Krishna, the Hindu God.

I made my way to Rawat Mishtaan Bhandaar near Sindhi Camp, a culinary hotspot in its own right. The famous *aloo-pyaaz kachori* (flaky, crisp deep-fried pastry filled with spiced potatoes and onions) was invented here, almost 150 years ago. I met the third generation of the Deora family, the owner of this famous eatery. He greeted me warmly and spoke passionately about his family's culinary legacy. The *aloo-pyaaz kachori* was made of, what he called, 'Jodhpuri spices' that included chillies, garlic, coriander, nutmeg and mace. The vegetables and spices used were grown on a field owned by the family. The produce came straight to the famous sweet shop to be used to make fresh *kachori*s.

I mingled with people eating there. Everyone was aware of how legendary the food was. They offered me food from their plates, things they thought I must try and some of which were their favourite food. Here, I came across the *mithi mawa kachori* (flaky, crisp deep-fried pastry filled with condensed milk). It was drenched in sugar syrup. I opened the *kachori* to reveal the soft crumbly filling made of *khoya* (dried whole milk solids). What I wasn't expecting was the curious combination of crushed peanut and the onion seed *(kalonji)*, a subtle twist to an ordinary plot. Interestingly enough, I also tasted my first sweet *samosa* (a triangular savoury fried pastry, usually with a filling inside)!

As always, I found my way to their kitchen. There, I met the men behind the magic. Three men sat cross-legged, together on a raised platform, shaping and filling the *kachoris*, preparing them to be fried into the crisp golden pastries. They too stressed on the fact that all the produce was grown by them and it was processed on the premises. They took a moment to show me how to fill and fold the *kachoris*. The rhythm with which their hands moved was definitely the key to the perfect shapes. Speaking of shapes, the *kachori* resembled a stuffed *parantha*, before it was rolled out into a flat plate-like shape.

I took my leave with yet another unique food memory. The afternoon was spent with a royal couple from the Bisau family. Eklavya and Natasha met me in the lawns of their palace and showed me how to make *dahi samosa maas* and dishes typical of Jaipur and the royal cuisine of their household. A very interesting preparation, *dahi samosa maas* was a complex mix of two very separate specialities of the region, *laal maas* and *keema samosa*. In case you are wondering, *laal maas* is a mutton curry, blood red in colour, because of the liberal use of red chillies. I also ate the *gatte ki sabzi*, a steamed chickpea dumpling coated in a light yoghurt-based curry. We dined in the Bisau family palace, which is now a full-fledged hotel, open to the public.

DAY 30

From the Pink City, I made my way to Udaipur.

Day 31
5 September / Udaipur

The 420 km from Jaipur to Udaipur was very pleasant. The journey on the highway was smooth and the arrival of the monsoon made the experience very enjoyable. I arrived in the City of Lakes to taste the famous *mirchi vada* (chilli cutlet) at Jayesh Mishthaan Bhandaar. Besides their famous snack, their *samosas* and *kachoris* were also very popular. I met Sanjay Bajaj who explained that even though the principal ingredient in the *mirchi vada* was a chilli, the *mirch* wasn't as spicy as one would assume. They were almost like jalapenos. These chillies were fat and bright green. The process involved deseeding them and then stuffing them with a potato mixture, similar to that of the Jaipur *kachoris* that I had mentioned previously. The only difference was the *amchoor* chutney (a spicy condiment similar to a dip made with dry mango powder) mixed into the filling. The chilli was then deep fried with a thick gram flour batter. The hot crispy *mirchi vada* was served with sweet and spicy chutney made of coriander and tamarind. Sold at a modest price of Rs. 20, it was a common breakfast item, popular amongst the residents of Chetak Circle, named after the famous battle horse of Maharana Pratap. I had come to realise that the quality of spices used in this region was exceptional. In fact, when in Udaipur, I suggest stocking up on local spices; hence, a short visit to the Dhan Mandi is a must.

The real reason I had decided to visit Udaipur was to experience the Fatehgarh Fort. Perched on top of a hill, just 20 minutes from outside Udaipur city, it is a very recent addition to the heritage hotel circuit, but surprisingly looks older than it really is. Mr. Jitender Singh Rathore, a member of the royal family of Kelwa, manages the fort. It boasts of a 360° panoramic view of the Aravallis. Before I go on to narrate my experience with the royals, I have to mention my meeting with the grandmaster of *pagdi* (Rajasthani turban) making, Mr. Mahinder Singh Parihar. He welcomed me with the traditional Rajasthani greeting, '*Khamma ghani sa*,' meaning hello. He had specially made a *pagdi* for me with the colours of the Indian flag, which I was going to wear to my royal dinner in the evening. Interestingly, he holds the record of making the longest *pagdi* in the world, with the cloth measuring half a kilometre in length.

Soon, it was evening and I felt lucky enough to be dining with the descendants of the Kelwa lineage. The dinner was at the fort which was made of antique stone and architectural elements that had been taken from abandoned buildings. I was served a Royal Mewar *thali*. As a general rule, Mewari cuisine focuses on fresh vegetables, mostly maize and its by products. Their dishes are originally slow-cooked on beds of coal. Amongst all the dishes that I had, the memorable one was the *ker sangri sabzi*: a subtle mix of dried berries and beans cooked in Mewar spices. This was followed by *maas ka sula*, a type of barbequed meat. A special vegetarian dish called *khada palak* was served. It had baby spinach leaves stir-fried with whole garlic, cumin and red chillies; this dish was rustic as well as delicate in taste. My favourite was the *gulab ki kheer* made of fresh rose petals, dry fruit and milk.

My contribution to this grand meal was the **Chocolate-Cashew** *Laddu*. Mewari cuisine uses a lot of dry fruits in their dessert and so does this *laddu* (Indian sweet made from a mixture of flour, sugar, and shortening, which is shaped into a ball). It was my chance to experiment and cook on the roof top of this gorgeous fort overlooking the city. This meal marked the end of my journey in Rajasthan. Whether it was *gulabo mirchi* or *gulab ki kheer*, Rajasthan was truly multi-coloured in every sense of the term.

CHOCOLATE-CASHEW *LADDU*
(Sweet cashew nut and chocolate balls.)

Ingredients

2 cups cashew nuts *(kajus)*
2 tsp rose water
3 tbsp water
¾ cup sugar
¼ tsp cardamom *(elaichi)* powder
8-10 strands saffron *(kesar)*
¼ cup clarified butter *(ghee)*, melted
1 cup dark chocolate nibs or grated dark chocolate

Method

1. Dry roast the cashew nuts for two minutes and allow them to cool.

2. In the mixer, make a coarse powder out of the cashew nuts.

3. Heat a pan, add the rose water, water and then sugar.

4. When the sugar melts and it reaches a string-like consistency and bubbles rise, it is ready. If the sugar syrup becomes too thick, add a bit of water to thin it down or the cashew nuts won't mix properly.

5. Then add cardamom powder, saffron, cashew powder and *ghee*. Mix thoroughly in the sugar syrup.

6. Switch off the gas. Let the preparation sit for 10 minutes.

7. Apply *ghee* on your palm and while the mixture is still warm make small balls.

8. Now coat these with chocolate nibs or shavings. Put this in the fridge for five minutes.

9. Once cooled, the *laddu*s are ready to be binged on.

Day 32

Today, I would be travelling from one end of the Thar desert to another end: the Rann of Kutch.

DAY 33
7 September / Dasada, Rann of Kutch

After the spicy food of Rajasthan, it was time for the vibrancy of Gujarat. I was on my way to the Rann of Kutch. By now, I had travelled almost 5000 km. Every 100 km, I could see a change in India. By that average, I had already seen 50 different shades of India thus far. I knew Gujarat had something new in store for me. It is believed that if you haven't seen the Rann, you haven't seen anything. That was the reason I was headed for Dasada village. The Rann of Kutch is a seasonal salt marsh, located in the Thar Desert in the Kutch district of Gujarat, India, and the Sindh province of Pakistan. It is reputed to be the largest salt desert in the world.

I got the opportunity to stay at the Rann Riders Resort, designed to resemble the villages in Gujarat. The most popular attraction of Dasada is the safari trail, through the 'Indian Wild Ass Sanctuary' of the Little Rann of Kutch, that stretched over 5000 sq km. The day we reached, our agenda was to explore Kutchi Cuisine, so I set out to meet the chef of the resort. He explained that Kutchi food was very similar to the food of the Jain community. There are no root vegetables in their cuisine and they follow pure vegetarianism. A few of the extremely popular dishes are *bajra ka rotla*, and *khichdi*, a simple combination of rice and lentils, made fancy with the use of accompaniments like, jaggery, butter, and *papad*. My personal favourite was the tomato *sev sabzi*. It was made of tomato, cooked like a spicy compote, and garnished with fried shredded gram flour bits. Another interesting accompaniment to the main meal was the garlic chutney that was very spicy and pungent.

Day 34
8 September / Mandvi and Rajkot

I woke up early that morning to experience the Dasada Wildlife Sanctuary firsthand. I was being guided by Mr. Mozaid, who was also the owner of the resort where I was staying. It had been raining for the past few days, so the sanctuary was a bright shade of green. The air was crisp and I stood tall in my jeep as we drove through the park. The sanctuary is said to have 2100 animals and I had the good fortune of spotting the wild asses, Siberian cranes and blue bulls. Close to the sanctuary were the salt marshes with large white pyramids of salt. I took some in a small bag for myself as a memento; as I looked around I noticed how barren, yet astoundingly beautiful, it looked. For those visiting Gujarat, this place is a must, and has to be seen to be believed. Salt is prepared out of saline sea water and the entire area is a major contributor to the entire salt production of the country.

After the marshes, I headed 150 km south towards the coastline; the destination was Mandvi, known for its silver sand beaches and the Vijaya Vilas Palace. The crafts of Mandvi are famous all over the world. Tie and dye, commonly known as *bandhani*, originated here. A highly skilled procedure, the designs are outlined on the fabric and the cloth is dyed in various colours. Thereafter, ornaments like small mirrors and shells are added to the fabric. I couldn't resist buying one for my mother. In exchange for showing me all the wonderful cloth work,

I decided to make a fruit biryani (I named it **Kashmir Ki Kali**) for Ismail Chacha, the owner of the tie and dye shop, who graciously took me around and patiently explained and answered my queries.

KASHMIR KI KALI
(Flavoured rice cooked with fresh fruits.)

Ingredients

2 tbsp clarified butter *(ghee)*
1 tsp cumin *(jeera)* seeds
A pinch of asafoetida *(hing)*
2 tsp fennel seed *(saunf)*, coarsely powdered
½ green apple
½ red apple
1 slice pear
1 cup guava, chopped
3 tbsp yoghurt, beaten
2 tsp red chilli powder
½ tsp garam masala powder
1 tsp dry mango *(amchoor)* powder
1 cup basmati rice
1 cup milk
½ cup water
2 tbsp sugar
Few strands of saffron *(kesar)*
1-inch cinnamon stick *(dalchini)*
1 bay leaf *(tejpatta)*
4 slices sapodilla *(chikoo)*

½ cup pomegranate kernels
¼ tsp cardamom *(elaichi)* powder
Few drops of Panadanas syrup *(kewra* essence)
Salt to taste

Method

1. Heat the *ghee* and when it is hot, add the cumin seeds.
2. When the cumin changes colour, add the asafoetida, fennel seed powder, apples, pears and guava. Sauté.
3. Add beaten yoghurt, chilli powder, garam masala, dry mango powder to the mixture and sauté for three to four minutes. Add the rice (that has been soaked in water for 30 minutes).
4. Pour the milk and water. Add salt to taste and bring to a boil. Then lower the flame so that it simmers. Add the sugar, saffron, cinnamon and bayleaf.
5. Cover the lid and cook for 12-15 minutes.
6. Switch off the gas. Remove the lid, add the sapodilla, pomegranate and cardamom powder. Finish with the Panadanas syrup.
7. Open the biryani up after an hour or so and enjoy with pickles and *raita* (an Indian condiment of yoghurt containing chopped cucumber or other vegetables and spices).

~

One of the reasons I had decided to come to Mandvi was the *dabeli*, a Gujarati burger made with a distinct potato masala stuffed in a soft *pav* bun. Served with many chutneys—tamarind, date, garlic, red chillies—it is filled with pomegranates, roasted peanuts and *sev* (fried shredded gram flour bits). What sets *dabeli* apart is its masala consisting of a secret list of ingredients. Some of the ingredients are red chillies, cardamom, cumin, cinnamon, coriander and black salt. I would still prefer to buy it from a local store, rather than making this tedious recipe. The flavour is a winning combination of all the essential ones: salty, sweet, spicy and sour. It was invented way back in the 1960s, in Mandvi, and was at that time sold at the time for six paisa!

After a long drive, of nearly 400 km, we stopped at Chokhi Dhani in Piragarhi, 14 km from Rajkot. Here, I saw a Garba performance. Garba is a traditional dance form performed during the Navratras. The dance takes the formation of concentric circles, and it is heavily influenced by the Dandiya Raas, a dance in which women are beautifully dressed in ethnic outfits and jewellery. The songs usually revolve around the stories of Lord Krishna. I met a few couples dancing who immediately pulled me in, made me change into an event-appropriate outfit and taught me few basic steps of the dance. This made me realise that not only is Gujarati food inherently sweet, but so are the people. After they found out that I was a chef, they made sure I sampled Kathiawadi cuisine. We all ate together on the floor from a big *thali* (platter), on being served the food. Unlike Kutchi food, this cuisine is hot, spicy and salty. One of the most popular dishes of this cuisine is *dal dhokli*, made of *arhar dal* (split pigeon pea legume), flour, nuts and spices. My favourite was *undhiyo*, a traditional dish made with legumes, vegetables, coconuts and coriander. The Gujaratis are very fond of their accompaniments. With the main course, I sampled the *chunda*, a sweet and spicy jam made of grated raw mango.

Thus, we called it a day at Rajkot.

Day 35
9 September / Ahmedabad

Our next stop was Ahmedabad, the former capital of Gujarat. It is ranked third in the *Forbes* list of fastest growing cities of the decade. No wonder Gujaratis love to make money. Located on the banks of the river Sabarmati, 30 km away from the state capital Gandhi Nagar, Ahmedabad is filled with passionate, outgoing people who love to celebrate life. They are very particular about the food they eat. Few of the best *thali*s in India are available here.

I had the chance to meet my old chef friend Pranav Joshi, who ran his own culinary academy in Ahmedabad. He explained how most restaurants in the city served only vegetarian food. He also mentioned that the Gujaratis love experimenting and have taken to loving fusion food. To pay tribute to the city I was in, I decided to make a **Spaghetti Moilee** for Pranav and his students at the academy.

Spaghetti Moilee
(Italian spaghetti tossed in south Indian curry.)

Ingredients

1 packet spaghetti
2 tbsp olive oil
½ tsp mustard *(sarson)* seeds
10 piece fresh curry leaves *(kari patta)*, plus more for
   garnish

1-inch ginger *(adrak)*, chopped
10 cloves garlic *(lasun)*, chopped
2 medium onions, sliced
4 green chillies, stemmed, deseeded and cut lengthwise
1 tsp turmeric *(haldi)* powder
1 cup assorted vegetables (broccoli, peppers, peas), blanched
100 ml vegetable stock
2 cups or 400 ml coconut milk
Salt to taste
2½ tbsp lemon juice
1 medium tomato, cubed
50 gm Parmesan cheese

Method

1. Bring salted water to a boil. Add the spaghetti and cook until it is tender. Drain and run it through cold water and keep it aside in a large serving bowl.
2. Heat the olive oil. When the oil is hot, add the mustard seeds. As they splutter, add the curry leaves and sauté for a few seconds.
3. Lower the heat and add ginger, garlic and onions. Cook until soft and translucent and the garlic turns golden; stir occasionally. Stir in the chillies, turmeric powder and the assorted vegetables.
4. Raise the heat to high and stir for about 30 seconds to a minute. Add the stock and let it come to a boil. Now add coconut milk to this mixture. Do not over boil after adding coconut milk. It might split. Add salt to taste. Reduce the heat to low, cover, and cook

for about six to seven minutes, stirring occasionally so it does not stick.

5.   Add spaghetti to this reduced sauce. Cook for another three minutes or till the time the sauce coats the spaghetti. Now, stir in the tomato. Finally, drizzle lots of lemon juice and Parmesan cheese and serve hot.

~

Pranav suggested that after a 'fusion' meal, we go out and have some *paan* (betel leaves prepared and used as a stimulant). Not just any *paan* but a Volcano *paan*. The reason why it is called so is that the conical stuffed leaf is made to sit flat, like a volcano, with a single clove at the top, which is then lit up, to resemble a volcano. *Paan* is a digestive, eaten after a heavy Indian meal. However, this *paan* had more to do with showmanship, a visual and gustatory experience, wrapped into one.

DAY 36
10 September / Ahmedabad

Today, I visited the Mahila Swashray Kendra in Ahmedabad. Here, fresh Gujarati breakfast items were made on a daily basis, by 110 strong independent working women. I met Madhav, who was overseeing the operations; he seemed very passionate about empowering women and making them self sufficient who could also support their families. I learnt how food had broken all social barriers and was a medium through which so many women were able to be proud employees of a morally-rich business endeavour.

The business was started by Madhav's uncle, Mr. Kalyan, and his two Jain friends, in 1985. I was then introduced to a few of the main lady chefs. They explained to me that Gujarati breakfast, usually consisted of *khakra* (thin crackers made from mat bean, wheat flour and oil), *khasta kachori* (flaky crisp pastry filled with a *moong dal* mixture and deep fried), *chakri* (wheel-shaped crunchy snack), *bhakri* (round flat unleavened bread), *gatiya* (crunchy and spicy deep-fried strands made from gram flour dough), *fafra* (wafer-like thin fried crispbreads), and *sev*. I was lucky enough to sample a few of these breakfast items. I really liked the *bhakad vadi*, a spicy snack made of gram flour and refined flour. It is usually fried and looks like pinwheel cookies. I also learnt that every household had their own version of the *khakra*, but the version here, at the Mahila Swashray Kendra, was very popular because of the dry chutney served on top of the *khakra*. The chutney is made of chickpeas and peanuts. The chutney was made with sautéed gram flour, yoghurt, green chillies and black salt. Madhav also explained that they were also thinking of baking these snacks, instead of frying, as a medium of cooking.

It was a delight to see so many women together in one place, preparing the food from scratch, weighing it, packing and storing. With such tempting food around me, I took permission from the head chef, a lady called Jasodha Behen, and set up a small station to make **Raw Banana** *Pakoras* (fritters) **with** *Khakra* **Canapés**, my own twist to this story.

RAW BANANA *PAKORAS* WITH *KHAKRA* CANAPÉS
(Raw banana fritter served on a bed of thin crackers.)

Ingredients

1 cup green gram lentil *(moong dal)*
2 medium green chillies, chopped
1-inch fresh ginger *(adrak)*, grated
A pinch of asafoetida *(hing)*
1 tsp cumin *(jeera)* powder
1 tsp garam masala
Salt to taste
1 big raw banana
3 whole *khakra*s
2 tbsp green chutney
Grated radish for garnishing
Oil for frying

Method

1. Wash and soak the green gram lentils for at least three to four hours so it is fluffy enough to make a *pakora*. Drain all the water out.

2. In the blender add the green gram lentils, green chillies, ginger and asafoetida and grind them. Add a couple of tablespoons of water if required for grinding it fine.

3. Transfer into a bowl and beat the batter well, so that air is incorporated and it gets fluffier.

4. Mix cumin powder, garam masala and salt in the batter. Check the consistency; it should be neither too thin nor thick.

5. Peel and chop raw bananas into small pieces. Mix it in the batter.

6. Heat three cups of oil in a frying pan.

7. Fry *pakora*-sized batter in this hot oil; shape them with your fingers as you drop them into the oil.

8. Let them fry for a minute. Then, with the slotted spoon, turn the *pakora*s around and let them fry; after a minute turn them back again.

9. Fry until they become golden brown. Take them out of the hot oil and dab the excess oil out.

10. Break the *khakra* into even bite-sized pieces. Put chutney on the *khakra*. Place a *pakora* on the chutney. Garnish with grated radish.

~

This little twist was appreciated by both Jasodha Behen and Madhav. After thanking them and wishing everyone good luck, I left with big bags of packed breakfast for my journey ahead. I finally understood what film star Amitabh Bachchan means when he says in his advertisement, 'Breathe in a bit of Gujarat.' It was already late afternoon by the time we left the Kendra. It was time to make it to Surat.

Day 37
11 September / Surat

Also called the diamond city, Surat is known for its flyovers! A lot of people don't realise that Surat is a hub for all things food. The cosmopolitan population and the street food culture bring together to the city, a unique combination of dishes and experiences.

The people of Surat are a fun loving, enthusiastic and energetic bunch. Interestingly, the street food culture overshadows the restaurant culture here. The celebration of eating on the streets of Surat can be experienced at Kamrej Chowk every weekend. The variety of food available on the streets makes one feel spoilt for choice. One such Surat speciality is the *lochu*. I decided that the first thing I should eat here is *lochu*. I stopped at Jalaram to try this speciality. It is a staple breakfast item and is a steamed paste made of gram flour, flavoured with garlic and other spices, served with oil and coriander chutney. It is garnished with onions and *sev*. It is a combination of warm soft textures. Most of the places that serve *lochu* run out of this delicious snack a few hours after opening!

After my delicious breakfast, I headed to the factory of Janta Ice Cream. I had heard of all the wonderful things they were doing there. Exotic ice cream flavours are what these people at Janta are famous for. This ice cream company echoes the sentiment of the people of Surat: the eagerness to innovate and use local ingredients to come up with interesting new food. It was shocking to see a green chilli ice cream and more shocking to find a okra ice cream, which was sweet and salty at once. Other flavours included ginger, coriander, lemon and mint. Before adding these flavours to the ice cream base, I was told, they were cooked in *ghee* and seasoned. I had the opportunity to try a range of flavours that were made there. I took a fancy to the ginger ice cream. I felt like I was using the creamy texture of the ice cream to experience the kick of pungent fresh ginger for the first time.

My experiences were really unique and inspiring. One common factor throughout my journey was that I was getting to meet people who fascinated me with their imagination and sometimes, made me question my own belief system.

One such person was Sanjay Shahu who ran a place called Bhai Bhai Omelette Centre at Nanpura Road. Might sound a bit unusual but this small restaurant had an interesting story behind its name. 'It is located in between a road that connects a Hindu and a Muslim colony. Years ago, when there used to be rifts in these two colonies, this omelette centre would be a common point to meet up. Hence, Bhai Bhai (*bhai*, in Hindi, means brother),' explained Sanjay.

This is no ordinary omelette centre; another selling point is that they have 100 dishes on their menu and each one has egg as the main ingredient. So, starting from soup to starters to main course, you can have all the 'egg' that you want.

A few interesting dishes at Bhai Bhai were *anda palak*, eggs with spinach and cheese. Served with buns on the side was *anda rogan josh*, the classic mutton curry with egg in it. This was absolutely drool-worthy! I have to mention here that the secret behind all these delicious egg specialities was the generous amount of butter used to cook all of them. They operated every evening between 6:30 p.m. and 11:30 p.m. and sold 2000 egg preparations every day. So, one could only imagine how tasty all those dishes were. The shop had only two main *tawa* counters from where main dishes were prepared; such was the precision. Technically, it meant that Sanjay took only 19 seconds to dish out a plate! Wow! Now that's really fast. I sat down with a family to enjoy a few of Sanjay's signature egg plates. Noteworthy was the Australian fry, which was made of half-fried eggs, green garlic and cheese. It was called 'Australian' because of the colour combination. I also had the egg *samosa*, which was a masala omelette stuffed with cheese. The coriander-mint chutney served with it made it special.

It was only natural that after having all this, I come up with something that could beat all 'egg'spectations. Since they didn't have a modern fusion dish made out of eggs, I helped them to add the **Indian Devilled Eggs** on their menu.

Indian Devilled Eggs
(Stuffed hard boiled eggs.)

Ingredients

6-8 boiled eggs
¼ cup garlic mayonnaise

2 green chillies, minced
2 tbsp fresh coriander *(dhania patti)*, finely chopped
½ tsp garam masala
2 tsp raw mango, finely chopped
1 teaspoon or more of lime juice
Salt to taste

Method

1. Shell the boiled eggs and cut each egg into two, lengthwise. Separate the egg whites and the yolks. Reserve the yolks.
2. Combine the mayonnaise and the yolk. Stir them together with a fork. Once the mixture is roughly combined, throw in the rest of the ingredients.
3. Taste the mixture and then adjust salt and lime juice.
4. Arrange the white halves on a serving platter and place or pipe spoonful of the yolk mixture into the whites.
5. Serve chilled, or at room temperature.

~

The beauty of travelling by road, without an itinerary, never knowing what's going to happen on the next curve, who you are going to meet, especially in India where water, food and people change every 100 km, enforces a change in the way one perceives life. I like to call myself a 'Sadak Chef.' This incredible Indian journey has taught me to overcome all my fears. There comes a moment when you start living in the present as you relish and truly feel the air you breathe in, feel the wind chasing you. That is a sign that you've attained the 'soul of a true traveller.'

Nasik, bordering Gujarat and Maharashtra, was where I was headed to next. My destination was the famous Sula Vineyards, to meet Ajoy Shaw, the chief winemaker there.

Day 38
12 September / Nasik

The 230 km stretch from Surat to Nasik is one of the most scenic highways that connect both states. Nasik is in the northwest of Maharashtra and is part of a golden triangle connecting Mumbai, Pune and Nasik. It is famous for its wine and has been deemed the wine capital of India over the last decade. Nasik is a very fertile belt with the ideal climatic conditions for the growth of vegetables and fruits.

I made my way to Sula Vineyards. This belt is famous for its grapes. The valley's first commercial winery, Sula Vineyards, established in 1999, is one of the biggest in India, covering 160 acres. Their most widely-produced variety of white wine is the Sauvignon Blanc.

Here, I met the Chief Winemaker, Mr. Ajoy Shaw, at Sula Vineyards. For someone who is not familiar with wine, it can be explained as the fermented grape juice that is filtered and bottled. Mr. Shaw said that India has the potential to produce wines that can compete with their European counterparts, and that it was only a matter of time. Some of the French varieties of grapes used here are Chenin Blanc, Sauvignon Blanc, Cabernet Sauvignon. I was lucky to see the barrels where the wine was stored and left to age; I also had the opportunity to do a small tasting class with the master himself. For those of us who are not familiar with the at-times complicated steps to tasting wine, I was enlightened about the correct way. Mr. Shaw mentioned that wine is meant to be sipped and enjoyed, not gulped! It is important to hold the glass up to the light and measure the clarity of wine. Then, the glass should be swirled and the aromas should be captured by deeply inhaling into the glass. Then, after sipping on the wine, you extend the mouth and absorb the flavours of the wine. It is important that you allow the wine to stay on your palate for a few delayed seconds.

The range of wines at Sula is quite wide, what is also interesting is that they make sparkling wine as well, which I had the opportunity to taste. They apply what they refer to as a 'champagne method' to produce this wine. However, they cannot label it as 'champagne' due to strict laws that protect the integrity of champagne from France. Sula is also popular for their wine tour; I hopped on a bicycle and rode around the vineyard. After the tasting session with Mr. Shaw, it was time for me to don the chef's hat. Cooking with wine is not a new phenomenon, but incorporating wine in the cooking of Indian food was my new local challenge. I set out to make a **Tomato, Dried Fenugreek & Wine Rice** using the Sula Chenin Blanc.

Tomato, Dried Fenugreek & Wine Rice
(Rice cooked with fenugreek leaves and Chenin Blanc.)

Ingredients (for the rice)

1 cup basmati rice
1 tbsp olive oil
1 tsp cumin *(jeera)*
½ cup dry white wine (preferred Chenin Blanc)

4 fresh tomatoes, puréed
1 tsp red chilli powder
¼ tsp turmeric *(haldi)* powder
½ tsp garam masala
1½ tsp roasted cumin *(bhuna jeera)* powder
2 tbsp dry roasted fenugreek leaves *(kasoori methi)*
Salt to taste

Method *(for the rice)*

1. Soak the basmati rice in water for 20-30 minutes. Thereafter, strain and keep it aside.
2. Heat the olive oil in a pan.
3. Add the cumin when the oil is hot and let it crackle.
4. Add the strained rice and stir for two minutes.
5. Add the white wine and raise the flame to high. Let it reduce for two to three minutes. Add tomato purée, red chilli powder, turmeric, garam masala, cumin powder, dried fenugreek and salt. Cook for two minutes.
6. Add one and half cups of water. Put the lid on and cook on low flame for 12-15 minutes.
7. Keep the pan aside thereafter. Uncover the lid after half an hour of resting it.

Ingredients *(for the sauce)*

1 tbsp olive oil
2 tbsp butter
6 cloves garlic *(lasun)*, finely chopped
1 onion, finely chopped

10-12 button mushrooms
¼ cup corn kernels
¼ cup dry white wine (preferred Chenin Blanc)
6-8 cherry tomatoes
1 tsp oregano
2 tsp chilli flakes
5-6 fresh basil *(tulsi)* leaves, torn
1 tsp freshly cracked peppercorns *(sabut kali mirch)*
Salt to taste

Method (for the sauce)

1. Add the olive oil and butter to the pan.
2. When hot, add the garlic and onion and cook till translucent.
3. Add the mushrooms and corn kernels. Cook on high flame for two minutes.
4. Add the wine and let it reduce for three to four minutes.
5. Add the cherry tomatoes, oregano, chilli flakes, salt and torn basil.
6. Cook for two minutes. Now, add freshly cracked pepper and serve with rice.

~

Over the lunch that I had cooked, I discussed how regional Indian dishes, like kebabs, curries, and biryanis can be paired with wine. After a pleasant lunch on the lawns, it was time to move on to Pune, 200 km away from Nasik.

DAY 39
13 September / Pune

Pune is a young city that prides in the large number of medical and management schools. This has earned the city the title of Oxford of the East. Pune not only has a strong pub culture, it is firmly rooted in tradition, resulting in it being a place of incredible mixes. My first stop was Good Luck Café. Dating back to 1935, Good Luck Café was the best place to understand the vibe of the city. The place had an unassuming décor and patrons that cut across all sections of the society, from cab drivers, to Bollywood stars, and unknown TV show hosts, like yours truly, all find their ways frequently to this small quaint eatery on Ferguson College Road.

Abbas Bhai, the current owner, spoke highly of the bun *maska* (bun and butter) and the *chai* (tea), which lived up to my expectation. The bun was soft, sweet and buttery. The *anda* (egg) chutney was a new experience for me. On probing about the recipe, the answer I got was unexpected and definitely movie-worthy. The special recipe was called Formula 44, inspired by a Naseeruddin Shah movie from the nineties. The chef who invented this dish, Mr. Arab, definitely had a strong Bollywood influence over him.

My next halt was at Bedekar Tea Stall at Narayan Peth. It was the city's most popular place to sample the Maharashtrian speciality called *puneri missal*. Missal literally means mixture with three main components: the *tarri*, or gravy, is a thin broth made of Maharashtrian spices and red chillies; the *ussal* is a mixture of sprouted lentils and the garnish, which is fancy in its own right, is made up of onions, *sev*, potato, coriander and *poha* (a kind of flat rice flake). The tea stall is run by a small family, who unlike some other places in Pune, have been consistent with taste and quality over the years. Kudos to the Bedekar family!

The *missal* is served with a slice of bread, instead of the standard *pav* (bun) accompaniment served across the rest of Maharashtra. Even after studying for three years in Maharashtra, I wasn't a big fan of *missal*. However, the experience at Bedekar changed my opinion of the dish and how it is made. Apart from *puneri missal*, you must also try the *gulkand* (sweet preserve of rose petals) and coconut *laddu*s there.

The day ended with me trying to figure out what 'Cad B' was. The outlet we visited was Ice Cream Magic at Kothrud which was close to famous universities like the Film and Television Institute of India. Popular among college students, this dessert-drink is a thick chocolate shake. They sell it for Rs. 40, and I did not shy away from indulging in this sinful treat.

DAY 40
14 September / Pune

The next day, I decided to visit Aarava Crafts, makers of traditional terracotta handicrafts. Ganesh Chaturthi was around the corner and I tried my hands at making terracotta idols of Lord Ganesha. My guide was Mrs. Swarnarekha who explained the delicate art to me, 'Simply put, terra means earth and cotta means baked.' She drew a parallel between food and the art of terracotta. She explained that just like how we knead dough, clay also requires the same patience and skill to form its final shape. I tried my hand at a few idols, and knew I was no Michelangelo. However, I really enjoyed being a part of the process. As a gesture of gratitude, I decided to churn some funky new age *golgappa*s (popular street snack consisting of a round, hollow puff pastry filled with spiced mashed potato, flavoured water, tamarind chutney, onion and chickpeas) for the skilful workers at Aarava Crafts. Instead of the traditional filling, it was filled with a fruit *chaat* tossed in yoghurt and the spicy water was replaced with some spiced-up fresh pomegranate juice. After eating they agreed cooking is an art too.

After my mid-day fling with terracotta, I went to meet an old friend and mentor, Chef Shailendra, at the famous Stone Water Grill. He is a molecular gastronomy expert and a TV show host himself and his skill and reputation precede him. I watched him deconstruct a watermelon and feta salad into the simple elements of molecular gastronomy. He explained how the process was not chemical and allowed chefs to experiment with textures and aesthetics of plate presentation. What was most exciting about my time with him was the beetroot-based dessert that he made. He used crushed waffles, nitro-frozen poached beetroot, charred meringue, and dehydrated oranges to make this dessert and called it the beetroot ice cream platter.

It is always inspiring to be around chefs from different walks of life, the traditional and the modern, by the roadside or in the tasting room. I am truly lucky to be able to experience this journey with so many wonderful people.

DAY 41

From Pune I headed to a place that had its three 'S's—sun, sand, and the sea—intact. Goa, here I come.

DAY 42
16 September / Panjim

It took us more than a day to reach Goa, India's smallest state by area. Part of the Konkan region, it is a very popular tourist destination for both Indians and foreigners. Interestingly, it is also India's richest state owing to the super successful tourism industry. Old Goa represents what remains of the former Portuguese Colony. The cuisine is a curious combination of Western influence and exotic Eastern ingredients. From coconut-based curries to fresh seafood, Goa showcases its Konkan style, while also bringing to the table traditional Portuguese dishes with heavy local influences.

My first experience in Goa was a little challenge I had set up for myself. Living in Delhi all my life I had always driven a car, but for those of you who know Goa, you would also know that the way to get around there is a scooter! It was my turn today to get on one and give it a go. My producer very graciously came to my assistance. After half an hour, and a slightly twisted wrist, I could proudly say that I was finally a biker!

I decided to take a small personal vacation within Goa (perks of being a TV show host) by taking a ferry from Panaji to Old Goa. It was my first ferry ride and I was smiling the whole way there. I visited the Basilica of Bom Jesus, one of the most popular churches in Old Goa. Being within its premises literally takes one back in time. Then, I took a jet ski to Fisherman's Wharf to sample their seafood specialities. This restaurant is on the banks of the Sal River. I must warn you beforehand; never visit this place for dinner without a reservation; it is popular! The restaurant serves authentic Goan food, with the tempting option of the 'Fresh Catch of the Day' preparations. That includes prawns, lobsters, red snapper and black pomfret. The ambience is what makes this restaurant special. The seafood display is very elaborate and is placed right at the entrance of the restaurant and is visually stunning. I chose to eat **Flaming Prawn Balchao**, which had generous amounts of palm vinegar, *feni* (spirit produced exclusively in Goa), ginger and tomatoes. I ate my meal in the company of a very cool Canadian couple. If they ever read this book, I want them to know that I would love to see them again!

Flaming Prawn Balchao

(Prawns served in a tangy tomato chilli sauce.)

Ingredients

600 gm medium-sized prawns *(jhinga)*
Salt to taste
2-inch piece ginger *(adrak)*, roughly chopped
15-20 cloves garlic *(lasun)*, roughly chopped
1 tsp cumin *(jeera)* seeds
12 dried red chillies
6-8 cloves *(laung)*
2-inch stick of cinnamon *(dalchini)*
1 tsp mustard *(sarson)* seeds
1 cup malt vinegar

½ cup oil
2 large onions, finely chopped
4 large tomatoes, chopped
2 tbsp jaggery
30 ml *feni*/vodka

Method

1. Devein the prawns. Wash thoroughly and remove excess water. Add salt and keep aside.
2. Grind the ginger, garlic, cumin seeds, red chillies, cloves, cinnamon and mustard seeds along with vinegar into a fine paste.
3. Heat the oil in a non-stick pan and sauté the prawns till all the moisture dries up. Drain the prawns and set aside. In the same oil sauté the onions till they turn soft and light brown.
4. Add the tomatoes and sauté on high heat till they turn pulpy and the oil surfaces. Add the ground masala and sauté for two to three minutes. Add the prawns and jaggery.
5. Check the seasoning and cook on low heat for five to seven minutes more or till the oil leaves the masala.
6. Last step is to do a *feni* flambé, so add *feni* and light the flame, so it gets that caramelised sweetness at the end, till *feni* evaporates.
7. Serve hot with rice.

DAY 43
17 September / Panjim

Today was the day to explore the spice trade of Goa. I travelled to Curti, in Ponda, where I met the people of Sahakari Spice Farm. The farm covers an area of 150 acres and has been around since the eighties. They use a balance of scientific growing techniques, with ancient mixed cropping methods, to grow their spices. They are also very conscious of their water management system and their farming techniques allow them to use their water efficiently. When they began farming more than 20 years ago, the land that they had acquired was barren. Today, they have a large variety of spice plants and cashew nut trees. What makes this farm special is that it does not look like a regular farm with rows of neatly manicured plants and distinct growing areas. The farm is integrated into the larger ecosystem of the surrounding habitat, where the plants grow in tandem with the natural foliage of the area. Being able to replicate this natural integrated system means that the plants are healthier, biodiversity is maintained and the life and health of the farm is prolonged.

The caretaker of the plants was a very kind local called Francis who took me on a tour of the plantation. First I saw green pepper. It was interesting to learn that one single fruit of the green pepper tree, at different stages of ripening, gives us different types of the spice pepper. Another spice that I saw and learnt about was bay leaf. Francis asked me to pluck a leaf, tear the stem away from the leaf, and differentiate the smells. I could smell cinnamon from the stem, while the leaf distinctly smelt like bay leaf. I was intrigued by the combination. Francis explained that Indian bay leaf or *malabathrum* (Cinnamomum Tamala, Lauraceae) is somewhat similar in appearance to the leaves of bay laurel, but in culinary terms, is quite different, having a fragrance and taste similar to cinnamon bark, but milder. For cinnamon, the tree is grown till 15 years of age, and then it is cut and dried, to make the spice ready to use. The other spices I saw were vanilla pods, cloves, chilli, curry leaves, turmeric and ginger. After the tour, they served me a traditional Goan meal, to which I added my own twist!

I used the spices from the farm to prepare a lively fruity dish **Pineapple Green Pepper Curry** for the friends I made on the tour.

PINEAPPLE GREEN PEPPER CURRY
(Pineapples cooked in coconut and green peppercorn curry.)

Ingredients

1 tbsp olive oil
1 tsp mustard *(sarson)* seeds
1-inch cinnamon *(dalchini)* stick
1 green chilli, sliced
10-12 curry leaves *(kari patta)*
10-12 green peppercorns, pounded
5-6 cocktail/Madras onions, finely chopped
1 tsp fresh ginger *(adrak)*, grated
1 tsp garlic *(lasun)*, finely chopped

¼ tsp fenugreek *(methi)* seeds
1 ripe pineapple, cut into small chunks
¼ tsp turmeric *(haldi)* powder
1 tsp rice wine vinegar
Salt to taste
1 tsp sugar
1 cup coconut milk

Method

1. Heat the olive oil and once done, add mustard seeds and let them splutter.
2. Add cinnamon stick, green chilli, curry leaves, green peppercorns, and onions. Fry for about a minute or two. Add grated ginger, garlic and fenugreek seeds. Sauté for another minute or so.
3. Add the pineapple, turmeric, vinegar, salt and sugar. Cook until vinegar is absorbed.
4. Now add the coconut milk and cook it on low flame for 10-12 minutes.
5. The curry is ready; serve it hot with steamed rice.

~

Before I talk about my visit to the famous Mum's Kitchen, I would like to talk a little about my eating habits. As a child, and till recently, I was a vegetarian. But being a chef doesn't allow you to take sides! So now I eat everything I am served. Goa was very intriguing to me as a lot of the food here was based on meat dishes that included pork, beef and chicken. The Portuguese influence here is so strong that these dishes have survived through time and become the identity of Goan food. Goa has seen a tourism explosion like no other state in the country has seen, and hence, the authenticity of the food has been diluted to some extent. I wanted to experience true Goan cuisine, cooked by locals, without any compromise. So I headed to Mum's Kitchen.

Mum's Kitchen, a growing movement headed by a gentle Goan by the name Suzie, is a must-visit for native-food-seekers like me. She began this kitchen with her mother-in-law's recipes, and added a few of her own. 'Mothers' from different parts of Goa have contributed and helped to compile the menu. Her effort is to sustain the genuineness of each recipe and to bring to the table her love for good food.

To give you a little background on Goan food, here is a summary of what I learnt at Mum's Kitchen.

The Portuguese brought potatoes, tomatoes, pineapples, guavas, and cashews from Brazil to Goa. Of these, tomatoes and potatoes were not accepted by the Hindus until the late twentieth century. The most important part of Goan spices, the chilli, was introduced to Goan cuisine by the Portuguese and became immensely popular. None of the above mentioned ingredients were used in Goan cuisine before the advent of the Portuguese. All the dishes I ate there were based around Portuguese traditions, especially since I was in a Catholic kitchen. First, I tried my hand at vindaloo. I was taught the true recipe and was informed politely that vindaloo has absolutely no *aloo* (potato) in it.

Suzie revealed, 'It is all about the spice mix. The spice mixture is a cooked paste that can be stored and used to make vindaloo with pork, chicken, beef, or anything else that one might like.' So to de-mystify this recipe, I shall break it into three parts.

Part one were the dry spices used, that included Kashmiri chilli for colour, *ghati* chilli for the spice, cinnamon, clove, spicy ginger, garlic, bay leaf, cumin, turmeric, pepper, tamarind, and the very special, palm vinegar.

Part two was the masala paste. The dry spices need to be ground together into a dry mix. After which onions and tomatoes need to be fried in coconut oil. Then, the dry ground spices need to be added to this onion-tomato mixture. After the two cook together, the entire masala is cooled and made into a coarse paste once again.

Part three was the curry which, I was told, depended on the kind of meat you were using for the curry. The meat had to be cut and prepared for marination. The marinade included salt, lemon juice and turmeric. Once the meat had been marinated, it was kept aside for about 15-20 minutes. The curry was a mix of the masala paste, water and the meat. And *that* was what vindaloo was all about! Phew!

Other dishes I tasted were *xacuti*, a curry made of meat, grated coconut, poppy seeds and dried red chillies. I also had *cafreal*, which is a dry but spicy chicken delicacy. The meat is smeared with a paste of chilli, garlic, ginger, coriander and mint. It is then shallow fried. Goans boast a heritage of desserts too. *Bebinca* is one of the most popular local sweets. It is a festive dessert made in abundance for

Christmas. This is a 10-layered cake made from a mix of refined flour, egg yolk, sugar and coconut milk.

I learnt a lot about ingredients that were unique to Goa, especially the palm vinegar and black jaggery. I was fortunate enough to take some back with me, to cook for my family. I firmly believe that it is these small, sometimes overlooked ingredients that characterise and differentiate regional cuisines from one another. Goa might be the smallest state, but it is definitely one of the most diverse and complex, as far as the cuisine is concerned. Before Goa is left behind, the people here definitely deserve a special mention. They believe in living life at a pace that allows you to stop and appreciate everything, especially the little things, around you. Life is slow and there is always time to relax.

Day 44
18 September / Udupi

On our way to Udupi, in Karnataka, we stopped along the highway to eat lunch and rest for a while. The reason I mention this stop is the buttermilk that I had then. It isn't uncommon in India to have a refreshing glass of buttermilk on a hot summer day. But this buttermilk, subtly flavoured with ginger, curry leaves and mustard seeds just blew my mind. Simplicity can inspire tremendous amounts of energy and positivity. I made my way to Udupi.

DAY 45
19 September / Udupi

Most of us don't know that Udupi is a small town in Karnataka. We see the word 'Udupi' on restaurant signs and don't usually correlate it with a town or a type of cuisine. This confusion is not uncommon. Udupi is mainly known for its Krishna temple, also called Krishna Matha. It is a pilgrimage spot for devout Hindus. Udupi cuisine has close ties to the temple. Hence, this was the place where I decided to learn about the cuisine.

Here I met Srinath, the public relations officer of the temple. It was interesting to learn about the dynamics of temple management. Here I was, thinking that the only person in the temple would be the priest. He explained that the Krishna Matha resembled an *ashram* (a hermitage, monastic community, or other place of religious retreat). Apart from the Krishna Matha, there were eight other temples in the surrounding area. The temples dated back to the thirteenth century. The founder of the temple, Sri Madhav Acharya, had very firm principles around the making and eating of food. Udupi cuisine comprises dishes made primarily from grains, beans, vegetables, and fruits. The variety and range of dishes is wide, and involves the use of locally and seasonally available ingredients. It adheres strictly to the *satvik* tradition of Indian vegetarian cuisine using no onions or garlic. Pumpkins and gourds were the main ingredients in the *sambar* (a lentil-based vegetable stew or chowder based on a broth made with tamarind) that was prepared with ground coconut and coconut oil. I was also told that the ubiquitous South Indian dish, *masala dosa* (a fermented crêpe made from rice batter and black lentils stuffed with potato masala), had its origins in Udupi.

Srinath gave me a tour of the 12 kitchens producing 70,000 meals a day. I wondered how they were managing that everyday? These were the very kitchens where the cuisine was born. To enter the kitchen, you had to be in traditional attire, which were the *janivaara* or the sacred white thread and the *dhoti*. They made 300 kg of rice and 300 litres of *rasam* (thin, spicy south Indian soup served with other dishes, typically as a drink) everyday. The food is meant to cleanse your body and mind. It is served traditionally on a banana leaf, and of course, you have to eat with your hands. The process of feeding all the visiting devotees is called *Anna Brahma* (*anna* means rice and Brahma after Lord Brahma, the creator). The food I ate was nutritious, delicious and simple. Future warning: eating *sambar* with your hands ain't easy; so, *practise*! Also, if you want to eat good Udupi food, a restaurant is definitely not the place to go to.

After a somewhat religious morning and a holistic lunch, I visited the Nadur Farm. This was a small village 30 km from Udupi. Here, the Kairana family was trying to promote goat farming and goat milk. Not a very common or commercially available dairy product, the aim of the farm was to revitalise the goat rearing industry and rejuvenate the local economy and rural development. I saw how the goats were stall fed a special feed that was processed on the farm. The milk was collected hygienically using an efficient technology. It was sold in 500 millilitres pasteurised packets and delivered fresh to Mumbai and Bengaluru everyday. I opened a freshly-sealed packet and tasted the milk straightaway. It was fresh and sweet which was surprising. Goat milk is generally known to have a sharp odour and a distinct taste, but this milk broke those myths for me. Nadur Farm is one of the best stall-fed farms in India; they are very careful about what their goats eat and how they are treated.

I used the milk to make a fancy dessert called **Beetroot Halwa with Rabri Toast**.

BEETROOT *HALWA* WITH *RABRI* TOAST
(Sweet shallow fried bread topped with reduced goat milk.)

Ingredients (for **Halwa**)

2 tbsp clarified butter *(ghee)*
500 gm beetroot *(chakunder)*, peeled and grated
3 cups goat milk, heated
½ cup sugar
½ cup dried whole milk solids *(khoya)*
½ tsp cardamom *(elaichi)* powder
4 drops rose water or essence

Method (for **Halwa**)

1.   Heat one tablespoon *ghee* in a pan. Add the beetroot and sauté on medium flame for eight to 10 minutes.
2.   Once it is tender, add the hot milk and keep stirring till it reduces and becomes thick.

3.   Add the sugar, mix well and cook till it reduces.
4.   Add the dried whole milk solids, one tablespoon *ghee* and cardamom powder and mix well.
5.   When the *halwa* is cooked and becomes thick, add rose water, mix well and keep aside.

Ingredients (for Rabri)

100 gm ready-made *rabri* (thickened sweet flavoured milk; in this case, made from goat milk)
10 strands saffron *(kesar)*
 3 tsp goat milk

Method (for Rabri)

1.   Mix the saffron strands in three teaspoon warm milk. After five minutes add the *rabri* to this saffron milk and simmer for two minutes. The *rabri* will get a beautiful saffron colour.

Ingredients (for Chocolate Almonds)

100 gm white chocolate
10 almonds *(badam)*
10 cashew nuts *(kaju)*

Method (for Chocolate Almonds)

1.   Melt chocolate on a double boiler. As soon as it melts, add the cashew nuts and almonds to it. On a greased tray, place these chocolate-coated almonds one by one.

2.   Keep it inside the fridge for five to seven minutes or until the coating sets.

Ingredients (for Toast)

10 bread slices
2 tbsp clarified butter *(ghee)*
2 tbsp sugar

Method (for Toast)

1. Cut the bread slices into bite-sized round or square shapes.
2. Heat two tablespoon *ghee* in a pan and add two tablespoon sugar to it.
3. Once it is hot and the sugar starts to melt, start cooking the bread slices until they're golden brown from both sides.
4. Assemble the dessert; spread saffron *rabri* on toast, place a small dollop of the beetroot *halwa* on top of it and garnish with chocolate almonds.

Day 46
20 September / Coorg

After Nadur, my next destination was Madikeri, 180 km
south. A hill station in the district of Coorg, this area was
extremely popular for large coffee plantations. Often called
the Scotland of India by the British, or the Kashmir of the
South by the rest of India, the aroma of coffee, cardamom
and pepper infiltrate Madikeri. I took the opportunity to
visit a coffee plantation called the Kaveri Coffee Estate.
Reena, from the family who owns the plantation, took
me through the plantation and showed me coffee plants of
different varieties and age. Her oldest plant dated back to
more than 50 years. The plantation had been converted into
a homestay, where guests could stay at the plantation and
take part in harvesting activities. I learnt that there are two
types of coffee: Arabica and Robusta. While the latter is well
suited for Indian climatic conditions and responds well to
hilly areas and heavy rain, Arabica grows in the plains and
does not require much rain. She explained how the coffee
fruit is harvested when it is green, it is then dried, extracted
and roasted, before it is powdered and sold.

My host was very soft spoken and knowledgeable. She
was also an exceptional cook. I had the opportunity to taste
authentic food of the district at the homestay. The cuisine
was called Kodava and was named after the local community.
This food was a mix of vegetarian and non-vegetarian fare.
Reena explained how rice is a staple, because of how widely
it is grown in the area. It is the foundation of their cuisine
and is served in many forms. A few of the rice dishes that

I tasted were *akki roti*, a type of crispy thin pancake of unleavened wholemeal bread cooked on a griddle, made from a combination of cooked rice and rice flour; *puttu*, a variety of steamed rice dishes; *kadam battu*, also called butter balls; *nu pattu*, rice threads similar to vermicelli. There was a typical chicken curry made with coconut and whole spices. Also, there was a sweet and sour pumpkin curry along with few chutneys to accompany the dishes. In my usual style, to thank her for her generous favour, I made **No Bake Coorgi Coffee Brownies** for Reena.

NO BAKE COORGI COFFEE BROWNIES
(Coffee-flavoured brownies prepared without an oven.)

Ingredients

¼ cup water
1½ tsp coffee powder from Coorg
½ cup sweetened condensed milk
2 cups cracker (biscuit) crumbs or around 20 whole crackers
¼ cup finely chopped roasted hazelnuts or almonds
¼ cup cocoa powder
½ tsp salt
100 gm dark chocolate, melted

Method

1. Make a coffee concoction by boiling ¼ cup of water and mixing the coffee powder in it. Strain after 10 minutes. Mix this with the condensed milk.

2. Line an eight-inch square baking dish with two crossed strips of parchment paper, letting the long ends hang over the sides of the dish. Grease lightly with butter.

3. In a large bowl, mix together the crackers, hazelnuts or almonds, cocoa, and salt. Pour in the coffee-condensed milk mixture. Pour in the melted chocolate and stir firmly to combine.

4. Empty this into the baking dish. Spread it evenly; if needed, cover it with a plastic wrap and press slightly with a pan or any heavy tool.

5. Chill it for an hour or until firm enough to cut. Remove the brownies from the pan. Cut the brownies into small squares. The brownies are ready!

~

After I left Coorg, and as I was entering the land of Ayurveda, Kerala, I decided to make a short detour to Calicut. I took some time off to visit the Kadavu Resort, an Ayurvedic retreat owned by a popular hotel chain. The resort is a gateway to the Malabar region, lush green palm hills flanked by bright blue water of the Chaliyar River. The general manager explained that it took a week to identify the body type of a guest who came for a healing treatment at the spa. After the assessment, the spa and Ayurveda treatment began. There was a unique diet pattern attuned to your body along with which you had to do various forms of yoga. All this was done alongside the river, to ease the pain.

This kind of spa treatment involved the use of essential oils, which were therapeutic in nature. With the abundance of spices and diverse medicinal plants in the area, this made sense. I opted for the *abhiyangam*, the full body massage, using clove oil. As much as I love travel, after being on the road for so long, this massage was just what I needed and two very strong masseurs did the needful. The humour of the situation wasn't lost on me, neither was the relief that the massage brought.

After the massage I found myself in Shavakar, Kerala. I have lately become a fan of strength training and regional martial arts. So my next destination was Valabhatta Kalari Academy, known for teaching the ancient martial art *kalaripayattu*. I saw young boys and girls of different age groups among the students practicing. The youngest was six! The guru here explained that the basic requirements were dedication, focus and time. The training stage was divided into four categories. First was physical exercise *(maithari)*, second was wooden weapons *(kolthari)*, third was the metal weapons *(ankathari)* and the last was unarmed combat *(verumkai)*. I saw them practising and I tried my hand at *kolthari*. I felt an immediate rush of adrenaline and I was filled with respect for all the students and their guru. There was one student, blindfolded, and he used a sword to slice targets—attached to other students—in half. Such was the precision of the training. Born and brought up in a devout Hindu family, I always like to seek blessings from my elders. I took a minute to touch the guru's feet and carry his blessings with me through the rest of the journey.

As I took leave from the academy, I took a moment to think about my journey. I had covered more than 9000 km by road and I was almost at the southern tip of my beautiful country. In retrospect, I had grown each day and learnt new things that I could write an additional journal! Having said this before, I must reiterate my amazement at the diversity in nature, people, landscape, traditions and cultures in India. It might take more than a lifetime to experience and explore our very own brand 'India.'

DAY 47
21 September / Allappuzha

It was afternoon as I arrived at God's Own Country. I was amazed, stunned, and in shock. For me, what I saw in the panoramic scene in front of me, surpassed my feelings that I had when I encountered Kashmir's beauty. This was ethereal!

My first stop was an eco-houseboat on the backwaters. Kerala had recently overtook the Taj Mahal in Agra as the number one travel destination on Google search trends. Now, after coming here, I realised that this piece of information just had to be true because of the beautiful beaches, backwaters, the mountain ranges, the wildlife sanctuaries, and of course, the spice trails. One of the main reasons for Kerala being so popular was the encouraging support of their government. They were the first to declare tourism as an industry in India. Kerala is widely known for its eco-tourism initiatives and I wanted to experience it first-hand. This was my first experience on the backwaters, an extensive network of 41 interlocking rivers, lakes and canals. I got aboard Pride Eco-houseboat run by Mr. Johnson. What was especially cool was that the houseboat had its own elaborate number plate. The houseboat was constructed with natural materials like wood, bamboo, coconut shells, husk and rods. Even the chair that I was swinging on was a cane chain. Mr. Johnson believed that when you are in the tourism business in Allappuzha you have to own a houseboat.

He made me observe the banks of the river and provided an insight into the lives of the people who were living along the river bank. There was a reason this area was called the Rice Bowl of India. The water level of the river was higher than the level of the fields along the banks, making it easier to irrigate and grow the rice, which actually required a lot of water to grow. Life along the backwaters was completely dependent on the river water. Even the foundation of the houses, of people living here, was built using sandstone from the riverbed. They worked on the rice fields and ate the fish they caught from the river. It was almost a self-contained environment. To take it a notch higher, they had ensured that tourists like me, not only got to enjoy the landscape, but also experience the culture and lifestyle of people living here. If you were of the creative kinds, you could use local ingredients, from the market on the backwaters, to cook for yourself, your family or friends. If you have the soul of a traveller, it is a must to spend a few days here enjoying the backwaters. Mr. Johnson was kind enough to lend his boat to me for the entire day and it was on the boat that I cooked **Kerala *Bhindi* Curry** for him.

Kerala *Bhindi* Curry

(Okra cooked in tamarind and tomato curry.)

Ingredients

4-5 tamarind *(imli)* pieces
1 tbsp coconut oil
1 tsp mustard *(sarson)* seeds
8-10 curry leaves *(kari patta)*
¼ tsp fenugreek *(methi)* seeds, crushed
2 dry red chillies

8-10 shallots, chopped
8-10 garlic *(lasun)* cloves, pounded
200 gm okra *(bhindi)*, chopped
3 tomatoes, puréed
¼ tsp turmeric *(haldi)* powder
1½ tsp chilly powder
2 tsp coriander *(dhania)* powder
Salt to taste

Method

1. Soak tamarind in warm water and squeeze. About ¼ cup thick tamarind water is needed.
2. Heat the coconut oil in a pan. Add the mustard seeds and let them splutter. Now add curry leaves, fenugreek seeds and dry red chillies. Then add the shallots and garlic. Sauté everything well till the shallots are translucent.
3. Add the chopped okra to this and sauté it for three to four minutes. Then add the tomato purée, turmeric powder, chilli powder and coriander powder. Sauté well.
4. Add the tamarind water, salt to taste and mix well. Add ½ cup of water and let it come to a boil. Simmer it for another 10-12 minutes with the lid on.
5. Once the okra is fully cooked, take it off the heat and serve with steamed rice.

~

After cooking, rest of my day was spent gazing into the horizon, watching the people in the paddy fields and wishing I had a boat of my own.

Day 48
22 September / Allappuzha

I woke up early to go to the local vegetable and spice market. I saw fresh beans, lemon, garlic, ginger, and different types of banana. An interesting ingredient that is a staple in Kerala is 'tapioca.' Seen in other parts of India mostly in the form of chips, I discovered its popularity here as an everyday vegetable. Also called cassava, it is made into chips along with bitter gourd and banana.

Continuing with my Allappuzha adventure, after the houseboat experience, I went to one of the most beautiful heritage houses I had ever seen. Built in the late 1800s, Pooppally's has been around for a long time. It is a family run eco-homestay, with large cottages spread out over a large plot of land on the banks and turns of the river. Therefore, you could enjoy the river on both sides of the property. Originally, trade and business took place on the river; it was the only way traders and merchants travelled, I was told. The original entrance to the homestay was through the 'back' of the river. For those of you who want to get married in a romantic South Indian destination, this is the place where you can plan your destination wedding.

This ancestral house was built by Mr. Pooppally Vavachen between 1892 and 1895. The bricks of the house still have the logo of the British Empire. Also, Sir Edmund Hillary visited the homestay many years ago. The cottages here are old wooden Kerala houses that were bought and restructured. The home stands secluded in a property of about three acres with varieties of fruit yielding trees and medicinal plants and herbs. It was home to more than 30 species of birds during the season.

I met with another member of the family who cooked with me in the afternoon. Lisa, the sister of Dr. Paul Pooppally, grandchild of Mr. Vavachen, told me how to go about the cooking. Before I explain what the food was all about, I want to give a little backdrop to Kerala cuisine. An essential ingredient of the cuisine is coconut. It is one plant which is used in all its forms. Rice and fish are also staples. Kerala's culinary history is tightly wound around the spice trail. Pepper, cardamom, cloves, ginger, cinnamon and chillies are found aplenty here. Interestingly, there's a large variety of meat on the menu like beef, rabbit, duck, seafood, and pork; these are common features on local menus.

Back to Lisa, a post graduate in the field of Food and Nutrition; she decided to teach me how to make a *karimeen pollichathu*. This was pearl spot fish, fried whole and finished in a banana leaf with a mix of spices. The recipe was her grandmother's. Gashes were first made on the fish so that the marinade seeped in. Then the marinade was applied; it had salt, pepper, turmeric, red chilli, nutmeg vinegar, and ginger-garlic paste. It was marinated for an hour after which the fish was shallow fried and prepared to be wrapped in the banana leaf. Once the fish had been removed from the pan, we used the same pan to cook the onions, shallots, ginger, garlic, and tomato, with a whole bunch of spices (coriander powder, turmeric, chilli powder, black pepper and garam masala) sprinkled generously into the pan. This masala was coarsely ground thereafter. After this mix was done, the fish was placed in the banana leaf and covered with this spice mix. The tightly sealed banana leaf was then placed in another pan with coconut oil. This was cooked for another four to five minutes.

The above mentioned activity done, she went onto speak about few other dishes of the region like *avial*, a thick mixture of vegetables, yoghurt and coconut that went very well with *appams*, a type of pancake made with fermented rice batter and coconut milk; *thoran*, almost like a cabbage stir-fry with grated coconut and mustard seeds; *pachchadi*, is made of any vegetable dish that is slightly pickled. While she prepared the fish, I decided to do a take on the classic *thoran*. I used raw papaya and served it as canapés on tapioca chips. I named it **Papaya Thoran Canapés**.

PAPAYA *THORAN* CANAPÉS
(Raw papaya stir-fry served on a bed of thin crackers.)

Ingredients

3 cups raw papaya, grated
2 tbsp coconut oil
½ tsp mustard *(sarson)* seeds
1 tsp cumin *(jeera)* seeds
8 shallots, finely chopped
2 dry red chillies
4 cloves garlic *(lasun)*, finely chopped
3 green chillies, chopped
6-8 curry leaves *(kari patta)*

½ cup coconut, scraped
¼ tsp turmeric *(haldi)* powder
12 tapioca chips
1 tbsp nutmeg *(jaiphal)* pickle, ground into a paste
Salt

Method

1. Clean the papaya and grate it to get at least three cups.
2. Heat the coconut oil. Once hot, add the mustard and cumin seeds together. After they start to splutter, add shallots, dry red chillies, garlic, green chillies and curry leaves. Fry till shallots are translucent.
3. Add the grated coconut, salt and turmeric powder. Stir for two to three minutes.
4. Then, add the grated papaya and mix well. Sprinkle some water to avoid the spices from sticking. Cover and cook on a low flame for five to seven minutes. Give a stir in between. The papaya *thoran* is ready.
5. Now, spread some pickle paste on the tapioca chips. Mount a heap of papaya *thoran* on the tapioca, the canapé is ready. You can garnish with a bit of grated coconut.

~

I had the lovely opportunity to eat lunch with the entire family. We shared experiences, food and stories about our travels. I had been missing the company of friends and family and this little meal made me feel at home again. The dishes were extensive: the pearl spot fish, beetroot *pachchadi* and *bhindi* and *cheru parippu*, the name for *moong dal* (green gram), all served with steaming rice. We then ate the fish that Lisa had prepared. I unwrapped the banana leaf and inhaled the beautiful aroma. It was soft, had soaked up all the goodness of the spices, and tasted delicious. Not to forget, the nutmeg vinegar did wonders. It was definitely one of the most memorable meetings. I took my blessings and walked away into the sunset, only to climb a coconut tree!

Helping me do my 'monkey' act were Pravin and Ravi. Ravi was nimble and agile. He climbed the tree like it was the easiest thing to do. His official designation was Toddy Tapper. Pravin was around for translation and ease of communication. Toddy is a natural alcoholic sap of some kinds of palm, used as a beverage in tropical countries. It is very potent and can easily make you feel light in the head. It is sweet, white and cloudy, similar to what milk looks like. I looked at Ravi and noticed that he had a well-armoured outfit, with many tools and equipment attached to his body. The knife, which looked like a cleaver, helped to cut the coconut flower, and he carried a bag called *labu katey* to collect the toddy. Then there was the *thalanya*, a wooden stick resembling a rounded hammer to pound the flower. At the risk of sounding pompous, I did actually manage to climb the tree and trust me, it is not easy.

Day 49
23 September / Munnar

After the backwaters, we headed for the Munnar plantations. This hill station is situated at the confluence of three mountain rivers: Muthirapuzha, Nallathanni and Kundala. The name Munnar, in Malayalam, is believed to mean three rivers. During the colonial rule, many British officials used Munnar as a summer retreat. It has several tea plantations, winding roads, and boasts of exotic species of flora and fauna. I have been to Mussoorie and Nainital, and a few other hill stations in the north, but they would have to struggle hard to compete with the beauty of Munnar. There is a constant scent of spice and tea that follows you around. It is an area where the density of sandalwood trees is very high. A visit to a tea plantation, that allows you to stay in for a few days, is also a must.

Another must-visit are the elephant camps abounding near the place. Just before entering Munnar, I went to one where I met an elephant, face-to-face, for the first time. There were options to ride the elephants and bathe them or take a shower with them. I opted for the last option, with an elephant called Saji. The whole experience made me feel like a little child once again.

Munnar was also where I was exposed to the art of Kathakali. It is the most stylised version of Indian classical dance and was developed in the seventeenth century. Kathakali is based on songs in Malayalam and Sanskrit from the tales of Mahabharata and the Ramayana. The movements of the body and the hands subtly convey the story and the emotions through the music. There are five elements in Kathakali: song, expression, dance, enactment and instrumental accompaniment. It takes seven years to study and become a dancer. The artiste's face is elaborately painted; the good characters have a green face, the ladies have a beige face, and the evil characters have red beards and black faces. Traditionally, a Kathakali performance is usually conducted at night and ends in the wee hours of the morning. Nowadays, it isn't difficult to see performances as short as three hours or less. Kathakali is usually performed in front of the huge *Kalivilakku* (*kali* meaning dance and *vilakku* meaning lamp) with its thick wick sunk till its neck in coconut oil. Traditionally, this lamp used to be the only source of light around the area where the performance happened. Enactment of a play takes place along with the accompaniment of music *(sangeet)* and instruments *(vadya)*.

The regimented training of a Kathakali artiste makes him focussed, and increases his skill and physical stamina, to prepare for his demanding role. The training can often last for eight to 10 years and is intensive. The story is enacted by the movements of the hands *(mudras)*, facial expressions *(rasas)* and body movements. The expressions are derived from Natyashastra (the tome that deals with the science of expressions) and are classified into nine sects in most Indian classical art forms. Dancers also undergo special practice sessions to learn control of their eye movements. After watching this performance, I spent the rest of the evening exploring a tea estate.

Day 50

I left Munnar for the picturesque beaches of Puducherry.

Day 51
25 September / Puducherry

Formerly Pondicherry, the city is fondly referred to as 'Pondy' sometimes. It is located 450 km from Munnar. The place looks like a beautiful slice of France that the colonisers left behind, on the Coromandel Coast of India. And the influence is quite strong, be it in their architecture or in the culinary field. You can feast on freshly baked baguettes and croissants for breakfast, celebrate Bastille Day and *parlez en Francais* (speak in French) with the locals. Saffron coloured churches, painted friezes and sculptured pillars of Hindu temples, road signs in French; a pleasing mélange is the word that can sum up this lazily beautiful town.

There are two sides to Puducherry: the French quarter and the Tamil quarter. The most beautiful part of the former is the promenade along the shore. I met Mr. Ashok from INTACH (Indian National Trust for Art and Cultural Heritage). He invited me to Le Café, an old French establishment, famous for its organic south Indian coffee, baguettes and croissants. The building, which is currently Le Café, used to be the old French passport office at the dock. Built along the promenade, the café remains open 24 hours a day. Life in Puducherry echoes its tourism slogan 'Give time a break;' quite an appropriate philosophy, if you ask me, for a break in this seaside town does take one into the slow lane. Mr. Ashok suggested I lose my car for two days and get a bicycle to ride around the city and that's exactly what I did. First, we pedalled to the French quarter where we visited one of the most popular churches called Church of Our Lady of Angels, built in 1853, in the Greeko-Roman architectural style. The pastel shades of peach and lime gave it a very serene appearance. It reminded me of Le Basilleque Church in the south of France. One of the Masses in this church is still conducted in French.

Then we visited Bharathi Park, a place which is perfect for an evening walk, and in the centre of the park stands the white Aayi Mandapam. The Park is surrounded by important administrative buildings in Puducherry. It is a treasure trove of 900 varieties of plants and was the location for the zoo shots in the famous movie, *Life Of Pi*. I got dropped off at the L'Orient Hotel; which earlier used to be the building for the public education offices. It dated back to the late 1760s. The emergence of most Puducherry hotels occurred around this time. Mr. Ashok told me that this hotel was one of the most popular hotels not only for their ambience but also for their food. Their restaurant was called Carte Planche. Set in a courtyard, this was where Tamil spices fused with French fare to create something curiously Creole. I met the chef at the restaurant and he explained this fusion by making a few dishes for me. He made vegetables in Creole spices (a mix of oregano, thyme, cinnamon, dill, cloves and cinnamon), started with white butter and finished with coconut milk. He showed me how tomato and vinegar could be used as souring agents instead of tamarind. Several Indian delicacies were given a twist of the French subtlety. Gravies were treated like sauces in the effort to make the cuisine mild. The food tasted pleasantly different, and the scope for this fusion to evolve still remains.

Because I was in this town I was immediately drawn to the bakeries, especially the exotic breads and the desserts. The variety of fresh bakery products was astonishing and their popularity heart-warming. One such bakery I visited was Baker's Street. The ambience reminded me of a cobbled French street, with small tables and chairs, perfect for a day out to sip coffee and read. They sold authentic French breads, cheese and chocolates. It couldn't get better than that!

I tasted the baguette, the macaroons, the caramel custard and a croissant. An odd combination to order, but a good French bakery is judged for its basics. Did they pass my little test? The baguette was dry and hard on the outside, and soft, fluffy and airy inside. The custard was my absolute favourite here. The deep amber glaze of the caramel made the custard look so yummy.

To fulfil my desire for chocolate, I had to dig a little deeper. I found myself at a chocolate shop called Choko La. It is an art to be able to handle chocolate well. They were very popular for their **Chocolate *Pakora*s** and for their 54 Degree Hot Chocolate that I had to try. I met the owner, Mr. Srinath, for whom chocolate making was not just a business, but a big passion. He explained the secret behind the 54 Degree Chocolate; according to him, the standard temperature to serve hot chocolate is 54 degrees. He served me the drink, complete with a chocolate stirring spoon and three cubes of chocolate.

I was instructed to dissolve the two cubes in the drink to balance the temperature and the texture. Their Chocolate *pakoras* were basically chocolate clusters...so really, it was just a *desi* way of selling it. I'll still pen the recipe down. You can make these *pakoras* with the ingredients that you love.

CHOCOLATE *PAKORAS*
(Chocolate clusters shaped like popular Indian fritters.)

Ingredients

1 cup + 3 tbsp melted dark chocolate
1½ cup mixed dry fruits (almond flakes, raisins and broken toasted cashew nuts)

Method

1. Mix one cup of melted chocolate with the mixed dry fruits gently. Don't overdo it or the chocolate will set quickly.
2. Line a baking sheet with baking mat or just butter paper. Place clusters of the chocolate nut mix with the help of a serving spoon. Drizzle some melted chocolate on each cluster from the top to give it a smooth finish. Transfer to the refrigerator and chill for at least one hour or until firm.

DAY 52
26 September / Puducherry

For all those who didn't know, the popular leather brand Hidesign is based out of Puducherry. The gentleman behind the scene is Mr. Dilip Kapur. He studied abroad and returned to open this establishment in 1979 and his first retail store in 1999, in India. The custom design factory definitely didn't look like a place where leather goods were manufactured. Instead, it looked more like a mix of a resort and a school. It had ponds, fountains, and lots of greenery. The factory employs a large number of women from the local community and has very strong ethical and moral principles. Mr. Kapur believes that the product is connected to the time and effort invested in the people and the place who then together bring the product to life. He gave me advise about using these same values when I opened my kitchen. The buildings were designed by Ray Meeker.

The generous man that Mr. Kapur was, he made a leather holster for my kitchen knife. I would like to take a moment here to thank him again for such a delicately made beautiful leather sheath. As a gesture of gratitude, I made **Apple & Banana** *Paniyaram* for him.

APPLE & BANANA *PANIYARAM*
(Sweet dumplings made from rice batter.)

Ingredients

½ cup apple, grated
½ tsp cinnamon *(dalchini)* powder

1 tbsp mint *(pudina)*, chopped
1 tbsp jaggery *(gur)*, chopped into small pieces
½ cup banana, finely chopped
1 tbsp chopped walnuts *(akhrot)*
½ tsp cardamom *(elaichi)* powder
1½ tbsp honey *(shehad)*
2 cups ready-made *dosa* batter

Method

1. Make two different stuffings for the *paniyarams*, one from banana and another from apple.
2. For the apple stuffing, mix the grated apple with cinnamon, mint and jaggery.
3. For the banana stuffing, mix the chopped banana with walnuts, cardamom powder, mint and half a tablespoon honey.
4. Heat a *paniyaram*, a special pan used for this dish to give it the ideal shape. (If you don't get this special pan, try making these in the oven with a tray that has interesting shapes or designs.)
5. Add a teaspoon of the banana-apple filling in different sections of the pan. Now top these up with a spoon of the *dosa* batter. Soon it will start to cook and swell up.
6. Once it swells up, quickly toss the *paniyaram* on the other side so that both sides cook evenly.
7. Once taken off the pan, coat the hot *paniyarams* with a little honey and serve hot.

~

As the evening set in, I decided I wanted to know more about the culture of Puducherry and the people who lived there. That is how I met Kasha, at Surcoufe Street. It was a store with an attached café, run by local women and owned by an American lady called Kasha, who had settled in Puducherry nine years ago. The store sold handicrafts, jewellery and clothes, all made by local craftsmen and artisans. The attached café on the roof was also operated by the local ladies, who cooked a fusion of Indian and world cuisine. They promoted a fair-trade system and worked to promote efforts of the local communities to sustain old traditional handicrafts. After having a long chat with Kasha, I tasted a few dishes and they spoke clearly about the thought behind the café: fresh vegetables and grains, refreshing drinks, abundance of greens. They had a European *thali*; basically, a French take on the traditional Indian *thali*. I personally loved the Indian enchilada. The tortilla was replaced by the *roti* and the stuffing was made with *masoor dal* (red lentil), onions and salsa. It was covered with cheese, baked and served with fresh cream on the side. It was amazing to see local women experimenting with this fusion cuisine and excelling at it. It was a lovely evening spent well at Kasha's.

Puducherry is a quiet city, so I went to bed early that night. The next morning I spent time surveying the stores and strolling on the quiet beaches. Puducherry turned out to be a chic shopping stop too. One can shop on the crowded Mission Street and visit the funky boutique Casablanca, filled with pottery, jewellery and exquisite linens. I bought a few knick-knacks for my family and spent the rest of my time at the beach, chasing the tide. It was nice to take some time off to rejuvenate and relax; the atmosphere in Puducherry was slow and made you want to stop time and dream for a little while.

DAY 53

After experiencing the quaint ex-French colony, I made my way towards Bengaluru.

Day 54
28 September / Bengaluru

It had been 307 km since Puducherry. I arrived in India's third largest city, now called Bengaluru. Since I had a small history with this place, I still prefer to call it by its previous name, Bangalore. I had arrived here back in the days…fresh out of college, with lot of hopes and dreams. Known as the Silicon Valley of India, it supports the rise of innovative entrepreneurs. I had worked at the flagship property of a luxury hotel chain. While I was working there, I did not understand or experience the cultural and religious vibe of the city. I was lost in the large crowds, making most of the vibrant pub culture and the large youth network.

Back in Delhi, in the small tight-knit community that I lived in, religion was, and still is, a way of life. Till today, my parents pray for my success—in life, in love, in marriage…and everything in between. My family and the Gods are pretty well connected. As for me, I have been like a parsley garnish on an elegant continental dish; nobody really cares what the parsley thinks! So, religion for me is more about learning how to have faith in a power that I cannot see. Keeping my faith intact, I stepped inside the halls of the ISKCON Temple.

This temple was inaugurated by Mr. Shankar Dayal Sharma, the then President of India, way back in May, 1997. Founded by Swami Prabhupada to promote Vedic culture and spiritual learning, this is situated atop Hare Krishna Hill. The temple is spread over seven acres and a whopping 32 crores was spent to build this up. The main feature of the temple was the gold-plated *dhwajastambha*, or the flag post, that was 17 metres (56 feet) high and a gold-plated *kalash shikara* (that signifies symbol of life) at the top of the temple, 8.5 metres (28 feet) high. The Sri Krishna *prasadam* was being distributed to all visitors during the *darshan* (auspicious viewing) hours. The temple operated 24 hours a day, but praying was restricted to the *darshan* times. I met Swami Vasudheva, who spoke to me at length on the philosophy, vision and mission of the foundation. People are drawn to ISKCON to discover Lord Krishna, the divine. The magnificent structure of the temple has 130 full-time missionary disciples, who work tirelessly to fulfil the needs of the visitors who come to worship and the Gods who rest there. I was told that the disciples start their day at quarter to four in the morning and perform a ritual called *jagaran seva*. This involves gently waking up the Gods with chants and prayers, followed by *baliya bhog*. It is a type of *kheer* offered to the Gods, before the first *aarti* (Hindu religious ritual of worship in which light from wicks soaked in *ghee* or camphor is offered to one or more deities). Does this make *kheer* the food of Gods? Perhaps. After all, it has pistachio, saffron, almond, cashew nuts, and 60 per cent dark chocolate in it. I am not drifting into a food fantasy here; ISKCON does use chocolate in their *prasadam*.

The ISKCON temple has an initiative called the Akshay Patra Foundation. They have taken on the responsibility to provide mid-day meals to children in government-aided schools across India. This programme runs across nine states in 19 different locations, covering 9000 schools, feeding 1.3 million children a year and two lakh meals being cooked on an average in a day. The foundation has generated a lot of admiration amongst the society and the leaders alike; with current US President, Barack Obama praising the efforts made by the foundation to spread their work around the country. Astounded by the numbers and quantities, I requested to be allowed into the kitchens, without any shoes of course. I met the head chef of the temple, dressed exactly like a priest; he walked me through the large kitchens and explained how the operation worked.

They start preparing their food at midnight. Pre-preparation leads into the actual cooking only by 5 a.m. I was also told that the food offered was not restricted to 'regular' temple food. We all know *laddu*, *peda* (a sweet usually prepared as thick, semi-soft pieces), and *kheer* are offered to the Gods, but at ISKCON, surprisingly, there is a bakery too, that prepares cakes and pastries especially for the offerings. It took me a minute to digest the thought and the pastry that I tried. Undoubtedly, the pastry and bakery goods are 100 per cent vegetarian, and 200 per cent pure. They also make muffins, cookies, tarts, puff pastry and bread. A total of 200 varieties of dishes are made everyday. I was inspired and overwhelmed when I found out about Govinda Prasadum, their fine-dining experience, where the food is prepared with the same *satvik* guidelines, with which their community eating rituals are prepared. For those who spend a day at the temple, this place is a must-visit for an early dinner.

Since I was at a temple and on a budget, I decided my contribution had to be special. I made **Blueberry Pedas** for the disciples. I made the *pedas* look like *diyas* (small cup-shaped oil lamp made of baked clay), garnished with mint leaves that played the role of the flame. They promised to place this on their menu, at the restaurant. Rest of the day was spent roaming around ISKCON. I wouldn't say it changed my perception about the intermingling of spirituality and religion, both being very different things to me, but it definitely showed me all the good things that could be done, in the name of God.

BLUEBERRY PEDAS
(Milk fudge stuffed with blueberries.)

Ingredients

7-8 saffron *(kesar)* strands
2 tbsp milk
4 tbsp clarified butter *(ghee)*
400 gm condensed milk
2½ cup milk powder
1 cup blueberry compote or blueberry jam
1 tsp cardamom *(elaichi)* powder
Mint leaves for garnishing

Method

1. Soak the saffron strand in warm milk and keep it aside.
2. Heat the *ghee* in a pan. Once heated, add the condensed milk to the pan. On medium flame, stir until both *ghee*

and condensed milk come together as one solution. Add saffron-soaked milk to it.

3. Add milk powder.

4. Keep stirring on low flame until the *peda* mixture starts to thicken.

5. It'll take approximately 15 minutes for the mix to be thick and fluffy. You'll see the *ghee* separating from the *peda* and a change of colour; an almost shade of camel.

6. Remove the pan from flame and allow the *peda* mixture to cool off until you can hold and roll the mixture. Roll out small (lemon-sized) balls and shape them like a *peda*.

7. Make a deep thumb impression, almost shaping it like a *diya*, leaving room for lots of blueberry topping to go in. Put a spoonful of blueberry on to the *peda* and finish off with a standing mint leaf.

~

Bangalore, this time around, had some interesting places for me to discover. I wasn't visiting the known eating joints or doing touristy things like I was doing while visiting the other cities. This trip had a special spiritual bent to it. After visiting the temple in the morning, the evening was spent at an old age home called Om Ashram that was specially set up for women. The people behind this *ashram* were dedicated to make life comfortable and stress free for the women staying there. One benefit of being seen on television is that you can do your share of good deeds by promoting awareness about such problems that our otherwise 'family-oriented' society faces. It was very humbling to spend the day with these women, who enjoyed my company and my 'apparently' quirky humour. They reminded me of my grandmothers. So, naturally, I took my blessings from each of them and cooked my *nani*'s (maternal grandmother) favourite **Palak Sai Bhaji** with brown onion rice.

Palak Sai Bhaji
(A green vegetable dish cooked along with spinach and pulses.)

This recipe is the regular version; reduce the garam masala, green chilli and chilli powder accordingly when serving it to elderly people who might not adjust to the spicy dish.

Ingredients

4 tbsp split Bengal gram *(chana dal)*
1 cup water
3 tsp olive oil
½ tsp cumin *(jeera)* seeds
½ cup chopped onions
1 cup chopped potatoes
100 gm colocasia root *(arbi)*
200 gm okra *(bhindi)*
100 gm cauliflower *(phoolgobhi)* florets
50 gm radish *(mooli)*
2 green chillies
4 tsp ginger-garlic *(adrak-lasun)* paste
2 tsp chilli powder

2 tsp coriander (dhania) powder
A pinch of turmeric (haldi) powder
4 cup spinach, chopped
¾ cup country sorrel (khatta palak), chopped
1 tsp raw mango (amchoor) powder
1 tsp garam masala
2 tsp garlic (lasun), finely chopped
2 dry red chillies, for tempering
Salt to taste

Method

1. Combine the split Bengal gram with a cup of water and pressure cook for one whistle. Drain the excess water and keep aside.
2. Heat oil in a pressure cooker and add cumin seeds.
3. When the seeds crackle, add onions, potatoes, colocasia root, okra, cauliflower, radish, green chillies and ginger-garlic paste and sauté for five minutes.
4. Add chilli powder, coriander powder, turmeric powder, salt and sauté.
5. Add spinach, country sorrel and cooked split Bengal gram and pressure cook for 15 minutes.
6. Allow it to cool and whisk the mixture well. Mash all the vegetables inside. Season it with raw mango powder and garam masala.
7. For the tempering, heat oil and once it is hot, add the garlic and red chillies. Let the chillies crackle and the garlic soften for a minute or two and then add this tempering to the dish.

8.   Serve hot with brown onion rice!

~

This dish is well suited for old people; it is nutritious and is mild when it comes to the use of spices.

Day 55
29 September / Bengaluru

Since this part of my trip had been a bit off-beat, bordering
on the spiritual side, I realised that after travelling so
many kilometres, I needed a quiet place to meditate
and truly understand the difference between spirituality
and religion. For the same, I went to the Art of Living
International Centre, located on the outskirts of Bangalore,
a place where many people from different walks of like,
and different parts of the world, came together. Founded
by Sri Sri Ravi Shankar, the foundation's centres are
located in more than 150 countries around the world.
They offer a variety of personal development and trauma
relief programmes. Majority of the staff here comprises
volunteers. The basis of these programmes is meditation,
yoga and breathing exercises. Thousands of people have
overcome complex issues of depression and aggression with
the help of the many programmes the foundation offers.
The Art of Living is engaged in a lot of social-service
activities globally; they offer their services in the areas
of conflict resolution, disaster and trauma relief, poverty
alleviation, empowerment of women, education for all,
and environment sustainability. The foundation focuses on
inner growth, so I felt it was the right place for me to
stop and rejuvenate before moving on.

I met Swami Param Dev, who gave me a walking tour
of the *ashram*. Greenery, water bodies, and birds surround
it, making it perfect for long, peaceful solitary walks. He
explained that the mission of the foundation is to bring an

unshakeable smile to every face in the world. I attended the Sudarshan Kriya programme, which is a yoga discipline focussing on breathing techniques that has a positive effect on the mental and physical well-being. In scientific terms, it improves the antioxidant levels, reduces DNA damage and cell aging. Also, every emotion is connected with a breathing pattern, hence, emotions can be influenced by selective breathing techniques, leading you to become the master of your mind and body rather than being a slave to them. I learnt all this in one session here at the *ashram*, truly impressed. Swami*ji* also informed me that the Art of Living has an Ayurveda centre that serves food for the soul. I made through the wilderness to the Panchkarma centre. Panchkarma refers to the five elements that make up our body. I met Dr. Nisha here who explained how important detoxification is for the body, and how Ayurveda helps revitalise, rejuvenate and refresh it. Food plays a vital role in the process of detoxification and healing of our beings. She quoted a line from a spiritual text that said, '*Pattiya sadi gada tasya kimo sadani sevame*' meaning, 'If there is a proper diet, there is no need for medicine.'

Diets are a subjective matter. What makes this science so specific and effective is that each diet is specific to the person's body type. Applying a process called the '*pith*' which involved an examination of my veins, my body type was identified. My *pith* turned out to be 'fire' which meant I was able to eat a lot and still feel hungry sooner rather than later. I was asked to stop eating so much spice, because it was adding to the fire. I needed to change my diet to light, spice free and full of dairy products. A very unique experience indeed; I walked around, visiting their kitchens and tasting the food they prepared for their patrons and staff. Everything was organic and meant to heal one's body. This trip definitely gave me a new perspective about our cuisine and style of cooking.

Coming back to my initial question, I realised that I couldn't really pick sides between spirituality and religion. There was a fine line dividing the two and sometimes, they meshed. I guess it was enough to say that I felt at peace. So, I gathered my peaceful thoughts and headed out for a lovely dinner.

I wanted to relive my food memories from my earlier days in Bangalore. So I first went to Anand Adyar Bhavan (popularly known as A2B), famous for their Mysore *pak*. The restaurant began its journey two and a half decades ago in Chennai, now spread across Karnataka and Tamil Nadu. I tried three different flavours of Mysore *pak* this time around: cashew nut, extra *ghee*, and low *ghee*. The way it dissolved on your tongue reminded me of butter. The nomenclature traced its origins back to the time when this dessert was made for kings (*pak* means royal). Apart from the Mysore *pak*, the standard Udupi items were also not to be missed. While looking around, I noticed the special *kara appam* maker with which I tried to make my very own domed *appam* (a type of pancake made with fermented rice batter and coconut milk). These *appam*s are served with three types of chutney, all coconut based, but with added flavours and ingredients. While one is served plain and simple, the others have tomato and coriander added to them, respectively.

After dinner, I called up an old friend; she and I frequented Corner House to feed our dessert fetish. Unassuming in its set-up, Corner House caters to a very large audience. The owner, Mr. Narayan Rao, met me and told me that the dessert death by chocolate—made from a generous helping of chocolate cake, three scoops of ice cream of your choice, whipped cream, cherries, and hot chocolate sauce—should be, in fact, renamed 'Life by Chocolate.' Corner House, as you would have guessed by now, was made up of many such desserts that combined all our different sweet cravings garnished with their special chocolate sauce. My favourite from the menu was the malt chocolate shake. Made with vanilla ice cream, dark chocolate sauce, the salty-malt flavour was because of the malt extract in it. What better way to end my Bangalore trip, than to smooth out my spiritual creases, with a sinful shake! These sins aren't really sins, wouldn't you agree?

DAY 56

I was now headed to the land of Nizams and of course, biryani; Hyderabad.

Day 57
1 October / Hyderabad

My journey went north to Andhra Pradesh. After 550 km, in the late afternoon, I entered the City of Nizams, Hyderabad. Established in 1591, the only way to describe the city is with the vocabulary of its architecture. In nineteenth century, when the Mughals took over, Hyderabad became the cultural hub. The Persian influence differentiates this city from the rest; it maintains the old Islamic glory in the patchwork of chaotic urbanisation.

Each Indian city has its defining monument; 'monuments' actually, but there is always that special one. Like Delhi boasts of India Gate, Hyderabad prides in the Char Minar. It is a monument, a minaret and a mosque. Getting to the top, via the dark winding staircase, was like walking through the film set of a horror movie. I was definitely spooked, until I got to the top. I climbed 149 stairs; I read, I re-read and I crosschecked. Each *minar*, minaret in English, had its own staircase. On what is called the 'upper floor' (another word for balcony), is the view of Laad Bazaar, famous for its pearl necklaces and all sorts of shiny imitation jewellery. I recollected that a famous chocolatier once made an impression of Char Minar out of 50 kg of chocolate; even the dessert world loves it!

After I spotted Laad Bazaar, I started my hunt for the famous Irani *chai*. Traditionally, it is a milky, sweet tea rather thick in consistency. What makes it unique is that the milk is boiled separate from the tea. The tea is brewed separately. They are then mixed by pouring the tea into

the milk. I enjoy this tea more because of my love for sweet tea, unlike the strong tea that many Indians prefer. So, whenever you visit Char Minar, a small tea break with assorted local biscuits should be on your to-do list.

Speaking of sweet things in Hyderabad, I would like to mention the *badam ki jaali*; *badam* means almonds and *jaali* means an ornamental lattice net. The design of the almond paste dough resembles the carved stone windows of the Nizam's old palaces. These almond *burfis*, with old Mughal designs, were being made by two very dynamic ladies. The older of the two, Nafees, was carrying forward an old recipe, given to her many years ago, by her mother-in-law. Now, she was working with her daughter-in-law, Nasreen, and carrying on the tradition. They had been in this business for 45 years, and they revealed that this way of preparing almond *burfis* went back to the Nawaiti people, when they migrated from Madras to Central India. Back in the days, cashew nuts and almonds were ground with the mortar and pestle as there were no machines or electric ovens to bake these desserts. They relied on kerosene to cook. They now had bulk ovens and grinders; but judging by the popularity, the taste has not changed much. The workspace was not much larger than an average living room, but it had the capacity to make over a lakh *jaali*s in a day.

As the first step, the dough is made using almond paste, and then, given a diamond-like shape. A sheet of silver *varq* was then laid on it and set aside. Another diamond-shaped dough was made to match. This one had the lattice design cut out of it, and pasted on top of the *varq* covered dough. That gave it the effect of an ornamental *jaali*. It was then baked and served. The fact that there was no additives in it, and that it was 100 per cent almond and sugar preparation, gave it a long shelf life. I tried my hand at this noble sweet; I made a chocolate *badaam ki jaali* by coating the *jaali* with melted chocolate and setting it.

What I am about to tell you next shows how Pakistan and India are still one when it comes to food. I am talking about a Sindhi migrant who came across in 1952, from Pakistan to Hyderabad with his fruit biscuits. I went to the Banjara Hills branch of a store, where I figured out that Osmania biscuits are a household name. These are the biscuits that the Hyderabadis love to enjoy their tea with. These are different from the regular fruit biscuits, and are a part of the wide range of other sweets available at the Karachi Bakery store. They still follow the old recipe and preparation methods, where everything is done by hand. The importance of being handmade is what makes this business special and successful. The fruit biscuits, which I would like to call tutti frutti biscuits, as clichéd as that might sound, tasted of cashew nuts and smelt like they had a whiff of *ittar* perfume. The flavour was elevated with a slight show of salt. This made the sweetness even more special.

A close second was the Osmania biscuit, which is the perfect accompaniment to that Irani *chai* I mentioned, much like the rusk and *chai* combination of the north. It is a soft tea biscuit that melts in your mouth and gets its name from the last ruler of Hyderabad, Osman Ali Khan. These biscuits don't crumble easily when dipped, have a hint of cardamom and saffron flavour and are unlike any other biscuit you would have tasted. Apart from this, Karachi Bakery is very famous for their plum cakes and a variety of other desserts, along with their *badam* milk. Pure full-cream milk, with saffron and ground almonds, broke the myth for me that good *badam* milk was only available in the North. I packed a kilogram of assorted biscuits to take home to my family.

I spent the whole evening eating sweets, and thinking of going easy on my tummy the next day. However, it was not meant to be as I was about to discover the history of the famous Hyderabadi biryani, with the master himself.

Day 58
2 October / Hyderabad

Today, I decided to abstain from any sort of food, all in anticipation of the biryani I was about to taste. biryani literally means fried or roasted. The meaning of the word definitely doesn't describe the complex make-up of this dish, which is the pride of the Muslim community. If I had to pick a place from where I would like to have biryani, Lucknow and Hyderabad would share the number one spot. To distinguish the two, Hyderabadi biryani is popular for being '*kacchi*' implying that the meat is raw, and is set as the first/bottom-most layer in the pot. In the tradition of Lucknow, biryani is made by cooking the rice and meat partially in separate containers and then layered together, for a final *dum*, which literally means to breathe in and conveys a slow cooking method for elaborate preparations like biryani where the lid of the cooking pot is sealed shut by wrapping dough around the circumference of the lid. The pot is then put on a slow flame. The trapped steam allows the cooking of meat and retaining of flavours.

Usually, foodies seem to have varied opinions and stories about biryani. As much as I love eating it, I have never claimed to be an expert. Today, I was to meet a man who while walking down the street, can catch a whiff of biryani being cooked and tell you if it is good or not. This biryani king's throne was located at Café Bahar at Basheer Bagh in Hyderabad. His name was Sayyed Hussain, who started his career at the age of seven as an assistant cook. Now, above 60, he still makes the biryani with his own hands, despite having a fleet of cooks who work for him. He revealed that he wanted to be a cook from the beginning and had to do the odd jobs around the kitchen to gain some respect. Even I believe that the best chefs are the ones who learn it the hard way. He told me that his guru was a man called Noor Mohammad. The way Sayyed explained about the kitchens, cooking, food, and especially biryani, it made me feel like his whole life has been about perfecting the art of making the best recipe. Biryani, it seems isn't about how much or how little, it is about each ingredient, right from buying the rice to the weight of the raw mutton. The weight of the goat has to be 9.5 kg, not a gram more, not a gram less. Even his saffron is sourced from Iran, something that could not be compromised, to him.

After he shared his stories with me, I met his son, Ali Asgar, who took me to the kitchen where 300 kg of biryani was being prepared. I stood next to a boiler that was cooking 40 kg of rice at the time, equipped with a specific rice temperature controller. Ali explained the practical aspect of putting together a biryani in such big lots. First, the rice should be washed until the water resembles clear drinking water. It is then drained and dried till there is no water left in the rice. Cooking the rice is another art form, a mix of science and art. When the rice is cooked, the grains at the bottom are cooked slightly longer than the grains at the top of the boiler. There is a difference of two minutes between the bottom and the top. This is done so that the rice that is layered at the bottom of the biryani comes from the top of the boiler. These grains would have cooked the least in the boiler and will cook the most in the biryani, because they will be covered with the water and juices of the meat that will go on top. The grains from the bottom of the boiler will be placed right on the top, because they have been cooked the most and will finish cooking at the top of the biryani with the help of steam. Therefore the rice at the bottom, with the meat, will be 20 per cent cooked and the rice on the top will be 80 per cent cooked. The meat is marinated for two hours with ginger and garlic, and then coated with *ghee*, yoghurt and spice for the final marination. I was lucky enough to witness the making of the famous **Hyderabadi *Gobhi Mussalam* Biryani** in this establishment, and I want to share the entire recipe with you, so that you can call yourself experts!

HYDERABADI *GOBHI MUSSALAM* BIRYANI
(A mixed rice dish cooked with whole marinated cauliflower.)

Ingredients

3 small or 2 big cauliflower *(gobhi)*
1 tbsp ginger-garlic *(adrak-lasun)* paste
1 tbsp lemon juice
2 cup basmati rice
15 strands of saffron *(kesar)*
¼ cup warm milk
4-5 green cardamom *(choti elaichi)*, only the seeds
1 inch stick cinnamon *(dalchini)*
1 tsp black cumin *(shahi jeera)*
6-8 cloves *(laung)*

8-10 peppercorns *(sabut kali mirch)*
½ cup fried onions
¾ cup hung yoghurt (two hours is enough for hanging the yoghurt)
2 tsp green chilli paste
Salt to taste
1½ tsp red chilli powder
½ tsp turmeric *(haldi)* powder
2 tsp coriander *(dhania)* powder
2 tbsp clarified butter *(ghee)*
10-12 mint *(pudina)* leaves
2 tbsp oil
1 cup refined flour *(maida)*
Water to knead the dough

Method

1. Remove the thick cauliflower stem. Don't separate the florets; cut the stem just enough to hold all of them together. If the cauliflower is big, cut it into half.
2. Marinate the cauliflower with ginger-garlic paste and lemon juice. Soak the rice in water for 30 minutes and keep changing the water, until it is not muddy and you can clearly see the rice. Also, soak the saffron strands in warm milk.
3. Meanwhile, prepare the biryani masala by grinding the above-mentioned quantities of cardamom, cinnamon, black cumin, cloves and peppercorns together. (If the quantity is too small grind in a big batch but use quantity as per this recipe).

4.   To the marinated cauliflower add fried onions (save some for garnish), hung yoghurt, green chilli paste, salt, chilli powder, turmeric powder, coriander powder and hot *ghee*.

5.   Mix this masala well and rub it over the cauliflower. Save the extra marinade in the same bowl, do not throw it away. Let the cauliflower rest for 10 minutes at least.

6.   In those 10 minutes, put rice to a boil with salt and mint leaves. Once it comes to a boil, put it on simmer. The idea is to partially cook the rice, so do not cook for more than four to five minutes. The science behind partially cooking rice a bit early is that it will cook evenly with vegetables or meats that you're cooking it with. Knead the dough by mixing flour and water together.

7.   Now take the pot you'll be cooking biryani in, ensure it is both deep and wide. Add a tablespoon of oil at the bottom. Put marinated cauliflower to this and spread the extra marinade evenly in the pan. Add two and a half cups of hot water. Now add top half layer of the rice that has been boiling for five minutes to this biryani pot and let it submerge in water. Add the leftover rice on the top of this; it will stay above water, as we have added only two and a half cups. The top half layer of the partially cooked rice is only 30 per cent cooked at the moment in comparison to the bottom half layer which is 60 per cent cooked, if you calculate technically from the time that rice went into boiling water and in the sequence it came out. Hence the top half layer will submerge in the water in the biryani pot (so it can cook more) and

the bottom half layer of rice will mostly stay above the hot water in the biryani pot, as it needs to cook lesser and steam will be enough to make it fluff up.

8. Add one tablespoon oil in a swirl in the biryani pot and in the same way add the saffron milk so it spreads evenly. Put it on high flame and shut the lid. Seal the pot from all sides by rolling a long strip of dough and sticking it on all sides.

9. Once the lid starts to get hot, lower the flame to medium and then finally to low. After five minutes, add burning coal on top of the lid; this is to prevent the water droplet formation beneath the lid because of the steam. The coal will make sure the biryani cooks evenly in the pot.

10. After 10 minutes, take the pot off the heat. Open it after 30 minutes only. Serve immediately with some fried onion on top. (You can follow the same recipe for mutton or chicken; marination and cooking time will vary slightly.)

~

Now it was time to taste the biryani; I sat down at a table and minutes later a huge plate of biryani was laid before me. If I didn't have such a massive appetite, my whole family would have to be here to finish the food on my plate. Every bite was testament to the 55 years of experience of Sayyed Hussain. What stood out was the fact that the spices were just enough to elevate the flavour of the rice.

The whole day was spent at Café Bahar, learning, eating and digesting.

DAY 59
3 October / Hyderabad

Hyderabad has two parts: the old city (my favourite) and the new city. I drove to the new city to meet Arun who has his own shooting academy called Shooting Stars in High Tech City. The history of archery goes back to ancient Hindu mythology. Arun's academy believes in the same principles of the ancient Indians. Spirituality and physical fitness is a very important part of being successful at this sport. I tried my hand at being Robin Hood; it worked two out of five times. When you travel, I suggest take time out to explore other dimensions of a city's culture. It is refreshing to see people who are passionate about learning and teaching what they are good at.

I also got a chance to visit an emporium where I met Prakashji who explained the intricacy of *kalamkari* paintings (type of hand-painted or block-printed cotton textile, produced in parts of India. The word is derived from the Persian words *kalam* (pen) and *kari* (craftmanship), meaning drawing with a pen) to me. Trying to understand more about this art, I realised the word *kalamkari*, comes from the word *kalam*, meaning pen. There is a special type of pen that is used to make these paintings, and in the past this art form has been used to depict various Gods. The most stunning among these paintings was called *The Tree of Life*, where the painting had been detailed with the help of *kundan* work (traditional form of Indian gemstone jewellery involving a gem set with gold foil between the stones and its mount). Each painting, I was told, took up to 15 days to make. Another reason why I came to meet Praksh*ji* was to be introduced to his cook, Abdul Hamid, who was an expert at cooking Hyderabadi dishes. I got to meet him later in the day and he taught me, step by step, how to make the famous **Baghare Baingan**. It is a brinjal recipe that belongs to Hyderabad. It involves peanuts, coconut, and sesame, a very unique blend of ingredients.

BAGHARE BAINGAN
(Eggplant curry.)

Ingredients

8 small brinjals *(baingan)*
Salt to taste
2 tbsp white sesame *(safed til)*
2 tsp cumin *(jeera)* seeds
3 tbsp peanuts *(moongphali)*, without skin
3 tbsp dry coconut
2-3 green chillies, slit in half
1 tbsp coriander leaves *(dhania patti)*, chopped
½ tsp turmeric *(haldi)* powder
¼ tsp red chilli powder
½ cup oil + oil for frying
1 tsp mustard *(sarson)* seeds
1 tsp black caraway *(kalonji)* seeds
8-10 curry leaves *(kari patta)*
1-inch long piece ginger *(adrak)*, finely chopped
10 cloves garlic *(lasun)*, finely chopped

2 tbsp tamarind *(imli)* paste
½ cup water
1 tsp honey *(shahad)*

Method

1. Take small brinjals and criss-cross them (dividing it into four quarters) from the bottom all the way till the stem or until 2/3 of the brinjal, so it is easy to cook them evenly and stuff them with spices. Apply salt on these and keep on the side for seven to eight minutes. Once the water is drained, strain these and half fry in oil, till it is tender but not cooked.

2. Separately roast the sesame; a teaspoon of cumin seeds, peanuts and coconut in a teaspoon oil each.

3. Make a paste by grinding the above along with green chillies and a little water. It has to be a thick paste. Take it out in a bowl. Add the coriander leaves, turmeric powder, chilli powder and salt to this paste and mix thoroughly.

4. Heat four tablespoon oil a pan. Add the mustard seeds, one teaspoon cumin and black caraway seeds to hot oil. Once they splutter, add curry leaves followed by ginger and garlic. Stir this for a minute or so.

5. Now add the roasted masala paste. Cook on medium flame till it changes colour to deep orange for five to six minutes. Add the tamarind paste, half cup water and honey. Once it comes to a boil, add the brinjals and then let it reduce for five minutes. This will enable the masala to seep into the brinjals.

6.   Take it off the stove when the gravy is semi thick. The dish is ready. Serve it hot with rice or *roti*.

~

It was very generous of Prakash*ji* to invite me to his house and share his recipes and his cook's knowledge with me. Luckily for me, Indians are very hospitable; all I needed to do was ask. As a farewell gift, he gave me a framed *kalamkari* painting to bring back with me to Delhi.

DAY 60

I left the City of Nizams with fond memories and with my stomach full of biryani. I headed to Vishakhapatnam.

DAY 61
5 October / Vishakhapatnam

I decided to drive east, to the coast of Andhra Pradesh, to Vishakhapatnam (also called Vizag for those of you who don't enjoy spelling). Over a distance of 625 km from Hyderabad, one does have to go a little out of the way to reach here. For those of you who enjoyed the movie *Avatar*, you will be intrigued to learn that life-size models of the character Neytiri and her 'Mountain Banshee' have been built in the new Municipal Corporation park, to spread the message of preserving the environment. Vizag is famous for its different tourist destinations, be it caves, beaches, valleys, hills or lakes, the city has it all. Vishakhapatnam has also been recognised as a Global City of the Future. Being near to the harbour, I decided to discover the fish market early in the morning.

At 6:30 a.m. I arrived at the Vishakhapatnam fishing harbour where the fish market opens from 6:30 a.m. to 9:30 a.m. On the way to the harbour, I saw a lot of wooden boats being built by hand. As the harbour came into view, my eyes took in the chaos, and the simile 'like a fish market' made a lot more sense. There were many boats docked along the harbour, and each boat owner had set up shop on the dock itself. They were unloading their fish straight onto their little makeshift tables and selling the fish fresh to the customers. It didn't feel like six in the morning; it felt like the stock market at midday! Amidst all this I was feeling a little lost. I found Mr. Panda who would be my tour guide for the day, to talk to some of the fishermen and translate for me.

My first stop was at Shakti Babu's boat. He was definitely an interesting man; his name had the addition '*babu*' which meant he had an important role to play. I found out that he was the vice president of the fishermen's union. He told me that the fishermen usually go out to sea for a period of 20-30 days and bring back all the catch. They carry ice for preserving the fish, oil for their boats, and food to survive for those days. Shakti Babu told me that they avoid exposing the fish to oil, food stuff and edible items to help preserve the fish till they reach the shore. There were about 500 boats in Vishakhapatnam and each could carry up to three tonnes of fish at a time. On an average, 30 tonnes of fresh fish was available everyday. River fish were sold separately on the roadsides in the city. I saw a few varieties of fish, the most popular of their catch being the Indian Mackerel, which is also sold in Kerala. I also saw shrimp, scampi, Bombay duck, and pomfret. By now, I was accustomed to the smell and chaos, and I began to notice the system in place and the order in which fish was being bought and sold. As a chef, it is very important for me to understand how to buy and select fresh fish. More so for lovers of seafood who live in landlocked places, like Delhi, a trip to the fish market is a must.

After an early morning start, Mr. Panda decided to show me a few historical sites and introduce me to the cultural heritage of Vishakhapatnam. First stop was Bhimli beach, believed to have originated in the third century. The first to land here were the Dutch, even before the

British. The beach is named after the figure from Hindu mythology, Bheem, who is said have rested here. The entire coastline is speckled with historical elements like the Dutch cemetery, the Buddha statue and the lighthouse. The Bhimli Beach is where the Gaushthani river joins the Bay of Bengal. If your smartphone has the panorama camera function, then this is the best place to use it.

Not far from the beach is a temple that dates back 500 years. This temple is called Sri Sri Naukamakali, and holds an idol of Kali, that the local fishermen pray to. She is said to be the mother goddess of the 14 fishermen communities. They believe that she needs to be placated if anything bad happens at sea.

After a long morning I got ready to meet Mr. V.V.N. Subhramaniam, a partner at Vijayawada Ramaiah Andhra Vegetarian Meals at Daba Gardens. They had been serving Andhra meals for 24 years, purely vegetarian as the name suggested. For a mere sum of Rs. 100, you could eat 32 traditional Andhra items, including accompaniments and condiments. It was one of those places that always fascinates a chef. Why? For a place with such a high turnover rate with such a complex regional menu, this restaurant's operation was smooth and well planned.

The restaurant was based on the *thali* concept; either steel or the traditional banana leaf, the choice was yours. At this point, even before I was served my food, my happiness had grown many times over. I noticed the blood red colour of the dishes that were served to me on my plantain leaf. This reflected the heavy use of spices in the food, very typical of Andhra Pradesh. I would describe the cuisine here as complex and multilayered, rather than subtle and simple like other parts of the country. The concept of Andhra *thalis* is popular all over the country, but experiencing it in the heart of the state was a great feeling. My favourite dish, among the many, was the *dal*, which had *gongura* leaves in it. The leaves are like wild spinach and are from the hibiscus family. They are slightly tangy and bitter. *Gongura* chutney is popular all over India. The North Indians like making *dal palak*, similar to *dal gongura* in Andhra. Another favourite was the *aratkaya*, a raw banana stir-fry. There were other authentic dishes like the *pacchadi*, the *mulgapodi masala*, *vada*, curd rice. I did count the 32 dishes that were on my plate and imagine my luck, Mr. Subhramaniam came up with another dish: tamarind or lemon rice, called **Pulihora**, in Telugu. The rice was not a simple dish, quite complex but easy to make. I proceeded to learn from Mr. Subhramanium. Extremely tangy and bursting with flavours this dish was made at every festival and auspicious occasion as an offering to God. I learnt here that even savoury items are served to the Gods!

PULIHORA
(Traditional sour rice preparation.)

Ingredients

1 cup rice, soaked in water
Salt to taste
2 tbsp sesame *(til)* oil

¼ tsp mustard *(sarson)* powder
1 tsp turmeric *(haldi)* powder
1 lemon-sized tamarind *(imli)* ball
1 tsp coriander *(dhania)* seeds
1 tsp mustard *(sarson)* seeds
1 tbsp black gram *(urad dal)*
1 tbsp split Bengal gram *(chana dal)*
1-inch ginger *(adrak)*, grated
½ cup peanuts *(moongphali)*, roasted
5-6 curry leaves *(kari patta)*
2 green chillies, slit lengthwise
2-3 red chillies, slit lengthwise

Method

1. Cook the soaked rice with apt amount of salt; add sesame oil to it and keep it aside. Mix mustard powder and turmeric powder with rice, with your hands or a spatula to ensure rice doesn't break.
2. Soak the tamarind in half-cup warm water for 30 minutes.
3. Roast and coarsely grind the coriander seeds. Keep aside.
4. Heat the sesame oil in a pan and let the mustard seeds splutter, add the black gram and split Bengal gram, grated ginger, peanuts, curry leaves, green chillies and red chillies. Once they turn golden brown in colour, add coriander seeds and tamarind water.
5. Let it reduce for 10 minutes. Once this mix becomes a thick paste add this to the turmeric mustard rice. Mix gently with a spatula or spoon.

6.   Serve hot with *papad*.

~

After a long eventful day as usual, I couldn't wait to get a good night's sleep, to digest my food, and be ready for a new day and all the new food experiences that were yet to come.

Day 62
6 October / Vishakhapatnam

Mr. Panda, who very graciously showed me around Vishakhapatnam the previous day, was taking me to see his very own labour of love. He worked in a pickle company that gave employment to rural-based communities. Mr. Panda managed the daily operations. He took me to see the factory and the line of products being manufactured there. The company made spices and pickles, out of which the powder of Guntoor chillies was the most popular. Guntoor chillies are from the Guntoor district in Andhra Pradesh and are also known as Andhra chillies; very popular because of their deep red colour that they induce into the food, and their high capsaicin level. The capsaicin level describes the intensity, or the heat, of a chilly. No wonder Andhra food is really spicy. If you recall, the lunch I had the previous day featured a member of the hibiscus family. '*Gongura*' was also present today at the factory. Being processed into relish and pickle, the versatility of this leaf was amplified by its many medicinal properties.

Besides *gongura*, there were many lines of pickles being made, out of which the emu pickle caught my attention. Mr. Panda told me that it is a very popular condiment that has caught on recently with the Andhra public. At first, I felt a little strange, as I had never eaten emu before, and this was probably be one of the only times I ate it. He then told me how various ailments could be cured by eating this pickle. Maybe I will eat it again after all! Apart from the emu pickle, I saw tomato pickle and chutney, ginger-garlic paste, and a wide range of other preserves that were being made and packaged.

I really pushed my luck and managed to squeeze out the **Gongura** Chutney recipe from them. So, if any of you manage to get your hands on some *gongura*, here is a recipe you can follow.

Gongura Chutney
(Red sorrel leaves dip.)

Ingredients

A bunch of sorrel leaves *(gongura)*
2 tbsp oil
1 tsp + ¼ tsp mustard *(sarson)* seeds
1 tsp cumin *(jeera)* seeds
2 tsp black gram *(urad dal)*
3 tsp split Bengal gram *(chana dal)*
2 tsp coriander *(dhania)* seeds
6 cloves garlic *(lasun)*
5-6 green chillies
1½ tbsp tamarind *(imli)* pulp
Salt to taste
2 dried red chillies
8-10 curries leaves *(kari patta)*
A pinch of asafoetida *(hing)*

Method:

1. Clean and chop the *gongura* leaves. Heat one tablespoon oil in a pan. Add the mustard and cumin seeds. When

the mustard starts spluttering, add black gram, split Bengal gram and coriander seeds.

2.   Sauté this mix until the grams are golden. Add garlic, green chillies and the chopped *gongura* leaves. In a few minutes the *gongura* leaves will be cooked. Switch off the flame and let it cool.

3.   Grind these ingredients while adding the tamarind pulp and salt to make a coarse paste. Take it out in a bowl. Heat half a tablespoon of oil in a pan to make tempering. Add one-fourth teaspoon of mustard seeds, red chillies, curry leaves and asafoetida. Add this tempering to the chutney. *Gongura* chutney is ready.

~

I bid farewell to Mr. Panda and thanked him for being so kind. I had a long journey ahead of me from Vishakhapatnam to Bhubaneshwar. I said goodbye and got back on the road. It would be 12 a.m. before I reach my destination.

DAY 63
7 October / Bhubaneshwar

A new day. A new state. I was now in Odisha, originally known as Orissa, I was in the capital, Bhubaneshwar. Called the Temple City of India, Bhubaneshwar was home to more than 1000 temples, most of which were built in the Kalinga architectural style. The state was famous for many art forms, handicrafts, sand artistry, sculptures and the classical Odissi dance. Out of all these I found the dance form Odissi most fascinating. I am a bit of a dancer myself and I have a special admiration in my heart for classical dance forms. What I find fascinating is the get-up and the pre-preparation that goes into the Indian classical dance forms. One of the eight classical dance forms in India, Odissi, is among the oldest. I happened to meet a classical dancer, Mamta, who ran her own school, where she had been teaching for almost 33 years. She had been dancing since she was seven years old.

Mamta explained that it was difficult to follow one's dreams when you were a classical dancer. She claimed that dedicating self to this art form and perfecting each movement took many years and the number of people who appreciated these classical dance forms were also dwindling. Being a classical dancer was not the most lucrative job she had, but the devotion to the dance form, and in turn, the devotion to God was rewarding. Odissi has evolved over the years. What separated this dance form from the others was the independent movement of the head, the chest and the pelvis. Much harder than it looks, this dance form is divided into five parts. The dance starts with a hymn invoking the God or Goddess. It then progresses into the dancers posing like sculptures, in tune to the music. From there, the dancers move into the actual dance form. I had the pleasure of watching a batch of Mamta's students perform a short recital for me. The dance finishes with *moksha* (In Hinduism and Jainism, release from the cycle of rebirth impelled by the law of karma), which is when the dancers declare complete devotion to the Gods through their movements. After watching them, I understood what Mamta meant about hard work, determination and precision. The dance performance was beautiful and was an outcome of the many years the dancers had spent mastering each movement and pose.

After this cultural stop at Bhubaneshwar, I began the longest stretch of my journey—850 km from Bhubaneshwar to the central-most point of India, Nagpur. It would take me a day and a half to reach this city via Raipur.

DAY 64

After taking a halfway stop at Raipur, I headed to Nagpur.

Day 65
9 October / Nagpur

I could proudly say that I had clocked in 2000 km over the last four days from Hyderabad to the geographical centre of India, Nagpur. It was a proud moment for me to realise that I had travelled by road and covered approximately 12,000 km to get there. The centre was marked by a '0' milestone and a sandstone pillar built by the British; a sculpture of four horses were near as well. The pillar was inscribed with distances (in miles) to various other Indian cities. Though Nagpur was not supposed to be on my travel map, I still found a way to make a small stop in this city, to taste the food and its famous oranges. Nagpur is the largest city in central India and you would be surprised to know that it has been deemed as one of the most successful cities of the future. High literacy rate, excellent health care, and lush greenery are the adjectives that describe the city that is Nagpur. As I drove through, these facts became evident to me.

Nagpur, being in the Vidarbha region, the cuisine and the food culture had the latter's influence. The cuisine was also famous as the Saoji cuisine of Maharashtra. I couldn't believe that being a vegetarian, I would put all my money down to catch a flight back here to eat that Saoji Mutton again. Saoji is actually a small Hindu community from Central India, specially the Malwa region. Saojis are known for their special blend of spices and the meat dishes that are prepared using them. This community is mostly non-vegetarian, which is quite unheard of for most Hindus. It is very typical of

Maharashtra to have small hotels with boards saying 'Nagpur Hotel' or 'Saoji Hotel,' meaning you will definitely find some excellent mutton dishes on their menu. I ran into a local family who had invited me to try their version of the mutton. I got the invitation through Facebook, where I am quite active (comes with the job profile)! I visited the family in Nagpur, who were part of the Saoji clan.

The family had set up a small arrangement in their garden, where I had a chance to taste their mutton and the traditional *lambi roti* (literally meaning a long flatbread, this is a crisp glutinous bread which is a speciality of the Dalit community of Vidarbha). The dough was very slack, and it was beaten and kneaded to make the texture like wet clay. The grandmother of the family was making this *roti*, sitting next to an upturned earthenware pot, placed atop a wood-fire. The pot was quite large and the *roti* was quickly cooked on the rounded surface of the pot, much like the popular *roomali roti* (extremely thin flatbread and usually served folded like a handkerchief). It is extremely thin and flaky and is used to dip in the mutton curry. When it came to the taste, it surpassed any other Indian bread I had had! Speaking of the mutton, I had a chance to see the whole spices separately to be able to relate the taste components. A fair warning, the curry is very spicy! The good part is that the spices are bursting with flavours and it makes you want to challenge your appetite and eat more! The spices were a blend of coriander seeds, cloves, peppercorn, cumin, and cinnamon. The three special ingredients in the mix are poppy seeds, powdered coconut and sorghum flour.

These three define the uniqueness of the spice mix. The spices are used for the **Saoji Curry**, which can be made with mutton or chicken. For the vegetarians, the curry is served with chickpea cutlets. I made this curry into a meal by cooking the curry with rice as a part of it. You can choose to cook the same recipe with mutton and without rice, just reduce the water.

Saoji Curry
(Spicy curry made from whole spices and dry coconut.)

Ingredients

2 tbsp oil
1½ tbsp poppy *(khus khus)* seeds
½ cup powdered coconut
1 tbsp coriander *(dhania)* seeds
1 tsp caraway seeds *(shahi jeera)*
4-6 cloves *(laung)*
12-15 black peppercorns *(sabut kali mirch)*
1-2 black cardamoms *(badi elaichi)*
3-4 green cardamoms *(choti elaichi)*
1-inch stick cinnamon *(dalchini)*
2 bay leaves *(tejpatta)*
6-8 whole dry red chillies
½ tbsp star anise or stone flower *(dagad phool)*
50 gm sorghum flour *(jowar atta)*
2 tbsp coconut oil
3 onions, chopped
2 tbsp fresh ginger-garlic *(adrak-lasun)* paste
300 gm boneless chicken

100 gm rice, soaked
500 ml chicken stock
Salt to taste

Method

1. Heat the oil in a pan. Make the Saoji masala by frying poppy seeds, powdered coconut, coriander seeds, caraway, cloves, peppercorns, black and green cardamom, cinnamon, bay leaf, dried red chillies, star anise or stone flower, and sorghum flour together. Fry until all spices release their aroma and the sorghum flour is cooked. Reserve the leftover oil and make a paste of this fried masala by grinding it with a bit of water.

2. Now heat the coconut oil in a pan and fry the onions in it until golden brown. Strain the oil and make a brown onion paste by grinding these fried onions.

3. Heat the leftover oils together and add the ginger-garlic paste to it. Now add the chicken on high flame and let it sear. Add the fried onion paste and the Saoji masala paste to this chicken. Add the soaked and drained rice. Sauté for two minutes. Add chicken stock and season with salt. Once it comes to a boil, let it all simmer together for 15 minutes. Serve the meal hot!

~

The combination of Saoji mutton and *lambi roti* is worth a trip to Nagpur, a must try before you die!

Nagpur is called the Orange City because of the oranges that grow here. It is also a major trade centre for oranges that travel to many parts of the country. The orange farm that I visited was about 20 km outside Nagpur, in a village called Hatla. Here I paid a visit to the owner, Manoj. He was an 'Udyan Pandit,' which basically meant that he was a master of horticulture, a title that he had worked hard to earn. Under his care were 250 small plants and 2500 big trees. These trees were of the Nagpur Mandarin variety. The Nagpur Mandarin is a table fruit and the skin comes off clean and the pulp can be eaten easily. It is very popular for this reason and for the sweet tangy flavour of the pulp. Another fact that Manoj told me was that the smaller the orange, the more concentrated the taste. Good things come in small packages, right?

Of course, I tasted a lot of orange juice. It was refreshing, sweet and very tasty. The skin had such concentrated aromas that my mind was buzzing with ideas of dishes that could be flavoured with the peel. I took the opportunity to pluck my own oranges, and prepared an **Orange Pesto Salad** for Manoj, right there on the field. People speak of wine tours in France and Scotch tours in Scotland...I had an orange tour in Nagpur. Why not! With this visit, my time in Nagpur came to an end. I was now getting ready to make my way to Madhya Pradesh on an overnight journey.

ORANGE PESTO SALAD
(Orange segments and greens tossed with basil pesto.)

Ingredients (For the Orange Pesto)

3 cups fresh basil (tulsi) leaves
1 cup grated Parmesan cheese
2 tbsp toasted pine nuts
3 tbsp Nagpur orange juice
2 tbsp olive oil
1 tbsp fresh lemon juice
8-10 cloves garlic (lasun)
Salt to taste

Ingredients (For the salad)

200 gm penne pasta, boiled
1 orange segment, skin removed (you can shape them like butterflies if you slit them half from the back side)
1 bunch lettuce leaves
1 tbsp melon seeds

Method

1. Combine all Orange Pesto ingredients in a processor. Blend until it becomes a coarse paste, scraping down sides of bowl occasionally. Season pesto with salt.
2. In a large bowl, toss together the boiled cold penne pasta, torn lettuce leaves, orange segments, melon seeds and orange pesto dressing.
3. Present in a white salad platter, garnish with shaved Parmesan and orange segments, that are made to look like butterflies, or melon seeds. Serve chilled.

DAY 66
10 October / Bhopal

Our day started late; with all the travelling, we needed to catch up on our sleep. The previous night I had reached Bhopal, the capital of Madhya Pradesh. Known as the City of Lakes, it is also popular for having the largest artificial lake in Asia. Bhopal was the second largest princely state ruled by the Mughals, which of course made a great impact on the food of the city. As a state Madhya Pradesh is fast developing for its agro food industries. As a chef it is very interesting for me to understand where a lot of these products come from and how they are grown. The state has a very fertile belt, with sufficient amount of rainfall and ample sunshine. The top quality wheat that gets circulated across the country is called *sharbati* wheat, also called grains of gold, which is one of the best produced in India. The soya bean industry in Madhya Pradesh is one of its biggest economies and accounts for over 5000 crores or 65 per cent of the country's yield. I decided to visit a new factory, run by a friend of my father's, where soya milk powder was produced and processed into different products. Since soya bean is very rich in protein, and is an excellent source of digestible protein, especially for those who are lactose intolerant, the company concept was a health-based project with which milk, tofu and soya *paneer* was made.

I took a small tour around the factory and saw how the tofu was being manufactured. I tasted interesting flavours of the tofu which were being prepared, as well as learnt how to make soya milk. I wanted to use the products and make a dish of my own, something that belonged to the state and yet also fitted in with the profile of the products I was going to use. Therefore, I decided to make **Tofu** *Kofta*. Indians are not accustomed to the taste of tofu, and I kept their preferences in mind while making this product. The *kofta*s (savoury ball made with minced meat, *paneer*, or vegetables) were delicious and the tofu was very easy to work with as an alternate for *paneer*.

Tofu *Kofta*
(Small cheese-stuffed tofu balls served in a thick gravy.)

Ingredients (For the Kofta)

1 cup tofu, crumbled
2 potatoes, boiled
2 tbsp chickpea flour *(besan)*
1 tsp green chillies, chopped
1 tsp garam masala
1 tsp cumin *(jeera)* powder
1 tbsp cornflour *(makke ka atta)*
2 tsp dry fenugreek powder *(kasoori methi)*, dry roasted and powdered
Salt to taste
Oil to deep fry
100 gm Cheddar cheese

Method (For the Kofta)

1.   Mix all the ingredients, (except the oil and cheese) to make a tofu *kofta* mix. Heat the oil for frying.

2. Divide the mixture into even pieces to make lemon-sized balls. Flatten this ball. Add a small cube of cheese in the centre and roll into a round shape again. Repeat this for all the *kofta*s.

3. Deep-fry all the *kofta*s, until each *kofta* turns golden-brown. Drain and set aside.

4. The cheese inside should have melted by now and you can pop in one before you can make the curry.

Ingredients (For the gravy)

2 tbsp clarified butter *(ghee)*
1 cup boiled onion purée
1 tbsp ginger-garlic *(adrak-lasun)* paste
1¼ tsp cumin *(jeera)* powder
1½ tsp coriander *(dhania)* powder
½ tsp red chilli powder
¼ tsp turmeric *(haldi)* powder
1 tbsp soaked cashew nuts *(kaju)*, made into a paste
2 cups fresh tomato purée
Salt to taste
½ tsp garam masala powder
2 tbsp fresh cream *(malai)*
Few coriander leaves *(dhania patti)*

Method (For the gravy)

1. Heat the *ghee* in a deep pan. Add boiled onion paste and ginger-garlic paste. Sauté for three to four minutes.

2. Add cumin, coriander, red chilli and turmeric powder.

3. Add cashew nut paste to this and sauté for a minute more. Add tomato purée and cook until the oil surfaces.

4. Add one cup of water, bring to a boil, then simmer for about 10 to 15 minutes or until you have fairly thick gravy.

5. Add salt and garam masala. Finish off with *malai* or cream. Switch off the gas. You can additionally add half a teaspoon of powdered dry fenugreek leaves (*kasoori methi*) as well.

6. Toss the tofu *kofta*s in this curry. Garnish with coriander and serve hot.

~

After leaving the factory, I set out to discover the cuisine of Bhopal. This was one of those rare cities where the Muslim and Hindu cultural mix was heavily reflected in the food. Hindu side of the cuisine was heavy on vegetarian food with *chaat*s being the most popular. *Poha jalebi* was one breakfast that one should not miss when in this part of the world. Most popular dishes from the Muslim side are meat based. Traditional dishes like *korma*, *sheekh* kebab and *rizala* till date are a hit. Most of the Muslim eateries are found in busy alleyways of small markets; the same story exists in Bhopal, where the best *korma*s, kebabs and curries are found in the busy heart of the city. So, it is interesting that how two entirely different cuisines coexist in the same city and you'll meet many people who enjoy both with the same passion.

Today, I was to meet a legend of sorts. He and his family had been cooking for the Pataudi family for generations. It was time to meet Chandu Bhai at his house. It was indeed an honour to be invited to cook and dine with him. He had previously been known for several years for the meat delicacies that he prepared, especially for the royal weddings that took place in Bhopal. His family had been cooking professionally for 250 years, almost when Bhopal came into existence. Chandu Bhai's grandfather, Khan Abdullah, catered for more royal weddings than any one of us could imagine. He handed me an 80-year-old photograph of his grandfather cooking over huge pots lined up in a row. As he put it, their speciality was the Nawabi cuisine. For me, he was a teacher, and what he said was worth remembering. He took out time to cook with me and he taught me how to make **Chicken Rizala** that had exceptional flavours. It was made of yoghurt and flavoured with coriander. The secret ingredient was the poppy seed that gave the dish the extra edge. This dish also happens to be very popular in Bengal.

CHICKEN RIZALA
(Chicken served in a thick white gravy.)

Ingredients

2 onions, roughly chopped
1-inch piece of ginger *(adrak)*
6 cloves garlic *(lasun)*
10 cashew nuts *(kaju)*
1 tbsp poppy *(khus khus)* seeds
1 cup thick yoghurt

½ kg chicken, cut into big pieces
Salt and pepper to taste
½ tsp nutmeg *(jaiphal)* and mace *(javitri)* powder
4 tbsp clarified butter *(ghee)*
2-inch cinnamon *(dalchini)* stick
4 cloves *(laung)*
2 whole dry red chillies
1 black cardamom *(badi elaichi)*
4 green cardamom *(choti elaichi)*
6-8 black peppercorns *(sabut kali mirch)*
½ tsp sugar
A few drops of Panadanas syrup *(kewra* essence)
A few drops of perfumed sweet essence *(mitha ittar)*

Method

1. Make an onion-ginger-garlic paste. Blend it nicely to make a smooth one.
2. Soak the cashew nuts separately and make a paste with the poppy seeds.
3. Add thick yoghurt to the chicken, along with onion-ginger-garlic paste, salt, pepper powder and nutmeg-mace powder. Mix and keep aside at least for an hour.
4. Heat the *ghee* in a pan. Lightly pound the whole spices (cinnamon, cloves, red chillies, black and green cardamom, and black peppercorns) so they release fresh aromas and add this to the *ghee*. Add chicken. Sauté the chicken in the pan until it seals its juices. Now pour in all the leftover or excess marinade.

5. Cook on medium flame for five to six minutes. Once the yoghurt is thick, add the poppy-cashew nut paste. Cook for a minute and pour half cup of hot water. Check the seasoning and cover. Let it simmer on low flame till oil starts to float on top and the chicken is cooked through.

6. Finish it with some sugar, Panadanas syrup and perfumed sweet essence. Serve hot.

~

We sat down to eat after spending time together cooking. The menu had vegetable *saloni*, chicken *rizala*, *laccha parantha* and *kheer*. The *rizala* was my favourite; it smelt good, tasted even better, and felt at home in my stomach. The yoghurt made the curry tangy, the cashew nuts made the curry thick and rich and the poppy seeds made the curry slightly sweet. As per the tradition in Bhopal, a *paan* is eaten after every meal; so, we too did the same. It was the perfect ending to my meal.

Meal done, friendship struck, lessons learnt and soon, it was time to leave. My next destination was Gwalior, the home of the Scindias.

DAY 67

Travelling from one region with a royal past, Bhopal, to another erstwhile royal kingdom, Gwalior.

Day 68
12 October/ Gwalior

Gwalior is one of the most popular cities of Madhya Pradesh, because of its historical significance. The city and its fortress have been ruled by several Indian dynasties: the Mughals, Marathas and the Scindias. I wanted to experience both history and culture together so I picked a destination where I could find a bit of both; I went to see the Scindia School, situated within the Gwalior Fort. On my way, I also explored the fort and the very famous Telli Ka Mandir. Literally translated, it means oil man's temple; the story goes that it was built by an oil dealer.

The fort overlooked the city and was quite expansive. The Scindia School is an Indian boarding school for boys, established in 1897, for children of the royal families. Presently headed by Jyotiraditya Scindia, it is still considered to be one of the 10 best boarding schools in India.

Before I met the principal, I headed straight for the mess. You will be surprised to know that this mess is unlike others and serves food that is fun for the children and is nutritious as well. I happened to arrive on the day when *samosa* was being served in the form of a money bag, thus making it visually appealing for the youngsters. The *kachori* was similar to the one available on the street, as they were stuffed with *dal*s, but the *saada aloo* was a 150-year-old recipe. It is potato lightly coated in a special sauce made of tomatoes, turmeric, *ghee* and asafoetida. The alumni of the school still return to taste this dish; such is the power of food! It was good to see that the children were well fed

and were happy to eat mess food; they ate anything from *dal*s and biryani, to butter chicken. On speaking with the mess in charge I found out that as *jalebi* (sweet made of a coil of batter, fried, and steeped in syrup) and *rabri* (a mixture of thickened creamy milk and bits of cream that is sweetened with sugar and flavoured with saffron and cardamom powder) are extremely popular in Gwalior, they are served in school on the weekends as a treat.

After having a heavy breakfast, I went for a long walk and saw the polo grounds and cricket field. How I secretly wished I had studied here! On meeting the principal, Mr. Sainik Ghosh, I got to know that students were also encouraged to cook and try their own recipes sometimes in the mess. He believed that the real fun of living in a boarding school was to be able to cook those midnight meals, on your own, using all the innovation one could! They had provided each dormitory with ovens and stoves to facilitate the midnight cooking. I was thinking about my college days and how I must have made 100 recipes out of Maggi alone.

I saw the brass band perform after meeting the principal. Very nice and tuneful. I spent the afternoon with students and walking around the grounds. Education in India has so much potential, why can't all children be educated like this? I was thinking to myself, if every little child of India had these facilities, learning environment and food, we would be the most powerful country in the world.

My Gwalior trip was a short one and I squeezed in all the little visits we had planned.

I now moved on to Agra, 120 km from where we were.

DAY 69
13 October / Agra

Gwalior to Agra was not a very long journey. I began my day with one of the Seven Wonders of the World in modern times. This wasn't my first visit, but I was excited and anxious as if it was the first time around. Before I weigh you down with facts that you might not remember, I want to give you a few personal recommendations for your visit. If you can manage to visit the Taj Mahal at night and see its beauty being reflected in the moonlight, then that image will remain with you for the rest of your life. It appears pink in the morning, white in the day and becomes ethereal in the moonlight. An identical Taj Mahal was supposed to be built in black marble instead of white. The base of it can still be seen across the river. However, after the completion of the Taj, emperor Shah Jahan ordered the right hand of the chief mason to be cut off so that no one could ever recreate the monument. Of course, there isn't any proof about this theory. According to one of the many other myths, the Taj Mahal is apparently sinking!

Built in 1653, even after more than 300 years, millions of people flock to this symbol of love every year. I revisited the tombs inside and the garden. I took a short break to rest against the cold marble of the structure and watched the world go by. Another point I want to make while we are on the subject is that everyone thinks of the Taj Mahal when they think of India, but just a few kilometres away is the equally grand Agra Fort. I didn't stop for a visit this time, I drove by one of the outer walls of this

94 acre historical monument, that was first built in the eleventh century.

Kalakriti, a store on V.I.P. Road, caught my attention and I just had to stop to have a look. It resembled an old fort, designed specifically to set pace with the mood of the city. The entire building resembled the famous Buland Darvaza; the door was studded with semi-precious stones set in intricate patterns. A very aesthetically designed handicraft emporium, this art gallery also housed jewellery, Taj-miniatures, furniture, and marble table-tops. The store was also the very proud owner of the Mini Taj. By that, I not only mean in comparison to the original one, albeit, it came with a sound and light show of its own. This Taj came out of the floor and took part in a very theatrical display, surrounding the original love story behind the monument. It took 10 years and 20 people to build this monument, and was not up for sale. I also learnt, while there, that *pacchakari* was the art of setting colourful stones inside intricate carvings on marble. Introduced to India by the Mughals in the seventeenth century, it was the name given to the carvings on the walls of Taj Mahal. Kalakriti had this same marble work done on table-tops, coffee tables and display pieces. I never got a chance to cook at the Taj Mahal, so I found an opportunity to cook for and serve the owner and his wife a special valentine platter. I wanted an excuse to sit at one of the beautiful marble dinner tables. I thought I could be a good son and send my parents a gift from Agra. However, it seemed I needed to work for a few more years before I could shop at Kalakriti.

DAY 70
14 October / Agra-Mathura

After a night filled with dreams about kings and palaces, I shook off the love cloud and headed out to eat.

I have had relatives who lived in Agra, so the roads were familiar to me. Every time they visited us in Delhi, they would bring the famous Agra *ka petha* (transparent soft candy, rectangular or cylindrical in shape, made from white pumpkin). I have a distinct memory of the colourful cardboard box bound by red string, with the words Panchhi Petha written in Hindi. Incidentally, fate had brought me to that very sweet shop today. Here, I met the third generation of the Goel family. I belong to the same caste as that of the Goel's, and I took an instant liking to them. This store that I was in was the original Panchhi Petha and there were many other imitations as well. According to Ankit Goel, the great grandson, the original stores always had a picture of his great grandfather, Mr. Panchhi Lal; hence, the name. The first store was set up in 1952, in a small space at Noori Darwaza. They believed that whoever came to see the Taj, wouldn't leave without a box of their famous *petha*.

It was finally time to eat and revisit childhood memories. I tasted the candied pumpkin in its full range of colours and flavours. The plain *petha* was a cloudy sugary white and was made in big squares. The first bite was what all Indian children loved about the sweet. It felt like a glutinous fleshy fruit and the sugar rush quickly kicked in. The *petha* industry has certainly become very creative; the sweets are now sandwiched with flavours like chocolate, coconut and *kesar pista*. My favourite was the *gulab laddu*, which had candied rose petals in its centre. There was an *angoori petha*, shaped like *angoor* (grapes). The shop was a bright island of colours, light and attractive displays.

After this stop, it was time to get on the road for Mathura. I bid farewell and took lots of pictures to show to my sister.

~

Mathura is not very far from Delhi; the driving time is only about three hours. Mathura is a holy city for the Hindus and is also called Braj Bhumi after the birth place of Lord Krishna. Again, this is a city I had been to many times, throughout my childhood. Narrow lanes, crowded markets, big temples; it paints an ancient picture of India. The city is filled with sounds of chanting from the temples, lending a very spiritual aura to the place. Since life in Mathura is best experienced in its tiny lanes, the only option I had was to walk and experience what the streets had to offer. Mathura is quite high up on the food quotient. Nearly everyone I know has a favourite from here, be it a *samosa*, *kachori*s for breakfast, or *bedmi* (stuffed lentil *puri*) *aloo* for lunch or *lassi* and dairy-rich desserts in the evening. You can get all these under one roof and that is the Brijwasi store. It is, without doubt, the largest food store in Mathura.

The best thing that happened, while I was there, was that I met up with Pulkit, a college friend of mine; he happens to be the third generation of the Brijwasi family. His grandfather began this business in the 1930s, on the banks of the river Yamuna. Today, that shop was one of their many manufacturing units. Most famous for their *pedas* (made from milk solids that are strained away from the whey, and cooked in sugar), Brijwasi now had a wide range of sweets and savouries. *Pedas* have a caramel colour that comes from the sugar being cooked. The main flavours added are cardamom, saffron and pistachio. It is said that *pedas* have been on the dessert table from the nineteenth century, and originated somewhere outside Mathura. The density, colour, sweetness, and milk content all depend on the person making it. This is explained by the fact that it is usually offered as *prasad* to the Gods. Each person has his or her own way of worshiping. Creativity sets apart different *pedas* in the city, however, all varieties instantly melt in your mouth, leaving behind a caramel milky flavour.

Pulkit didn't wait for me to ask; he lined up all the varieties for me to taste. The plain one was the best. I asked him what was the secret behind the taste, to which he replied, 'Blessings of Lord Krishna.' I drank a whole glass of the saffron pistachio milk and I could not believe how creamy the milk was and how pure the saffron. It was like an instant energy shot in one tall glass.

The first floor was a food court where they served me a *thali*. The food was vegetarian, cooked without onion and garlic. It had an assortment of *dal*, vegetables, *paneer* and yoghurt. As a starter they served *dhokla*, a steamed gram flour cake and *pakoras*. *Puris* were served instead of *rotis* and the meal was more than substantial at a very reasonable cost. Pulkit made sure I had so much food that it could pull me through till dinner. It was one of those days where all I did was eat. Tomorrow would be dedicated to knowing about the religious leanings of Mathura.

DAY 71
15 October / Mathura

I would like to believe that there are two ways of looking at religion: either with boring, objective eyes, or with an adventure and flair for story telling. My grandfather, a big Krishna devotee, was the reason I used to visit Mathura. I even went with him to a wedding once, where I (a fat 14-year-old) was dressed up as Lord Krishna, surrounded by girls who were much too pretty for me, dancing to the chants. I had saved that picture in my head for a very long time.

The Raas dance is part of the traditional story telling of Krishna. It is known as Raas Leela and *katha* (story telling form) is believed to have evolved from here. *Raas* means aesthetics and *leela* means storytelling. The dance originally has Krishna surrounded by *gopi*s (women who herd cows) devoted to him. Today, extracts from the original Raas Leela are performed by dancers at temples. At one such temple I met a pandit who arranged a dance performance for me, which was enacted by the dancers while the pandit*ji* sang. The dancers had painted their skin in various colours and their dresses were adorned with peacock feathers. They danced and swayed to the chants and songs; after a while I felt serene. I had a moment with pandit*ji* where we talked about beliefs and the meaning of being devoted to Lord Krishna. The only way I felt like I could do my part was by cooking, even if it was just for my grandfather's sake. I made his favourite, **Saffron *Pakwaan*.**

SAFFRON *PAKWAAN*
(Traditional flatbread from Sindh, flavoured with saffron.)

Ingredients

10-12 saffron *(kesar)* strands
2 tbsp milk
½ cup whole wheat flour *(atta)*
1½ cup all purpose flour *(maida)*
1 tsp cumin *(jeera)* seeds
1 tsp carom *(ajwain)* seeds
A pinch of asafoetida *(hing)*
½ tsp crushed black pepper *(sabut kali mirch)*
Salt to taste
Water to knead the dough
2 tbsp clarified butter *(ghee)*
Oil to fry

Method

1. Soak the saffron in warm milk.
2. Sieve both, the whole wheat flour and all-purpose flour together.
3. Mix the flour with cumin seeds, carom seeds, asafoetida, crushed peppercorns and salt.
4. Rub the flour with *ghee*, just like we do for short crust. It'll have a coarse breadcrumb-like texture now.
5. Add saffron milk with sufficient water to knead a semi-soft dough. Let it rest for 15-20 minutes.
6. Divide into small equal portions (*roti*-size dough balls).
7. Roll it out like *roti*s. With the help of a knife or a fork make tiny impressions on it. Please do not miss this important step.

8. Heat the oil for frying. Fry the *pakwaan*s on medium flame until they are crisp and have a nice golden colour.
9. Serve the *pakwaan*s with hot *dal* or a vegetable curry of your choice. Or you can eat them as it is.

~

It might sound clichéd, but the air made my *pakwaan* richer, more flavourful and definitely delicious. The other reason I decided to make this *pakwaan* was that it was used as *prasad* in my house, as an offering to the Gods; a tradition started by my grandfather. When it was time to eat, we sat together on the floor and pandit*ji* said a small prayer before we began. I never pray before I eat and I almost reached out for the food before I caught myself. Pandit*ji* had an acquired taste. He tasted the food at the place where he performed his rituals, and only then did he decide where he would pray. After the first bite, he smiled and approved. He told me my grandfather would be very proud, and I remember, at that moment, my eyes did moisten up a bit. I spent the rest of the day walking along the banks and wandering in the streets. I recalled my earlier visits and the things I had done then. I added this visit to my bank of memories for Mathura, as I had done with my earlier visits.

Day 72

From the land of Krishna, I was now heading towards the hills and plains of Dehradun.

DAY 73
17 October/ Dehradun

I had been in central India, on the plains, for a while. Throughout my journey, I had been reading Ruskin Bond and now as I headed to Doon Valley, the stories were almost coming to life. Dehradun lies on the foothills of the Himalayas, nestled between two of India's mightiest rivers, the Ganga and the Yamuna. Located very close to Mussourie, Dehradun has inspired many artists, writers and poets into creativity. Of course, my interest lied in the culinary heritage of the area. As I walked the streets, I realised that since the British arrived in 1816, very little had changed. The corner shops still made jams, preserves and cheese, very much in the English style. My first stop was a cultural one. I went to Rio Resorts, where I met Mrs. Gosai who had arranged a cultural programme for me, followed by a Garhwali cooking lesson. She told me that she followed me on television and promised me that if I ever paid her a visit, she would teach me the lesser know techniques of the mountain cuisine.

Her company had been set up with the aim of preserving their culture and cuisine. She was a small portly lady and her sari was a bright red that stood out against the dull green hills. The group of ladies, who were about to perform their traditional dance were all housewives from the area, who had come together to form a society to preserve their dying culture. The dance revolved around Goddess Parvati and the song was sung in Garhwali, one of the 325 languages recognised in India. They wore a long skirt worn with a blouse and a *chunni* (a long scarf that women wear around their head and shoulders) draped over their heads. Around their necks they wore beautiful silver ornaments called *hansuli*. The area was rugged and mountainous, none the less, the flora and fauna that grew here, were suitable for the cuisine. The ladies had intricate knowledge about wild edible plants and their usage in the making of the food.

The two popular cuisines of Uttaranchal were from the Garhwal region and the Kumaon region with lot of commonalities between them. The principles of fresh, local, organic and nutritional food have existed here throughout time. What I loved here was the generous amount of *ghee* used in the food. Being a cold area, the *ghee* provided the warmth that the winter chill took away. As we stood outside and cooked, I waited desperately for the food and some of that warmth. They ate thick *rotis* stuffed with *dals*, leafy greens and vegetables. Mrs. Gosai took time to tell me about a little grey seed, called *jhangora*, which they use to make a *kheer*. Apparently, this seed has the power to dispel the supernatural. It also has medicinal properties and provides a lot of energy to the person who eats it. *Jhangora* is a type of millet that grows in the region. She told me I was still a growing boy and I should eat this millet to be strong. She also showed me how to make a **Moong Dal Pakora**, made during an auspicious occasion or a festival and also the *jhangoora kheer*. This had to be my lucky day. The culture and cuisine here were new to me and Mrs. Gosai taught me well. I spent a long day enjoying the scenery, the weather and the food.

MOONG DAL PAKORA
(Fritters made from grounded pulses.)

Ingredients

2 cups skinless split green gram *(dhuli moong dal)*, soaked
  overnight
Salt to taste
½ tsp dry mango *(amchoor)* powder
½ tsp turmeric *(haldi)* powder
½ tsp red chilli powder
¼ tsp asafoetida *(hing)*
½ tsp caraway seeds *(shahi jeera)*
2 green chillies, finely chopped
1 tbsp fresh coriander leaves *(dhania patta)*, finely chopped
Green chutney as required

Method

1. Coarsely grind the soaked skinless split green gram
   with salt, dry mango powder, turmeric, red chilli
   powder, and asafoetida.
2. Add caraway seeds, green chillies and chopped
   coriander to this and mix well.
3. Heat sufficient oil in a wok.
4. Grease your palms and shape the mixture with your
   fingertips to even-sized *vada*s. Slide them into the
   oil, a few at a time, and deep fry till golden and
   crisp. Drain on absorbent paper. Serve hot with
   green chutney.

DAY 74
18 October/ Dehradun

It was a completely different experience waking up in Dehradun than waking up anywhere else. The weather was perfect, the slight chill in the air made me cling to my quilt for few moments longer. The view from my window was more than just scenic. It was like a misty picture postcard from the middle of the mountains. I had my ritual cup of tea and my morning rusk. I dunked the rusk in the tea and waited for it to soften slightly before I got my morning dose of stimulants. That brought me to the bakery culture in Dehradun. Ellora's is the most fitting example of the baking tradition in the city. It was right opposite a very popular school on Rajpur road. Although, you don't need the address since everyone knows exactly where it is, just ask anyone for directions if lost. The bakery bestsellers are stick jaws, plum cakes and rusks. Mr. Gulati met me at the bakery and allowed me to question him incessantly about all the desserts and the history behind them.

Their plum cake recipe was 200 years old; that explained why this bakery had been around for so long. As we chatted, we exchanged stories about food and life, and he happened to mention that Chef Sanjeev Kapoor was a friend and still ordered from Ellora. I also met Mr. Gulati's son, Drone, who showed me around the kitchens, and told me that the family had not let go of the old methods of baking, whether it was the machinery or the utensils. Standing outside the bakery, judging by the smell of bread wafting through the air, one wouldn't think that the ovens were over 35 years old. It reminded me of my trip to Italy and the time where I was hanging around a bakery with a wood-fired oven. The walls were made of brick, that wasn't painted over, and the smell made me want to eat everything I laid my eyes upon. The oven at Ellora could bake 100 loaves of bread at a time. The long-handled pizza peel was a large, long fat spoon like tool that was used to shuffle the many loaves of the bread in the oven. The bakers wore thick gloves, while old-school ceiling fans cooled the rest of the bakery.

I went to the next floor to see the old plum cake recipe come together. Of course when I tasted, it fulfilled the rich, crumply and moist requirements of a good cake. Mr. Gulati said that the fruit is macerated in alcoholic syrup for six months and the cake, if well kept, lasts for almost a year. The rusk was actually what I was looking for. I chanced upon a fresh batch and grabbed a few for my tour around Ellora. Just the fact that they tasted like cardamom with the sweetness of crisp buttery toast made my visit worthwhile. My last experiment was with stick jaws. Incredibly sweet, the buttery toffee stuck to each tooth in my mouth and kept me occupied for a good 10 minutes. I bought some cake for the rest of the trip and headed off down the road. I had decided that this day would be dedicated to the British cuisine and culture, and what was left of it in India.

I made my way from Dehradun to Mussourie, a mere 40 km by road, and an hour and a half by one's watch. Mussourie is called the queen of the hills. The British influence here is evident, especially on the architecture and the food. I had been here for a few summer holidays, like every other kid from Delhi. Mussourie has always been very popular for the entertainment on the Mall Road and the cable car rides. This was my first trip where I was going to make an effort to fish out all the little store-owners who made cheese, jam and peanut butter. Right up until the sixties, the British lived here, and consequently left behind a lot of their eating habits with the locals. I found a place called Sister's Bazaar, where I went into one Prakash Store to sample all of these Brit traditions that had survived over time in a little hill station in India. Of course, I wasn't surprised that everything was remarkably delicious. The owner offered me a small space to cook, near the store. I couldn't resist the offer to use the peanut butter and jam. I made cookies. I just had to. It was nice to literally taste a piece of Mussourie's history. I overdid it and ate the cinnamon roll sandwiches, muffins, butter cookies and peanut butter biscuits too. It dawned on me that I had eaten much more than I should have. I stayed in Mussourie and rested until the sugar wore off.

Around dinner time, I rose from my stupor, and wandered around Mall Road that was buzzing with action. It was completely tailored to the clientele that visited this place. Video games, bangle shops, small hotels and restaurants filled the streets. Couples holding hands walked the streets, while I looked for more food. One of the most popular places on the street was a lovely omelette centre. How could I not go in? Khursheed Bhai met me and introduced himself; he has been in charge of the place for 20 years. The restaurant had opened in 1918. Khursheed has been given star ratings and reviews by magazines and newspapers. He was a favourite in and around the area.

Here, I learnt how to flip a cheese omelette. The bread was toasted with cheese in a pan and then coated with egg. The secret trick was the turmeric and the green chillies. He gave me a fantastic tip to cook eggs with only chopped green chillies and not use any salt. He claimed that the eggs tasted both salty and spicy with just the chillies. I returned the good feeling by making a **Schezwan Cheese Omelette**.

SCHEZWAN CHEESE OMELETTE
(Omelette cooked with spicy Schezwan sauce and cheese.)

Ingredients

4 eggs
Salt to taste
Pepper to taste
2 tsp oil
4 slices small bread
2 tbsp Schezwan sauce
2 cheese slices, cut in half (Add as many as you like and
   make it four cheese slices if you're a cheese lover.)

Method

1. Take a bowl and crack open the eggs; season with salt and pepper. Whisk well to combine.
2. Heat oil in a non-stick frying pan. Pour half of the egg mix in and spread it out.

3.   Place four slices of bread over the egg. Pour the remaining half of the egg mix over the bread and spread well.

4.   After a few minutes, once the egg is cooked from the bottom, flip over and let the top side cook.

5.   When the other side is cooking, spread some Schezwan over the bread. Place cheese slices over it and fold them over like a sandwich. Flip again and cook until the cheese melts.

6.   Serve hot. DO NOT SERVE IT WITH KETCHUP!

~

So here I was trying to impress this egg expert who had been around doing his thing for 20 years. Hot and steaming, I brought my classic omelette for him. He politely refused; turned out he was a vegetarian! The person who earned his bread and butter by making eggs had never tasted his own dishes. It made me wonder how strangely this world runs sometimes. My omelette was hungrily snatched up by my director and producer, who rated it on behalf of Khursheed. The verdict: *'kabil-e-tareef!'* This marked the end of my Dehradun journey. In the middle of the mountains, I found the perfect balance between traditional local cuisine and British cultural heritage that had been left behind for hungry travellers like me. Next stop: Lucknow.

DAY 75

From the hills, I climbed down for the plains of Lucknow.

Day 76
20 October / Lucknow

I was now in Lucknow, 550 km from Dehradun. I had taken a day to reach there, but it felt like I had 'time-travelled' to a different period in history. Lucknow resembled an urban version of a city in the Persian Empire—a crossway for merchants, traders, poets, and food lovers to exchange fragments of history. A citadel of Awadhi cuisine, Lucknow was a serious stop on the culinary map. Their traditions date back hundreds of years, and every recipe has an elaborate, often royal, story behind it. Most of Lucknow's cuisine gets its influence from the Mughals, who spent some time in Persia after their defeat in the Third Battle of Panipat in 1761. The Mughals introduced their own style of cooking, adapted from the experiences in the Persian kingdom. The Nawabs of Awadh, who were the deputies of the Mughals, settled here in Lucknow and evolved this style of cooking further.

There are many heritage strolls that you can take when in Lucknow. However, the only one that I wanted to do was to find authentic Awadhi food. I have friends who make day-trips to Lucknow just to eat. Tunday Kebabi is a shop that has expanded over the 109 years that they have been in business. They serve fresh kebabs on the streets of Aminabad. The old houses, the crowds, and the charm of the *chowk* (in south Asia, an open market area in a city at the junction of two roads) befit this kebab story. The queue to buy a few kebabs usually extends long past the corners of the store. Their latest addition is a small seating area in the basement, which makes it easier to eat if you are not in a hurry. I was more curious about their history and their legacy. I met the third generation of the Tunday Kebabi family, Mr. Muhammad Osman. His grandfather, Mr. Murad Ali, opened this shop many years ago. Being handicapped, Mr. Murad Ali had only one arm, therefore the nick-name Tunday came to be associated with his shop, where he made kebabs with one hand. Osman Bhai told me that his grandfather was the fastest kebab maker there ever was; people with two hands didn't stand a chance. As if that wasn't enough, he also revealed that the kebab is claimed to be made with 160 different spices.

Another story goes that there was a nawab who lost all his teeth and commanded his subjects to produce the softest kebab. The person who achieved this feat would have royal patronage for the rest of their life. Mr. Murad Ali created the secret recipe and won that honour. I had a chance to eat a replica of that very same kebab. The story helped build my appetite. I reached for the kebab, which fell apart in my fingers. The kebab couldn't keep its shape if touched by hand; it was so soft that when you put it in your mouth, it melted away into a warmth of flavours. I could feel the flavours of cardamom, cinnamon, and Panadanas Syrup (*kewra* essence) blossoming in my mouth. The minced meat was ground with fat and spices over and over again until it was so fine that it needed to be held together with a powder of *dal*, nothing synthetic or flavourless like cornflour.

It is the love of spices that rules the kingdom of flavours. Now, as a chef, there was obviously no question about how delicately-made this kebab was. There was a solid reason why it was so popular and that itself vouched for its authenticity. However, even I found it hard to believe that the kebab is made with 160 spices in the recipe. Perhaps it is this myth that adds to its hype and to a slight extent, makes it the legend it is. After eating kebabs for lunch, I decided to wash it down with some liquid marijuana.

Thandai literally means a cold drink. Often confused with milk, this is made with the liquid of ground dry fruit, water and an array of spices. Once again, I met the fourth generation of Pandit Raja ki Mashoor Thandai. This gentleman had quite a formidable personality. Vinod Kumar Tripathi, a.k.a. Raja, literally meaning king in Hindi, met me at the front of the shop to introduce me to *thandai*. Before we could even begin the conversation, he let me know that the who's who of the country had been to his shop. *Thandai* could be either made with milk or water. The spices and the *bhang* are added (or not) depending on how you want to spend the rest of the day. For those of you who are of the sober variety, *bhang* is a preparation from the leaves and flowers buds of the cannabis plant, consumed as a beverage in the Indian subcontinent. Basically, you drink your 'joint' with milk and spices.

The spice and dry fruit mix that goes into the drink has a few essential components: poppy seeds, saffron, cashew nuts, almond, pistachio, pepper, cardamom and dry fennel. A mortar and pestle are used to grind these spices. It has a small mix of medicinal herbs *(jadi booti)* to give strength to the people who consume the concoction.

All these are strained through a muslin cloth while milk or water is passed through to extract their respective flavours. That *is* the secret behind the *thandai*. Mr. Tripathi used a copper mug and a glass to mix the drink and make it frothy; the showmanship involved was a part of the experience!

Roadside eating joints, serving *kulfi falooda* (Indian dessert consisting of a conical-shaped ice cream with rose syrup, vermicelli, psyllium or basil seeds, tapioca pearls and pieces of gelatin with milk or water), *shahi tukda*, and biryani, seemed to crop up after every few metres. I spent the whole day in Aminabad where I even went to a nawab's house to eat.

Day 77
21 October/ Lucknow

I began my day with breakfast that was fit for a king...
king of the roads, that is. The breakfast culture is different
in each region of India, much like the eating habits and
customs. Here in Lucknow, where 'what to eat' is an
important decision of the day, I stopped at Bajpaiji's Special
Kachori at Hazrat Ganj. Situated in the heart of Lucknow,
this is a very popular area for restaurants, bazaars, and
handicraft stores.

I ate my breakfast with people staring at me in the
market's busy square. Bajpai*ji* had a special style of making
his *kachori*, very typical of the state. It was almost like a
cross between a *puri* and a *kachori*, where the outer shell
was very crispy, but not hard. This was made possible
by adding semolina *(sooji)* to the dough. Unlike a *puri*, it
doesn't balloon up on frying, but still manages not to be
flat. In fact, this is optional and is usually made of *dal* and
spices. My grandfather is from Uttar Pradesh, so I had
set the standard high for Mr. Bajpai. *Kachori*s from this
area are my idea of comfort food. I have grown up eating
various types of *kachori*s, which also makes it one of my
favourite food, ever. The shop was tiny and there were
five people huddled inside a room, sitting cross-legged.
Their jobs were well defined. One chopped and boiled
potatoes, while another kneaded and flattened the dough.
One man was only frying the *kachori*s while the other
was serving them hot, to the eager customers. The fifth
one in the room was collecting cash and taking orders;

it was a full-fledged business that successfully ran out of a hole in the wall.

It was chaotic to get to the head of the queue to place an order. The consolation was that the *kachori*s were extremely affordable and once you had eaten them, the rest was forgotten. The regular order size was four *kachori*s in a *pattal* (a cup made of dried leaves) for a reasonable sum of Rs. 20. When I cracked the first *kachori* open, the steam that came out rushed the aroma of the stuffing straight to my nose. It goes without saying that the spices and potato where of very good quality; and their judicious use made the *kachori*s almost delicate. The pickle and raw onions served as accompaniments made for 'a wholesome experience.' I couldn't have been more satisfied.

After Hazrat Ganj I made my way towards *Chawal-waali Gully* (literal translation being 'the rice street') in Nakhas. If you thought you would get rice aplenty here, well then, you are wrong! Despite the name, everyone in the gully is in reality, famous for making *sheermal*; hence it is also popular as the *Sheermal Gully*. A Persian word, *mal* is Arabian for material and *sheer* is Persian for milk. It is a sort of rich, sweet, saffron-flavoured bread. It is baked in an Iranian tandoor made of iron and is built into the ground. I went to the oldest *sheermal* shop in Lucknow. It was also the place where the *sheermal* was invented by Mohammadus Jaanashin in 1830. I met his great great grandson, Mohammad Umar of the sixth generation who ran the Ali Hussain Sheermal Shop. I was told that more than 10,000 pieces of *sheermal* were made here every day. He also told me how the taste of the *sheermal* had not changed since the 1830s. It was a little hard to believe, but however, I didn't waste any time, and went to grab a fresh piece that had just come out of the oven. It was bright orange, and was shaped like a horseshoe. I could taste *desi ghee*, cardamom, dry fruit powder and most of all, saffron, which was bought in all the way from Iran. All these ingredients were mixed with the refined flour while being kneaded. There was also an additional taste that I could not quite put my finger on. I asked Umar who told me that they had a secret ingredient that had been passed down for generations. Even the cooks were not aware of the secret ingredient. The price of the *sheermal* depended on the amount of spices and dry fruits used to make it. On the streets, the *sheermal* was sold for Rs. 10. I found this concept of costing the *sheermal* very interesting. It catered to everyone's pocket and taste, without compromising on quality. I ate a *sheermal* priced at Rs. 20.

Apart from the *sheermal*, I tasted various other breads that were made here, like the *taftan*, the *bakar-khaani*, *tabarak*, and *salona kulcha*. The most popular item after the *sheermal* was the *taftan*, which tasted best when had with tea and cream. Now that made me think, 'What could be best paired with *sheermal*?' I learnt that it was best served with kebabs. I couldn't resist the opportunity once again to leave my mark and contribute to the shop. I got my production team to set up a makeshift kitchen, to make my own version of the Tunday Kebabi, which I named **Chandan** (Sandalwood) **Ke Kebab**.

CHANDAN KE KEBAB
(Hung curd patties scented with sandalwood.)

Ingredients

3 cups hung yoghurt
100 gm cottage cheese *(paneer)*, crumbled
1 tbsp ginger-garlic *(adrak-lasun)* paste
2 green chillies, chopped
1 tsp red chilli powder
Freshly ground mix of 4 cloves *(laung)*, 8 peppercorns
    (sabut kali mirch), 1 tsp cumin *(jeera)* seeds, 1-inch
    cinnamon *(dalchini)* stick and 4 small cardamom *(choti
    elaichi)* [Note: Take 2 tsp if you grind in a big batch.]
Salt to taste
¼ cup finely powdered dry fruits like cashew nuts *(kaju)*,
    almonds *(badaam)*, pistachios *(pista)*
1 tbsp fresh mint *(pudina)* leaves, finely chopped
10-12 saffron *(kesar)* strands, soaked in 1 tbsp warm milk
1 tbsp cornflour *(makki ka atta)*
1 tbsp refined flour *(maida)*
½ cup breadcrumbs
3 tbsp clarified butter *(ghee)*
1 small sandalwood *(chandan)* stick

Method

1. Take the hung yoghurt in a bowl. Add crumbled
    cottage cheese, ginger-garlic paste, green chillies, red
    chilli powder, freshly ground spice powders, salt, dry
    fruits, chopped mint, saffron, cornflour and refined
    flour to it. Mix well.

2. Keep it aside for 15 minutes.
3. Make a small patty with the hung yoghurt mixture, almost the size of a cutlet. Now coat these patties with breadcrumbs.
4. Heat the *ghee* in a pan and add grated sandalwood or the whole piece as it is. Simmer it for five minutes. Let it stand for 30 minutes. The *ghee* will absorb the beautiful aroma of sandalwood. Strain it.
5. Now, shallow fry these kebabs in this sandalwood *ghee*.
6. Serve them hot with *sheermal* or any other Indian bread that you prefer.

~

I came across the information that the *sheermal* made here, travelled as far as the United States, the UK, the Middle East, Japan, Pakistan and other countries. I had to make sure my kebabs matched up to the level of quality established here and the only judge was Umar. He tasted my kebab and said that he had never imagined that a vegetarian kebab could taste so good. He asked for another piece and I couldn't help but smile. He asked me for the recipe and I had a mini heart attack! This was definitely my lucky day. It was dusk when I went to meet Pankaj Bhadouria, the first winner of the TV show *MasterChef India*, at her culinary academy in Hazrat Ganj.

DAY 78
22 October / Lucknow

Today was the beginning of the Bakra Eid celebrations in Lucknow and I was excited to be a part of it here in the city itself. Let me start by talking about the Bakra Market. We saw floating markets in Kashmir, the organic markets in Punjab, and now a goat market in Lucknow. Like any good goat market, there were more goats here than people. This market had been set up for people who wanted to buy goats for Bakra Eid. Buying and sacrificing a goat is part and parcel of the festival. There were various breeds available and were priced depending on weight, height, and other parameters. The price started from Rs. 5000 and would go up to rupees three lakh. The fanciest goat I saw was surrounded by people bidding for it. It was dressed up and decorated. It was priced at Rs. 1.5 lakh because the goat was born with 'Allah' and 'Mohammad' written in Urdu on its ears! I have a feeling there was some tattooing involved, but no one cared what I thought. Thereafter, I made my way to the house of Nawab Masood Mir Abdullah, last of the Nawabi lineage of Awadh, who had invited me to celebrate Bakra Eid with him.

Nawab Abdullah was present in his house with his brother Nawab Jafar. They greeted me with the traditional *aadaab* and *khushamadeen*. I entered their house, which had an antique old world feel to it. I sat across from them, as they explained the reason behind the celebration of Bakra Eid. They spoke with the typical *Lakhnavi* accent, a mix of Hindi and Urdu. They were also dressed in *chikan-*

embroidered *kurta*s for the occasion, with the customary *taquiyah* (an Urdu word for short-rounded skullcap) on their head. They spoke slowly while chewing on their *paan*. After I settled down and took in all this visual information, Nawab Jafar began the story of Bakra Eid.

'Almost 5000 years ago, Janabe Ibrahim, who was a messenger of God, had a vision that he was sacrificing his son for Allah. Janabe Ibrahim blindfolded himself and lay his son down on a rock. As soon as put the knife to his son's neck a voice from heaven said, "Ibrahim, I have accepted your sacrifice, there is a goat *(dumba)* behind the tree *(darakht)*. Sacrifice that instead and we will let go of your son's sacrifice." Since then this sacrifice was termed as Bakra Eid. Goat is sacrificed, cooked and then distributed.' The entire goat is consumed in some way or the other, which was a daunting thought for a preferred vegetarian like me.

I forgot to mention the ornamental silver tagine-like centrepiece on the table. Called *peerha* or *paan ki gilori*, it had *paan* wrapped individually in silver cones. I was also offered a *khazdaan*, a decorated version of a spittoon. The *paan* spiked my appetite and I mustered up the courage to ask what we were going to eat. They told me all the food being prepared was in my honour and being cooked on a wood-fire. Before I was taken for my meal, I was told that dressing well for the meal was an essential part of eating. I also learnt that I had to understand and imbibe a few mannerisms before I ate in the company of the nawabs. I met with Nawab sahib's wife, who gave me a whole new *chikan*-embroidered outfit to wear, complete with the *taquiyah*. They managed to get my size right and the lady, Begum Almas, had created that especially for me. Finally, I was ready to partake in the elaborate banquet that had been set up for me.

We went to a beautiful lawn outside, where I saw at least six of the dishes being prepared. On the menu were *pasanda* kebabs, Lucknow biryani, mutton *korma*, and *raan*. The *pasanda*s were being grilled on an open fire and were being basted with *desi ghee*. *Pasanda*s have been on the menu since Shah Jahan's time; very creamy, soft and flavourful. *Pasanda* means to like, it also denotes a prime cut of the mutton leg. The biryani was being made on the other side of the lawns. Nawab *sahib* said that authentic biryanis could be only had from Hyderabad. The Lucknow biryani was actually a constructed *pulao*, with multiple layers of rice and *korma*. All the breads I had seen in the alleyways of Lucknow were now at the dinner table. With such delectable food being cooked in front of me, I definitely had to jump into action. I put on my chef's hat and decided to make *Dal Sultani*. It is special because of the tempering of *paan*.

Dal Sultani
(Creamy lentils flavoured with betel leaf.)

Ingredients

1 cup split pigeon peas *(arhar/toor dal)*
Salt to taste
1½ tsp cumin *(jeera)* seeds

1 tsp red chilli powder
8-10 strands saffron *(kesar)*
½ cup yoghurt
½ cup full cream milk
½ cup cream
4 cloves *(laung)*
4 green cardamoms *(choti elaichi)*
2 tbsp clarified butter *(ghee)*
5-6 cloves garlic *(lasun)*, finely chopped
2 green chillies, finely chopped
10-12 fresh mint *(pudina)* leaves
2 betel leaves *(paan)*
2 charcoal pieces

Method

1. Soak the *dal* for 20 minutes. Strain and add to a deep pan. Add a cup of water with salt, cumin seeds and chilli powder and bring it to a boil. Now let it simmer for 15-20 minutes, until it is cooked.

2. In the meanwhile soak saffron in one tablespoon warm milk. Whisk yoghurt, cream and milk in a bowl together. Crush or blend cloves and cardamoms together.

3. Once the *dal* is cooked, let it cool down. Now mash and pass it through a sieve or you can simply blend it to a fine paste.

4. Heat the *ghee* in a pan. Once hot, add garlic to it. Once garlic is lightly golden, add green chillies and the mashed *dal*. Cook it at medium flame for two minutes. Add the yoghurt cream mix, half the mint,

clove cardamom powder, and saffron milk. Whisk nicely. Let it cook on low flame for five minutes so that everything mixes together nicely.

5.   Burn the charcoal by placing it over a high flame (till red hot).

6.   Place the betel leaves on the top surface of the simmering *dal*. Switch off the burner.

7.   Place the hot burning coal on top of these betel leaves.

8.   Drizzle the hot coal with a few drops of *ghee*. Immediately cover the saucepan tightly with a lid and keep it aside for seven to eight minutes.

9.   Remove the charcoal with the help of a tong and discard the betel leaves.

10.   Give it a final mix and serve hot, garnished with mint.

~

With the cooking done, it was time to celebrate Eid. Nawab *sahib* and his family joined us in the celebrations. Just like every other part of India I have seen, the whole family came together to celebrate and eat. The evening was filled with food, poetry and conviviality. Definitely one of the best Eid celebrations of my life; this experience was up, close and personal.

Day 79

I left Lucknow and its graceful *andaaz* (style) to go towards the land of Hindu spiritualism, Varanasi.

DAY 80
24 October / Varanasi

Holiest of the seven sacred Indian cities in India, Varanasi, also called Benares, is built on the banks of the river Ganga. Also called the religious capital of India, Varanasi is home to *sadhu*s (holy men or ascetics), saints and devotees of Lord Shiva. Varanasi is most famous for its *ghat*s (banks), and the temple ceremonies that revolve around the Ganga. A few of the ancient Indian poets and writers lived in this city and their works were greatly inspired by the life in Varanasi. The *ghat*s are also a place where Hindus come to cremate their loved ones and then disperse the ashes in the holy river. So not only is this ancient city a place of worship and spirituality, it is also a place when life completes a full circle. Hindus believe that to liberate your soul, after death, it is important for your soul and body to become one with the Ganga. You have to be careful here though, emotions can be played with, and the cremation can become a business affair. Be careful when you visit, it is always best to know a local or travel with someone who knows the whereabouts.

On a lighter note, the best part of the day at the *ghat*s is the grand *aarti* (a Hindu religious ritual of worship in which light from wicks soaked in *ghee* or camphor is offered to one or more deities). Thousands of people gather at the steps to attend it and the priests stand on an elevated platform to perform their prayer in the view of the crowds amid the electrifying sounds of bells and conch shells. Devotees let *diya*s and flowers float onto the river, carrying their prayers far out into the horizon. Offerings are made to the priest, in the form of coconut, milk, money, jewellery, and gold.

The ritual is worth attending just for the sights and sounds that can spiritually overwhelm your senses, all at once. I sat on a small boat, taking it all in, watching the evening *puja*, strangely moved by the human and divine synthesis unfolding in front of me. You can hire a boat from the *ghat*, to observe the sunset and the imminent celebrations.

I woke up at 4:30 a.m. and hired a boat to go on the Ganga. I decided that this day was important because I was going to cook, while floating atop the river. Many artists and poets have been inspired by this place and have created great pieces of art. I wanted to use the inspiration to create a dish worth the *ghat*s of Varanasi. My producer, Anshul, first laughed off the idea. He then took up the challenge to execute the whole scene on a boat. There were two cameras, one on my boat and one on a boat floating next to me. It was a mini adventure, which turned out to be pretty successful. Even though the sunrise looks almost the same every day, this sunrise was special for all of us. We started shooting as the sun rose and the first light of the day blessed my cooking and my dish.

After absorbing the first few rays of the sun, I got down to cooking on my little boat. Even though my boat was stationary, the waves kept hitting my boat, making chopping slightly difficult. I was preparing **Kuliya Ki Chaat** (*Kuliya* means cups). Still very inspired from the previous night's *puja* and watching all the *diya*s floating by, I wanted to shape the vegetables like tiny buckets resembling a *diya*. After cooking in the mountains, on a houseboat, on the highway, in a temple, at royal palaces, I think cooking while floating on the Ganga is a first.

KULIYA KI CHAAT
(Vegetable and fruit cups stuffed with Indian snack.)

Ingredients

2 cucumbers
2 tomatoes
1 pineapple
2 apples
1 cup pomegranate kernels
½ cup sprouts
1½ cup hung yoghurt
¼ cup roasted crushed peanuts
¼ cup *aloo bhujia* or *sev*
8-10 juliennes ginger *(adrak)*
2 tbsp tamarind *(imli)* chutney
1½ tbsp green chutney
2 tbsp lemon juice
1 tsp chilli powder
2 tsp roasted cumin *(bhuna jeera)* powder
2 tsp powdered sugar
1 tbsp chaat masala
20 mint leaves
Salt to taste

Method

1. Clean and cut the cucumbers and pineapples into even cylinders (1.5-inches tall) and core out the centres to make buckets. Bottoms should remain sealed.
2. Half the tomatoes and core them out to make buckets as well.
3. Cut quarters of half an apple and then scoop out triangular pockets from the top side (the side with the skin).
4. Now store all these fruits and vegetable baskets in chilled water. Make at least 16 buckets in all.
5. Prepare the filling for these baskets by whisking hung yoghurt and sugar together. Add cumin powder, chilli powder, mint, salt, tamarind and green chutney to it.
6. Now, toss this yoghurt mixture with pomegranate kernels, sprouts and roasted peanuts. The filling is ready.
7. Stuff the chilled fruits/vegetables with this filling.
8. Now top them with *aloo sev*, lots of lemon juice and chaat masala. Quantities for these three are subjective to your taste.
9. Garnish with ginger julienne.
10. Serve chilled.

~

As you can imagine, the rhythm of the river, the ebb and flow, slowed my general life speed down to 20 km per hour. I was feeling happy and content.

After collecting memories and blessings, I carried my culinary journey forward, into the streets of Varanasi.

People of Varanasi are known for being proud of their local street food. Apparently, it all 'originated' here. There could be no better city in India for a foodie to excite his or her taste buds. But, be warned, this city is purely vegetarian; all your experiences will be 'chicken free.' The city as a whole avoids eating meat, because they believe 'dead meat gives you dead thoughts.' On one side are the banks and on the other are winding streets with unending options of snacks, sweets, *lassi* and flowers. My first stop was Jawahri Ki Kachori. It was not easy to find, though if you ask around, everyone knows and helps. The set-up was very similar to that of Mr. Bajpai's in Lucknow. The cooks of the shop were sitting cross-legged on an elevated platform of the store, while patrons were waiting in line for the *kachori*s, which were actually a version of *puri*, served with *aloo sabzi* (potato curry). The interesting part was that there was a *pattal* for the *sabzi* and *puri*s served separately on a leaf. An enthusiastic gentleman came forward to show me how to hold both the *puri*s and *sabzi* with my left hand, while eating with my right hand.

I struck up a conversation with Sudhir, the gentleman who helped me figure my *kachori*s out. He told me that the shop was the oldest in Varanasi. It had been around for ages and that he visited the shop almost every week. These breads were stuffed with *dal*. Also, they were absolutely dry, versus being the usual oily *puri*s that one eats with *sabzi*, which was one of their biggest USPs. The *sabzi* had three distinct flavours: *saunf* (fennel or aniseed), *kasoori methi* (dry fenugreek leaves), and *elaichi* (cardamom). Even better was the little surprise in the *sabzi*; the jackfruit *kofta* took me by surprise. It was delicious. Like Sudhir said, the *puri* had an *urad dal* (black gram) stuffing, making it a *kachori*. After shamelessly devouring four, I still felt hungry. My stomach was full but my heart was not content, something all of us have heard in the Hindi saying, '*Peth bhar gaya, par neeyat nahi bhari.*'

Luckily for me, it took all but one second for me to be distracted by the *kadhai* on my left. The *kadhai* was full of hot oil and it had a massive honeycomb-like *jalebi* inside it. The difference was that it was called *jaleba*, only because of its size. It was all of two kilograms, frying solo in the *kadhai*. These are made of fermented gram flour that is piped in concentric circles into hot oil. Once they become fluffy and crispy, they are soaked in sugar syrup *(chashni)* that has been flavoured with saffron and cardamom. Another surprising fact about the making of the *jaleba* is that they don't weigh out the portion that they are going to fry. It is a free flow feeling that decides the size of the *jaleba*. They then break it up, into rough pieces and see it by the plate. For Rs. 15, I had one of the tastiest meals I had ever had.

As if by default, my next instinct was to drink *lassi*. My stomach had grown a few inches and my body struggled to make space for my next visit. I went looking for it and found Mr. Blue Lassi Wala. As a chef, I immediately was trying to decode the use of blue in the shop title. I was thinking it was grapes, or some fruit syrup, or even the colour. As soon as I reached the shop, I realised that the blue was to denote the colour of the shop, and not the colour of the drink. Mr. Vikas Yadav, the present owner of the shop, told me that his shop was the first in Varanasi. His grandfather, who was a TV actor, set this shop up 70 years ago.

He has been deemed one the best *lassi wala*s in the country. The recipes haven't changed, the shop hasn't changed, and even the taste remains the same as it was initially. He had 70 different varieties of *lassi*. Vikas used all old school equipment to make his *lassi*. He used a brass urn in which he churned the liquid using a wooden spoon with a flat bottom that he rolled between his palms. He mashed the fruit into the *lassi* using this spoon. The ingredients were home-style thick yoghurt, sugar, two layers of fresh *malai*. He garnished his *lassi* with whatever fruit was mixed in it, with an addition of pistachios. Unlike a lot of shops in the city, this one had an adjacent area for seating. Watching him make *lassi*, sitting in a small area of the shop, was picture-worthy. You would be surprised how many foreigners were patrons of the shop. The ratio was almost 8:2; once inside, it was hard to understand whether I was in Varanasi or Venice. Let me also mention that you need a spoon to have your *lassi*. Once the first few dollops are ingested, you could start sipping on the thick *lassi*. It isn't too sugary, but the sweetness comes from the fruit added. Once you start drinking it, you almost forget about the *jalebi*. I tried the pomegranate *lassi* and the banana chocolate, after which I could not do anything else. It was a lovely day: I cooked, I ate, I ate, and I ate. Now it was time for a nap and to digest whatever I had stuffed myself with since the morning.

Day 81
25 October / Varanasi

Not only a food haven, Varanasi is also known for its art and artisans. I found one such artist, who once was a Japanese chef, and now played the didgeridoo (a 5000-year-old instrument) in a small shop. People called him Mithu, but his actual name was Mithun. He believed that the didgeridoo was like a mobile phone that allowed you to connect with your ancestors. It was made of recycled materials like matchsticks and trash wood. He spoke at length about life, music and art. He seemed a bit divorced from reality, but nonetheless, he was spiritual, kind and genuine. One of the prime reasons he came from Japan was to find peace and play his didgeridoo!

He took me to the *ghat* to play his music and get me to try playing the instrument. The way to play it was by vibrating your lips to the sounds—di-ji-ri-du—with your lips pressed against the mouth of the instrument. I shut my eyes and listened to the music. If one paid attention, one could differentiate each note and feel the unique sounds emanating from the instrument. For me this experience was special because, usually, I am very good at motivating myself and chasing my dreams. When I met Mithun, I saw a man who was a cook and who felt like there was a void in his life. Unperturbed, he gave up that life to start another filled with music. No fear, no regrets, only positivity. One might question about how he earned a decent living? The answer is that he also ran a small restaurant on the side to make money that would fund his musical hobby. Perhaps, someday I will be able to be so successful and so content with my life that I will be able to leave the culinary world for the guitar, something that I have always wanted to play. Perhaps. I ate lunch with him, a simple meal that we had prepared and exchanged notes about cooking.

In Varanasi, whether it is breakfast, lunch or dinner, all meals end with the *paan*. When it concerns the city and its *paan*, the stereotypical connection for every Indian is Amitabh Bachchan and the famous song picturised on him, 'Khaike Paan Benares Wala.' I decided to listen to this gem of a song while completing the rest of the journey. This song of the eighties is still immensely popular because of the common-man connect with the pleasure of eating *paan*. To learn more about the Varanasi *paan* culture, I went and visited Keshav Paan Bhandaar in an area called Lanka. The reason for their success is credited to the purity of all their ingredients, which are sourced locally. I met Mr. Chaurasia, the owner of the shop. He explained that the *paan* leaves were not from Varanasi; instead, they came from Magadh, a region in Bihar. The best leaf was called *magai* that came from Gaya in Bihar. That region is not only popular for the leaves, but also for the *gulkand* that is an essential part of the *paan*. The *magai paan* leaves were soft, and I could feel their warmth as I bit into the stuffed leaf. It also melted in the mouth immediately. The relationship between Varanasi and *paan* came from the fact that Bholenath (Lord Shiva) resided here. Bholenath had a liking for two things: *bhaang* and *paan*. Both were consumed here as an offering to the God.

If you want to know how a *magai paan* is made, then here's what you need to do. First, you take the *magai paan* leaf and spread *kathechu*, also called *catechu*, a paste made from acacia extract, rich in iron and calcium. Then *chuna* (edible limestone paste) is applied. Next comes the cardamom, and then a special *paan masala* called Shankar Shambhu, a type of sweet betel nut. Next comes my favourite ingredient, *gulkand*, followed by a sweet chutney, which is usually fruit flavoured. Last is the menthol; only a pinch is added because of its strength. Well, this is how Mr. Chaurasia prepared my *paan*. The actual magic was how he folded it into a neat little green pyramid. It took him a millisecond to neatly stuff all the ingredients into place, fold the leaf, and present it to me. Me, being the dramatic foodie that I am, asked for the *paan* to be fed to me, as a gesture of goodwill.

As I began to chew on the *paan*, the leaf softly gave way to the juices of the stuffing. The *paan* was fresh; the bitterness of the leaf balanced the sweetness of the *gulkand*. The fresh effect of menthol was definitely the first flavour that hit me.

After Surat, Varanasi had been a very rewarding experience. The people had been humble, welcoming and very knowledgeable about food. I spent the rest of the day wandering the streets, talking to some locals, cherishing the last few moments in the holy city. Before you ask, I didn't watch the sun set.

Day 82

Travelling from the holy city of Varanasi to Maner, Patna.

DAY 83
27 October / Maner, Patna

After Uttar Pradesh, I was supposed to drive straight to Kolkata. I decided to drive through Bihar, briefly. From Varanasi, it was a journey of 750 km to Kolkata, via Patna. Luckily for me, Patna was en route, where I eventually stopped to taste a few delicacies.

Patna, the capital of Bihar, was the first stop on my journey to Kolkata. I was surprised to know that the history of Patna dated back to 600 B.C. In ancient India, Patna was a place where higher knowledge was imparted to young students. No wonder, even today, some of the brightest minds come from here. Just before I entered Patna, about 20 km west of the city, I stopped at a small town called Maner, a famous tourist destination because of the mausoleums and the *dargah*s (the tomb or shrine of a Muslim saint). There is yet another reason why foodies would have heard of Maner; Maner *ke laddu* was as popular as the Agra *ka petha*, and the Mathura *ke pede*. Maner Sweets was situated at the entrance to the city. The *motichur laddu* was special here. One of the reasons the *laddu*s here got popular was thanks to yesteryear actor Shatrugan Sinha. In one of his movies, he asks someone if they had tried the Maner *ke laddu*. It helped that Shatrugan Sinha was from the area as well. The other reason is that the crew of Aamir Khan's popular television show, *Satyamev Jayate*, stopped here to try the *laddu*s. Hence, I had to stop and try.

The well-spoken gentleman at the counter, Rajeev, the owner and a postgraduate in marketing and business, now ran the family business, with a vision to expand his business across the country. The original *laddu*s dated back to the time of Aurangzeb, when he was trying to conquer India. He, of course, took his chef along with him when he travelled. When he was in this part of the country, it was his chef who invented this *laddu*; that's how the story goes. Another reason why they are so popular is because of the river Son, which is said to have sweet water. Rajeev's grandfather was also an actor who had acted with Shatrugan Sinha in the same movie which led to the *laddu* becoming famous in Bihar and all over India. By now, my curiosity levels had gone through the roof, and I asked Rajeev if I could see how the *laddu*s were being made. Kilos and kilos of *laddu*s were being made here. Wherever the eyes looked, there was *laddu* everywhere.

The process was actually very simple. First, a thin batter of gram flour *(besan)* was made using the sweet water of the river Son. The *chana dal* (split Bengal gram) used was also called Bombay Gold. The mixture was then passed through a large eight millimetre perforated strainer. It was then tapped on the edge of the big *kadhai* which had hot *ghee* in it. The tapping made the *besan* fall like droplets into the oil. These droplets were commonly referred to as *moti* (pearls). The *moti*s needed to be fine, and once fried they were removed from the *kadhai* and added to a thick sugar syrup flavoured with saffron. It was then cooked for five to 10 minutes, after which it was left aside for the granules to soak up the syrup. Once the granules fluffed up, they added cashew nuts, pistachios, melon seeds and *kewra* water. The mixture was then rolled gently into a small ball. I was lucky enough to try the whole process on my own. Considering the fact that I made my first *jalebi* when I was 12, I felt confident about making my own *laddu*s. The owner, Rajeev, agreed that I was quite skilled at making them. I was feeling quite pleased with myself, the *laddu* turned out very well. Just like the *motichur laddu*, they crumbled in your hands, melted in your mouth, and left a long lasting flavour for you to remember.

Day 84
28 October / Patna

It had been a journey of 260 km to Patna, and the next day was to be filled with a whole lot of new experiences to add to my *handi* (an earthenware or metal pot used in Indian cooking). Kolkata-Bihari cuisine is predominantly vegetarian, but because they live by the rivers, there are a few fish dishes on the menu. A few dishes they swear by are *sattu* (powdered and baked pulses and cereals), and yoghurt. The first dish I tried in the morning, on my long journey towards Kolkata, was *litti chokha*. Found at every kilometre, it is so common that some people eat it for lunch and dinner, both. If you don't like this dish, I doubt you would survive in Bihar. Definitely the common man's food, *litti* is a hard pastry-like dumpling, smaller than a tennis ball, baked on a coal fire. It is made of white flour and filled with *sattu* and spices. *Sattu* is primarily made of gram four. According to my grandfather, *sattu* gives heat to the body. It is also one of the healthiest dishes you could eat. It gives strength to the body and helps the laborious workers of Bihar afford a healthy meal. Sometimes, it is even dissolved in milk and had in the morning like a *desi* malt powder.

It might sound boring and bland, but it was very tasty because of the spices used. The main ones used were: roasted cumin seeds, dry mango powder, carom seeds, finely chopped green chillies, onion, coriander, ginger, chilli, pickle masala, and garlic. The *sattu* was then stuffed in the *litti* casing, and then shaped into a tennis ball.

Traditionally, it is baked on an open coal fire, but there were options of cooking it in the oven, or deep-frying it. *Litti* was traditionally had with *chokha*, a stir-fry of brinjals or potatoes. I ate this interesting meal for breakfast. Not realising initially how filling or energy giving they were, I had four of them. You definitely need to have a body and stomach of steel to eat these. I ate mine from a street vendor near one of the railway stations. There are no personal favourites, you can go anywhere, and find a decent plate of *litti chokha* for yourself. It reminded me of the *dal bati* I had in Rajasthan. I spent the rest of the day travelling to reach my ultimate destination.

I wasn't bored of my Bihar delicacy, and stopped on the highway to eat some with fish curry.

Day 85
29 October / Kolkata

As I moved towards a new side of the country, the landscape and the lifestyle changed slightly, and so did the scenery. We were clearly moving into West Bengal.

I was trying hard not to succumb to the pressures of my travels. I almost caught a terrible flu, I seemed to be a few sizes smaller than my clothes, and I had an irreversible tan. I hadn't shaved for days and I did look quite unwell. In fact, I not only got the flu, but I gave it to my director as well. With such tight schedules, there was no stopping and resting. I was a man on a mission; to complete 100 days of India, non-stop. A difficult drive health-wise, I must say.

The road was very smooth from Patna to Kolkata. We managed to reach Kolkata at 4 p.m. in the afternoon, checked into the hotel, took a medicine for fever, and slept for four hours.

I never did actually wake up for dinner; my first half day off since we left Delhi!

DAY 86
30 October / Kolkata

I woke up early, hungry and sick. For a second, I actually did ask myself if I could finish this journey. My crew asked if I wanted to fly back. It all seemed too good to just let go off because of a fever. No, I wasn't going to go back, I was going to go find some good old Chinese chicken soup.

Before that, I want to formally welcome you all to Calcutta, or Kolkata. Well, I prefer the latter over the former...for reasons I can't explain. The capital of West Bengal, it used to be the capital of India during the British rule. This was pretty clear considering the architecture, the roadways and habits of the people. The place reminded you of a different era altogether with the tea-drinking habits, the way the locals spoke English and the general aura of the city. As far as the cuisine went, fish meant everything to Bengalis. I cannot imagine a single traditional meal without fish, and the staples: lentils and rice. The Bengalis are also known for several creations that are popular across the globe: *kathi* rolls (skewer-roasted kebab wrapped in a *parantha* bread), *kala jamun* (dark brown sweet balls made from cottage cheese and whole dried milk, deep fried and coated with sugar), and *rasgulla* (Indian sweet consisting a ball of cottage cheese cooked in syrup).

There is also a thriving Chinese community in Kolkata, that continues to live in China Town. Geographical proximity to China has, over the years, resulted in a large Chinese population in Kolkata. Of course, this has also led to the evolution of the Bengali Chinese menu and a whole array of dishes such as sweet corn soup, manchurian, chilly chicken, all heavy with the use of MSG (mono sodium glutamate a.k.a. ajinomoto)—the villain of Chinese food. There are still places in Kolkata that serve authentic Chinese food, out of which the most popular is Tiritta Bazaar. It is very popular for its fish ball and prawn ball soup. At 6 a.m. I found myself in the market following my nose to the nearest soup shack. I met an acquaintance there, a freelance journalist called Anshuk, who helped me get better with a Chinese breakfast! The bazaar was open from 6 a.m. to 8 a.m. People bought and sold everything available here in these two hours. It was right at the entrance to Old China Town, a broad road with shops lining the two sides of the street. For the late party goers and insomniacs, this was a great place to have breakfast to close an eventful night. Both steamed and fried momos were served with a sweet chilli sauce on both sides of the road, flanked by *bao* (also called *baozi*, it is a type of steamed bun with fillings, in various Chinese cuisines, as there is much variation as to the fillings and the preparations) and sausages, vegetables and soup. For a second it did look like a Chinese town, until you heard them speaking in Bengali.

Anshuk was one of those people who fell in love with this market and suggested we start the morning by having a warm bowl of soup. The soup stall was run by a middle-aged lady, who was a bit cranky at first. She was not especially interested in me or my questions about her family history. All interviews are not planned, and some don't go very well. Anshuk explained that as a community, they had been through a lot, and generally liked to be reserved and private. I quietly took my fish soup and went to a corner. The soup was not thickened with cornflour, nor heavily laden with MSG. The fish ball was made of surmai, and the soup was clear, with some serious restorative properties. These recipes had been handed down generations and that was very evident by the simplicity of the dish and the flavour of the broth. There wasn't much place to sit or stand, and the vendors had not set up fancy shops. I had two bowls of soup that gave me the energy to go on for the rest of my day.

It was time to take a deep breath and go get some real breakfast. I moved around the market and surveyed the various other dishes on sale; different types of chicken, pork and shrimp dim sums (all of which I tried and loved). Pork sausages were hung from store ceilings; I tasted those as well. I was most happy with my big *bao* as they call it, which was stuffed with chicken, egg and spring onions. The *bao* was slightly sweet and the chicken stuffing complemented the soft springy texture of the insides. I still wasn't full, so I went in for the rice dish that looked like a *churro* (a fried-dough pastry, predominantly choux-based snack), and was called *lathi* (stick). For those who really didn't care for Chinese breakfast, there were a few *aloo-puri* stalls in a corner. I ate till it was time for the market to shut down, and there was literally nothing left to eat. It was humanly impossible to eat for the next few hours; so instead, I decided to explore the Kumartuli Market.

Traditionally a potter's quarter, Kumartuli is where clay idols of Hindu Gods and Goddesses are made. In recent years, this area has become very popular because of the idols of Durga that are made for Durga Puja every year. Kumartuli is even on the tour map of Kolkata city. Filled with extremely skilled artisans, who model clay with their hands, and follow a traditional technique which hasn't changed for many years, they get really busy for a whole month before Durga Puja. A well made sturdy idol is about 10-feet tall. They first make a brass frame in which they fill straw, and tie it into the base shape of the idol. They then make a mud and clay mixture and coat the hay that is tied using string. Once coated, they begin to carve in the intricate designs. Surprisingly, they don't use any references and just model the idols freehand. It takes about 10 days to complete the whole process. These idols are, I was told, exported to 90 countries across the world, and the artisans produce 20,000 deities throughout the year. I tried designing one of the clay idols and made a complete mess. It obviously required great skill, patience and practice, like cooking.

After my visit to the market I went to the Victoria Memorial, another popular tourist stop. The entire building was made of marble. I would recommend everyone to take the tonga ride and go to the memorial. I actually took a detour and went behind the memorial to eat *chaat*, and drink masala aerated drink, made with lemon and chaat masala. My version was spiked with green chilly. If you are not planning on going to Kolkata any time soon, try this at home; it is very refreshing in summer.

After my morning soup and mid-day snack I was feeling a tad bit better. I decided I would spend the evening exploring Kolkata's street food culture that is very famous all over India. The street food had the daily specials common to all the metro cities: *chaat*, *bhelpuri*, *pucchka* (called *gol gappa* in Delhi and *pani puri* in Bombay), *samosa*, chowmein; but the most popular was still the *kathi* roll. Though everybody had their own personal favourite, Decker's Lane had some of the best street food in Kolkata. Me being the enthusiastic chef that I am, I requested one *kathi* roll owner to let me take over his stall for a while. The idea was to see if I could generate more revenue for him by making my own version of the *kathi* roll. A typical one is almost a shallow-fried flaky *parantha*, with or without egg, which is then stuffed with various fillings like *paneer*, chicken, mutton, vegetables. Known to be extremely oily and greasy, it tastes absolutely divine. The idea was to create a new roll, an experiment that would fit in with the taste of Kolkata.

I sold eight pieces of my **Thai *Kathi* Roll** by pulling people off the street and making them sample my experiment. All of them agreed to pay after having the roll. Nothing gives a chef more joy than that.

THAI *KATHI* ROLL
(Thai noodles wrapped in a flaky flatbread.)

Ingredients (for the Thai noodles)

3 tbsp sesame *(til)* oil
1 tbsp crushed red chilli flakes
200 gm noodles
1 tbsp ginger-garlic *(adrak-lasun)* paste
3 spring onions, finely sliced
1 tbsp crushed peanuts *(moongphali)*, optional
1 cup shredded carrots *(gajar)*, coriander *(dhania patta)*,
capsicum *(shimla mirch)*, cabbage *(patta gobhi)*
2 tbsp low-sodium soya sauce
1 tbsp rice vinegar
1 tbsp honey *(shahad)*
½ cup torn basil *(tulsi)* leaves

Method (for the Thai noodles)

1. In a pan, heat sesame oil and red chilli flakes on low heat for 10-15 minutes. Pour the oil through a strainer and discard the pepper flakes.
2. In a pot of boiling salted water, cook the noodles according to the package directions. Drain the noodles and set aside.
3. Heat the sesame oil in a large frying pan or wok, add ginger-garlic paste, spring onions and peanuts and toss well. Now, add all the vegetables and sauté for a minute. Add soya sauce, vinegar and honey. Give a gentle mix and add boiled noodles.
4. Toss the noodles till it coats the sauce and finish with torn basil leaves. Filling is ready. (You can even serve it like a dish right away).

Ingredients (for the Kathi Roll)

2 cups refined flour (maida)
4 eggs
Oil for frying
Salt to taste
Pepper to taste

Method (for the Kathi Roll)

1. Knead the flour with sufficient amount of water and some salt. Divide the dough into equal balls for a parantha.

2. Make round layered paranthas with it. Basically, once you roll the dough ball like a roti, spread some oil over it. Then, first fold it like a paper fan and then roll it from one end to another (like a carpet) and tuck in the loose end at the centre of the circle. Flatten it out again as a roti. You'll see several layers in it.

3. On the side, beat the eggs with little salt and pepper.

4. Now, on a hot griddle half cook the parantha from both sides with a little oil. Remove it.

5. Heat half tablespoon oil in a frying pan or on the same griddle and add one beaten egg to it, spread as the same diameter as the parantha.

6. Carefully place the half-cooked parantha over the half fried omelette and allow it to cook for two more minutes; turn around the parantha and cook the other side for one minute. Kathi roll parantha is now ready.

7.   Add a generous amount of Thai noodle filling to
     this *parantha*.
8.   Roll the *parantha* and cover half of it with an aluminum
     foil or kitchen paper and tuck the paper well so that
     the roll doesn't open up.
9.   Serve hot.

~

That was enough food, in one day, for a sick person.
I decided not to push any more boundaries and went
back to the hotel to rest and re-energise myself for the
next day's events.

DAY 87
31 October / Kolkata

Now that we had experienced the street food of Kolkata, this day was about the traditional meals of the city. For a traditional Bengali *thali* I visited Kewpie's; here I met Rakhi, the owner. This was a small restaurant on a corner street with an entrance under a flower creeper. Rakhi had given up her career in Bombay to open this restaurant in Kolkata. A lot like how Mum's Kitchen came into being in Goa. This was actually Rakhi's old house that had been converted into a restaurant.

Before we began eating, Rakhi agreed to share her great-grand-aunt's recipe of mustard cauliflower, called **Monoma**, named after her aunt. Cauliflower had gained a new respect in my eyes. Though the dish was a bit laborious to prepare, it was done so lovingly by Rakhi.

MONOMA
(Cauliflower cooked in a mustard flavoured gravy.)

Ingredients

2 cauliflowers, cut into medium-sized florets
Salt to taste
2 tsp yellow mustard *(rai)* seeds
1 tsp black mustard *(sarson)* seeds
1½ cups yoghurt
1 tsp gram flour *(besan)*
2 tsp sugar
1 tsp turmeric powder

1½ tsp red chilli powder
1 tbsp ginger-garlic *(adrak-lasun)* paste
4 tbsp mustard oil *(sarson ka tel)*
2 tsp *panch phoron* (whole spice mix of mustard, cumin, fennel, onion seeds and fenugreek seeds, all in equal measure)
2-3 green chillies, slit lengthwise
Fresh coriander leaves *(dhania patti)* for garnishing

Method

1. Rub the cauliflower florets with little salt and turmeric powder and keep it aside for 20 minutes at least.
2. Soak both the mustard seeds in one-fourth cup hot water for 10 minutes; then blend them to a fine paste with a bit of salt.
3. Whisk the yoghurt, gram flour, sugar and salt together, so that the yoghurt doesn't split when it is put in a hot pan.
4. In another bowl, mix together turmeric, red chilli powder, ginger-garlic paste with a little water.
5. Heat half the mustard oil in a pan, fry cauliflower florets until they're almost cooked and have a nice golden brown colour.
6. Heat the rest of the mustard oil in a pan; let it reach a smoking point. Reduce the flame to medium. Now add *panch phoron*. When the spices start to crackle, add ginger-garlic-spice mix and green chillies and sauté for two minutes.
7. On low flame add the yoghurt mix. Cook this with spices for three to four minutes until it thickens.
8. Add mustard paste, mix nicely and cook for two minutes.

9. Add fried cauliflower florets into this paste.
10. Add half cup of warm water and sprinkle chopped coriander leaves. Cover the pan and let it simmer for five minutes. Check the seasoning and as the gravy coats the cauliflower, take it off the heat and serve it with hot rice.

~

Rakhi explained that a traditional Bengali lunch started with bitter flavours, and ended, like all others, with sweets. One of the popular bitter dishes was called *shukto* made with a spice called *radhuni*. It had a mix of vegetables like sweet potato, drumsticks, brinjal and beans, and had a creamy texture. This was followed by lentils. It was a *chana dal* (split Bengal gram) preparation called *cholar dal*. The *dal* had cashew nuts, and the special *panch phoran* spices. The *dal* was made with *ghee* and was finished with coconut; two things that really made the *dal* stand out. *Panch phoran* has five primary spices: fenugreek *(methi)* seeds, fennel *(saunf)* seeds, cumin *(jeera)* seeds, onion *(kalonji)* seeds, and mustard *(sarson)* seeds. The vegetable that was served after the *dal* was *baingun bhaja*, which was basically fried brinjals. Similarly, other vegetables could be made into a *bhaja* depending on the season. They were fried and then coated with spices. If the meal was a non-vegetarian one, the meat followed. Here, it was usually fish. I ate prawn *malai* curry, paired with chutney and *papad*, and lastly, the dessert. Usually all this was eaten with rice, or *lucchi*s (extremely light *puri*s). For dessert I had *mishti doi*; made with yoghurt that was sweetened with jaggery.

I knew I was in for a treat and my decision to skip breakfast was a great one. One of the new ingredients I discovered during my meal was *gondhoraj*. It is a type of lime particular to this region of Bengal. Called *gondhoraj*, that literally means aroma king, it is served with the meal, and enhances the flavour of food. It was nice of her to invite me for a meal, and learning about the food of her family couldn't have been easier, all thanks to the elaborate *thali*.

After lunch I travelled around the city, on the tram, looked at the old buildings, and wandered around absorbing in as much of Kolkata as I could. My last stop was K.C. Das; a temple for dessert lovers. I was told that this was the place where *rasgulla* was invented in 1868. It was made of *chenna*, or in simple language, fresh cottage cheese. This Indian dessert not only filled your stomach, but also quenched your thirst. It was soft, springy and filled with sugar syrup. Hats off to the person who invented this dish, because the technique is very difficult to imitate. I must admit, I am not a fan of tinned *rasgulla*s. The *rasmalai* was to die for, or rather, to live for. The quality of the saffron used was top notch, and the *malai* just melted in my mouth. The milk was creamy and pure. My recommendation would be to go straight for the *rasmalai* when you visit this shop in Kolkata.

On this sweet note, I closed my visit to Kolkata and was glad that I no longer had fever. This was also the day I found out that I would be a part of the *Limca Book of Records* for being the first chef to travel 100 days by road, in search of good food.

My chef trainer would usually joke and tell me, 'You need to marinate yourself long enough before you hit the tandoor.' He would usually use this quote to teach me how important timing was and that success only tasted better when you have invested enough time, money and hard work in it.

The same joke would be applied to my acting skills. After a rigorous 40-day training in voice exercises and mirror rehearsals, I got my act straight. Under the guidance and supervision of my director, I began to befriend the camera. Slowly, my earlier barriers, in articulating thoughts in front of the camera, disappeared. Words, actions and expressions began to fall in sync.

The best part about this creative exercise was I stopped pretending to portray a certain image for the camera. I returned to being myself, it was all me and my audience could see me just the way I am.

DAY 88 AND 89
1–2 November / Siliguri to Gangtok

I was on the road for the longest stretch this time as my next destination was Sikkim in Northeast India, very far from Kolkata. The Northeast is geographically, culturally and socially a very special part of India. Squeezed between Nepal and Bangladesh are the seven sisters: Arunachal Pradesh, Assam, Manipur, Meghalaya, Mizoram, Nagaland, and Tripura; and together with the Himalayan state of Sikkim make up the exquisitely beautiful Northeast. I was making my way towards Sikkim and then aimed to go to Assam, to sample the culture and cuisine there.

The main connection to the Northeast is Siliguri, at the tip of West Bengal. Siliguri has an airport and is a convenient place to land and continue onwards to the east. The airport has a very famous restaurant where we stopped for lunch to eat fish cutlets with mustard chilli sauce. The road led us from New Jalpaiguri to the Tista river valley. This was the landmark or the fork in the road, which led to Darjeeling, Gangtok or Kalimpong. We took the road to Gangtok, which was up and around the hills and through the valley. On the way up, I stopped at the Tista Bazaar where I ate fresh, steamy delicious momos with a cup of tea. They were very particular about serving the local chilli paste with the momos. The momos were quite big and stuffed generously with cabbage and chicken. I washed down my meal with hot tea and a small *narangi* (orange) for dessert. I felt delighted to be there.

Back on the road, we reached a junction with a board that said, 'Welcome to Sikkim.' There was a checkpoint for verifying the IDs, unlike any other city in the country. We were headed towards Gangtok, to begin our journey of the Northeast as well as to end our journey of India.

DAY 90
3 November / Gangtok

Sikkim is heavily influenced by the neighbouring Nepal and China. The people are an indigenous mix of tribes that thrive in the heartland of the Himalayas and mostly follow Buddhism or Hinduism. The most popular tribes are the Lepcha, the Sikkimese and Nepalese. I feel that one of the best ways to explore a culture is by attending a wedding and taking part in the ceremonies. Most of us have been to a Hindu, Muslim or even a Christian wedding, but attending a wedding in Sikkim is a rare affair. I had the pleasure of being invited to a *khim gyapa*, a Bhutia wedding. One of the main communities of Sikkim, the Bhutias are a matriarchal society. So, while I was at the residence of the bride, the groom arrived laden with gifts for the girl's family. The boy's family was greeted with silk scarves called *khara*s. Two kilograms of pork, a bottle of wine and cookies made of rice powder called *zhedro* were presented to the bride. I realised how food was such an important catalyst for cultures to express emotions, celebrate special occasions and also exchanged as gestures of welcome.

I was given the ritual butter tea similar to the one that I had had in Ladakh. Along with butter rice, *deshi* (fried pastries) and *khapse* (local biscuits), it marked the beginning of the celebrations. The wedding ceremony was conducted by the Lama monks who recited the chants. Once this was over, there was breakfast that included *gyatho*, which is a popular Sikkimese dish made from long egg noodles. The mincemeat of your choice was added with whatever vegetables you wanted to have. The noodles were prepared fresh using flour; the process was long and particular to each family. *Thukpa* is the poorer version of *gyatho*, which is richer with more variations. The cherry on the cake was the chilli (that looked like a cherry itself), that was served with the *gyatho*. It was called *dalley*. The paste of this chilli was added on top of the *gyatho*, and the oldest lady of the house told me that anybody who visits them needed to be well fed. That, I found, was the general feeling across India: Guests were God.

The tea cups, the bowls and all the crockery were very ornamental with intricate designs and paintings that were very typically Tibetan. Another remarkably striking feature of the ceremony were the outfits of both the ladies and the men. The outfits were multi-coloured and resembled the Japanese kimonos. What caught my attention was the biscuit called *khapse* or *zhedro*, prepared for festivals or important ceremonies. The dough is usually made with rice flour, butter, eggs, and sugar. The interesting part came when it was time to shape the dough before deep-frying it. It could be left flat or made into lattice like designs. Fried and sweet, it was a very lethal combination and was almost begging to be eaten! I got a lot of ideas when I was eating the *khapse*. To describe it, I would say it was a cross between *shakker para* and the Mexican churros. I spent a lot of time there eating, talking and celebrating with the gentle people of the Bhutia community. The family made me comfortable and fed me till I couldn't eat any more. I love how food takes the physical form of generosity.

The day began on an exceptional note, but thanks to my producer, the day was getting better. I had the chance to meet and cook for India's football legend Baichung Bhutia. I immediately went online and checked out about Baichung's choice of food. I met him at the Paljor Stadium where he played football and coached the United Sikkim Football Club. The club is one of the top clubs in India, all thanks to Baichung and his inspiring career that put football on the world map in a cricket-crazy country. It is his passion and love for the game that has kept him motivated all these years. I think the secret is to just follow your heart. Talking to him, I also realised that it took him a lot of hard work and dedication to be where he is. Later in the day, I joined Baichung for a match. His team was playing and to add to the evening's general cheerful spirit, his team won.

I cooked for him after the match, after doing my own little research about his preferences. His children loved chocolate and he loved momos, so I decided to make **Chocolate Football Momos**. Sometimes, you think of things on the spur of the moment and don't really have a follow-up plan. The football design, however, turned out quite well and the kids loved the momos!

Baichung was one of the most celebrated people I had met on my journey, so like all social media junkies, I took pictures and tweeted all about my day.

CHOCOLATE FOOTBALL MOMOS
(Deep-fried chocolate dumplings presented like a football.)

Ingredients

250 gm refined flour *(maida)*
A pinch of salt
¼ tsp baking powder
½ cup green apples, chopped into small cubes
1 cup chocolate, chopped into small cubes
1 tsp cinnamon *(dalchini)* powder
¼ tsp cardamom *(elaichi)* powder
¼ tsp black pepper *(kali mirch)* powder
½ cup chocolate sauce
Oil to deep fry

Method

1. Knead the flour, salt and baking powder with water into a hard dough.
2. In a bowl gently toss apples, chocolate, cinnamon, cardamom, salt and black pepper together. Freeze this mix.
3. Now take the small balls of dough, flatten them into small rounds, put some frozen chocolate filling in between and seal folding the edges and shape it into a round like a football.
4. Steam these for five minutes.
5. Then deep-fry these until they're well cooked and golden. Make the football design pattern on this fried momo with the help of chocolate sauce.
6. Serve hot with chocolate sauce on the side.

~

The end of the day was culturally significant, as I decided to meet the Shering Lepcha. He wanted to introduce me to the Lepcha community and the viewers of my show. The community is one of the most marginalised in the country and is on the brink of extinction as a group. He greeted me by saying, '*Thumri moh,*' meaning welcome. He told me that he organised festivals to promote the arts and crafts of his community. These festivals would help educate the general public about the Lepchas. Shering said that they are considered an ancient tribe and that he was trying to preserve the cultural heritage of his people. They believed that they were the most loved offspring of Mother Earth, and their origins could date back to the beginning of time. Such ancient cultures shouldn't be forgotten or ignored. I was invited to watch a band perform folk songs. The musicians where dressed in *dumpra* which was a lot like the Scottish kilts. The ladies too wore a similar skirt called the *dumdem*. They explained how their food was very similar to the Sikkimese food culture.

I had thoroughly enjoyed exploring the links between culture and food in a new land, while making new friends and listening to new music. Gangtok was proving to be a beautiful beginning of my journey through the Northeast.

DAY 91
4 November / Gangtok

Early in the morning I went up to the Tashi Viewpoint to watch the sunrise. It was breathtaking to be in the east where the sun rose earlier than other places of the country. I was filled with the energy from the first light of the day and to keep up the good feeling I went to the Rumtek Monastery. To my eyes, it seemed like an outburst of different colours that was peaceful and powerful at the same time. From the monastery the view of the city was incredible. What really struck me was how quiet it was up there. I almost missed the noise of the city down below. In all honesty, if you have seen one, you have seen them all.

My roommate from college days, Aditya, owns a hotel called Tashi Delek, which in Sikkimese means welcome. It is right on the Mall Road. The narrow Mall Road was flanked by shops on both sides and the striking bit about the architecture on that road was that the big shops were always behind the small shops. The entrance to the shop was narrow and long, which finally opened up into a square. Aditya introduced me to Sonam, an expert on the local food. She was known for her catering business that served traditional food for ceremonies. I had the opportunity to cook on the terrace of the hotel at the back, which overlooked the valley and the rest of the city. On a sunny day, when the visibility was clear, you could even spot the Kanchenjunga. It was one of the most spectacular views after my experience in Varanasi.

Sonam was looking extremely pretty; she was wearing a dress called the *baku*, made of Chinese silk. She gave me a quick lesson about Sikkimese basics. They used a lot of onions, ginger, garlic, turmeric, fresh chillies and mustard seeds. The food was not overloaded with spices, and based, more broadly, on a variety of vegetables that were both wild and grown in Sikkim. She explained that broths eaten with rice made up most of their diet. Few of the dishes that were popular were the *gaythuk*, *thukpa*, momos and the *khapse*. There were many names that I can't quite recall, and don't remember, even though this was my third visit! The ones I do remember were *prok gyari*, cooked with tender bamboo shoots; *sael roti*, cooked in a tomato masala, unlike the Sikkimese version that looked like thick onion rings made from fermented rice batter, that was deep fried. Another ingredient that she introduced me to was the *churpi* momos. *Churpi* is a type of cheese that is available both fresh and dried. It is slightly crumbly with sharpness in its taste. My mind was working overtime thinking about all the dishes that I could use the cheese in!

After giving me a brief lesson about Sikkimese food, she cooked with me and taught me how to make a typical dish eaten at her home; **Sikkim Chicken Curry**. This was very simple, so simple that it actually took me a while to adjust to the fact that there was barely anything in it!

SIKKIM CHICKEN CURRY
(Wild chicken cooked in a flavoured broth.)

Ingredients

1 kg chicken (local country chicken with bones), cut into
  medium pieces
1½ tbsp ginger-garlic (adrak-lasun) paste
Salt to taste
½ tsp turmeric (haldi) powder
2 tsp chilli powder
2 tsp lime juice or vinegar
3 tbsp mustard oil (sarson ka tel)
3 onions, diced
5 green chillies, each sliced into two.
4 tomatoes, roughly chopped
¼ cup yoghurt
1 tbsp cumin (jeera) powder
Coriander leaves (dhania patti) for garnishing

Method

1. Marinate the chicken with ginger-garlic paste, salt,
    turmeric, chilli powder and lemon juice for two hours.
2. Heat the mustard oil, bring it to a smoking point,
    and then reduce the flame to medium. Add onions
    to this and cook until translucent.
3. Add the green chillies, followed by tomatoes. Cook
    for another three to four minutes.
4. Lower the flame and then add yoghurt, followed by
    cumin power. Reduce this for two minutes.
5. Add the marinated chicken and let it seal for three
    to four minutes.

6. Top it with two cups of warm water; bring it to a boil and then let it cook for 25 minutes on simmer. Season with salt.
7. Keep checking, as you need to cook it till the bones separate from the meat easily (check with a fork).
8. Garnish it with coriander leaves and serve hot with rice.

~

After learning the recipe, we all sat down together to eat lunch. Along with the chicken there were *churpi* momos and *sael roti*. Another dish that stood out was called *chaang*. It was an alcoholic beverage that was fermented and made with cereals. Drunk from a bamboo pipe, it is also called Sikkimese beer, and has fermented seeds of millet in it.

After this lovely meal with a lovely view, I thanked Sonam for her time and patience. I spent the evening walking around Gangtok and exploring the nightlife. The weather was perfect. Sikkim Super Lotto was very popular; I placed my bet and even won!

I want to thrown in my two cents to all travellers who would like to explore India and its hill stations. Sikkim is a fascinating, unique and beautiful destination that you must visit.

Day 92

I spent the day travelling from Gangtok to Guwahati, Assam.

DAY 93
5 November / Guwahati

I arrived in Guwahati and somehow it made me feel like I had taken the road less travelled. This was going to be the last state that I would visit as part of the show. Assam is known for its silk and tea estates, it has a very rich culture and heritage; however, it has been politically unstable. We took a while to reach our destination because of the state of unrest. I reached at noon and it had taken me a day and a half to just get there. The saving grace was that the road I took was picturesque with tea estates on both sides.

A little later after my arrival I met Chef Atul Lahakar, who has done more for Assamese cuisine than anybody else has from the state. He runs restaurants to promote local Assamese cuisine and has written many books about the same. I was glad that he could fit me into his schedule that day and that I got the chance to cook and eat with the master himself.

Atul took me from Guwahati to Sonapur, a small village on the outskirts of Guwahati. He wanted me to experience traditional methods of cooking, with local fresh ingredients, in a unique surrounding. He gave me a small brief about the food. He explained that rice was very important and there was no use of *rotis*. They used few spices: cumin, coriander and black pepper. Assam's 70 per cent of the population are tribal, who cook without oil and spices. They rely a lot on the natural herbs and local ingredients that are available in the wild. They like to preserve their meats by smoking them over fire. The dry meat or fish is then used as chutney by mixing them with fresh spices and flavourings. He also mentioned something that really caught my attention: the use of a hollow bamboo as a cooking vessel.

Coming from north India, the tastes here were very different from anything that is available to us or that we are used to; especially foods that are preserved using fermentation, smoking and drying. Chef Atul and I sat ourselves down at a small cooking site that he had set up. It was made of a few stones and between them, there was a fire burning and a wok made of bell metal resting, slightly elevated over the fire. There were also a few sticks that were arranged over the fire with stands, to roast meats. We sat down in front of the fire, with banana leaves beside us, with all our raw ingredients on display. On my right was a stone *silbatta* (grinding stone), with a wooden mallet to crush fresh spices. The *silbatta* could be used to make a paste, or could be used as a surface to flatten fruit or spices.

The two dishes Chef Atul and I were going to prepare today were **Fish Outenga**, which was river fish cooked with a vegetable particular to Assam, called outenga or elephant apple. It was a very simple recipe that used freshly pound turmeric, which closely resembled ginger. On tasting the recipe, I realised it reminded me of raw mango that had been cooked in a curry. The flavour profile was subtle; I could identify all the ingredients, and I was not bombarded with spices. The curry gave each ingredient the turn to shine.

FISH OUTENGA
(Fish cooked with elephant apples.)

Ingredients

6 pieces (300 gm) rohu or any fresh-water fish
2 tsp mustard oil *(sarson ka tel)*
1½ piece of elephant apple or outenga, cut into small pieces
Salt to taste
2 green chillies, slit
2-inch ginger *(adrak)*
8-10 cloves garlic *(lasun)*
1 tsp turmeric *(haldi)*
2 tsp rice powder
1 full stem of roselle leaves *(tenga mora)*
A few sprigs of fresh coriander *(dhania patti)*

Method

1. Wash the fish well; apply some turmeric and salt, and keep aside.
2. Heat a bit of mustard oil in a deep pan. Add pounded and crushed elephant apple pieces and sauté for a minute with a bit of salt. Add four cups of water to this. Bring it to a boil and then put it on simmer. If you don't find elephant apple, you can add raw mango to this recipe instead. After 10 minutes add green chillies and pounded ginger and garlic (not chopped). Let it simmer for another 10 minutes. Add turmeric powder.

3.   Once the elephant apple is almost cooked, add marinated fish to this reduced stock. Let the fish cook for five to seven minutes. Handle it delicately. Add rice powder and crush and sprinkle roselle leaves with your hand. (If you can't find this, add any local fern available in your area).

4.   Cook it for another minute or so; garnish with coriander. Serve it hot with rice.

~

The second dish we made was the chicken cooked in a hollow bamboo, also called **Sunga Kukura**. I got a few tips from the chef; he said that the bamboo should be fresh and rich in moisture. This helps the food inside to boil and prevents the shoot from burning. The bamboo shoot was also lightly smoked to add to the flavour. The chicken is marinated with fresh turmeric, ginger, garlic, coriander, fermented bamboo shoot water, and fermented bamboo shoots. The chicken is then stuffed into the shoot and then sealed using a fresh turmeric leaf. The shoot is then put in the fire, standing up, to cook for about 40 minutes.

BAMBOO CHICKEN A.K.A. *SUNGA KUKURA*
(Chicken cooked inside a roasted hollow bamboo, sealed from the sides.)

Ingredients

1 kg chicken, with bones or boneless, whatever you prefer

2 tbsp fresh turmeric *(haldi)* roots, grated or finely chopped

1½ tbsp fresh ginger *(adrak)*, grated or finely chopped

8-10 cloves garlic *(lasun)*, finely chopped

3 green chillies

2 tbsp coriander leaves *(dhania patti)*, chopped

1½ tbsp fermented bamboo shoot juice

Salt to taste

1 tbsp dried bamboo shoot (optional)

2 big pieces of bamboo, fresh, tender and edible (both sides are usually closed; get it cut at a 45 degree angle from the top and you'll see the hollow)

2-3 turmeric leaves to seal the bamboo hollow

Other

A place to light up a wood-fire or a set-up to burn the bamboo.

Method

1. Marinate the chicken with turmeric roots, ginger, garlic, chillies, coriander leaves, fermented bamboo shoot juice, salt and dried bamboo shoot. If you're not adding fermented bamboo juice add a bit of lime juice or oil to mix all the ingredients together. Marinate this for two hours at least.

2. Now roast the bamboo hollow from outside for two minutes so that fresh flavours are released within the hollow.

3. Fill this hollow with half the marinated chicken. Add two and a half cups of water. Fold the turmeric leaves and push the chicken down and make sure that the

leaves do not let the steam escape. (It basically acts like a cooker.)

4.   Cook this on open fire for approximately 40 minutes. The outer side will turn dark grey and you will be able to smell that it is cooked. Remove from the flame and serve hot with steamed rice. The time for cooking may vary depending on the size and quality of the bamboo.

~

At the end of all the cooking, we sat down to enjoy the fruits of our labour. On a fresh banana leaf was the Assamese *dal*, made of only cereal water and salt. Not my favourite choice on the platter. What saved me was the fish outenga. The fish was tender and the flavours unique. The chicken was soft and the bamboo had acted as the perfect pressure cooker. I thanked him for my first Assamese experience.

I had spent a lot of time travelling through India and had learnt from different people—chefs, mothers, housewives, shopkeepers, *mithai walas*, *namkeen walas*, and cooks—about different styles of cooking, different types of food, and of course, different cultures. This was another unforgettable experience to add to my diary, my memories and my life.

DAY 94
6 November / Guwahati

Yesterday was dedicated to the traditional food of Assam. So, today I took a small detour from my culinary journey to explore the cultural side of Assam. I was invited by the Assam Kala Kendra to learn about the energetic, fast paced dance, Bihu. Brisk movements and deft hand gestures describe this beautiful folk dance the best. The dance is attached to the Bihu festival, which celebrates the onset of spring and marks the harvesting season. This festival is dedicated to nature, rebirth and fertility. Both men and women participate in the dance and wear traditional Assamese clothing called the *muga mekhela*, which is a two-piece garment that has red floral designs embroidered on them and resembles a sari. The men wear the *dhoti gamosa*. The most important part of the costume is the *gamosa*, a thin towel with a red border that is tied on the head with a fluffy knot. The *gamosa* is tied on the head while dancing and later hung around the neck during the prayers.

I could see a lot of bright red during the group dance. They enacted stories, forming different types of circles and formations. The dance was accompanied by traditional music. The lyrics ranged from welcoming the Assamese New Year, celebrating the life of farmers, history and to even modern life. Besides the common *dhol,* the other instruments were made from hollow bamboo, like the *toka* (a bamboo flute that could be as big as a didgeridoo). I joined in for the last bit of the dance and all I was clap my hands. I had to do it really fast, keeping rhythm with the music. I did make a complete fool of myself as I couldn't keep up with the change in pace, mood and rhythm, but I tried my best! I admired the skill of the dancers for being so agile and graceful.

I spent the morning with them and then we all joined to eat a light Assamese breakfast. We had the traditional farmer's breakfast which includes *poita*, a fermented rice preparation with yoghurt, chillies and mashed potatoes. It was a high-energy start for farmers to eat *poita* and set out to the fields. It was a lot like curd rice, but sour because of the fermentation.

I left the dancers after breakfast to find an interesting spot for lunch, with my thoughts solely revolving around planning and preparing for my meals. Unfortunately, I couldn't make it to Nagaland on this trip, but I had managed to find food from Nagaland in Guwahati at a place called Naga Kitchen. I spent lunch time there, eating with the owner, Romeo. He introduced me to Naga food by giving me a few tips. Nothing was fried and most of the dishes were boiled. Just like Assamese food, they did not use a lot of spices and used pickled, fermented and preserved food instead. Their favourite meat, and very common on the menus, was pork. All the meats were smoked, whether it was pork, fish, or chicken. Nagaland has about 30 tribes that all speak different languages and have different cultural habits and of course, a unique cuisine.

Lunch began and I was served a platter of different smoked meats called *ith akuni*, a kind of fermented soya beans. Only someone familiar with *akuni* would not be taken aback by its pungent smell. I tried eating it, without smelling it, and it actually tasted good. The second dish I tasted was smoked fish with *anishi*, which was made of dry fermented yam leaves smoked over fire. There was also a soup that came for the main course called the mixed vegetable. It was literally vegetables with salt that were boiled with water. That was the only vegetarian dish available, so if you are a vegetarian, maybe Nagaland isn't the best place to be in. If I had to pick one of my favourite dishes from the afternoon, it would have had to be the smoked fish with the *anishi*. If you are a pork fan, the dry pork with bamboo shoots would appeal to you.

One very special feature about Nagaland is that it is home to *bhut jolokia*, the world's second hottest chilli with a count of 10 lakh Scoville units. I was told that the chilli might be hard on the palate, but it is easy on the stomach. I mustered up my courage to eat this chilli. I decided to taste the paste of the chilli by dipping the tip of a spoon into the bowl. It wasn't as bad as I thought it would be; I survived and it didn't trouble my stomach either. That was my experience at the Naga Kitchen. I didn't want to judge it, just experience it. It was a better idea to just absorb everything I had learnt.

DAY 95
7 November / Guwahati

Today was my last day in Assam, and soon after the sun set, it would be time to head home. That made it mandatory for me to start the day on a sweet note, just for good luck. I went to Lakshmi Mishtan Bhandar in Beltola. Here I met Arnab, the owner. The shop was founded by his grandfather in 1942. I was looking for a particular variety of Assamese sweet called *pitha*. I had never seen or tasted it before. From what I had gathered, it was like a flat Assamese crêpe made of only rice flour and stuffed with a kind of *kheer*. There were many varieties of it; some were made of palm syrup, others had sesame, and some had jaggery in them. I also found savoury *pitha*s with different stuffing that were fried, boiled or even steamed. I ordered two; the plain version with *kheer* and one with palm jaggery called *ghila pitha*; this was fried. Both were delicious and reminded me of dessert crêpes that I have had at a continental restaurant. The *pitha* is usually accompanied by tea, and the shop was set up in such a way that the guests could pick up the *pitha* of their choice with their tea, and stand at the little counters.

My next point of interest, while I was still in Assam, was tea! I had been surrounded by garden estates and plantations throughout my trip, whether it was Dharamshala or Munnar. Most of the tea here was grown in the Brahmaputra valley. The climate and altitude was perfect for the production. So much so that 150 years ago it was one of the most famous tea production spots in the world. Both sides of the river have fertile banks suitable for tea production.

I am not a tea drinker, or a coffee addict for that matter, but my family drinks a lot of both. If I had to choose, and I couldn't avoid it, I preferred sugary sweet, milky tea, like most Indians. After my travels I could see how important a cup of tea was for someone's mental peace. Tea stalls in our country are little hubs for conversation, political debates and camaraderie. Like all food and beverage products, tea has a huge variety in terms of quality. We can buy anything from boxed tea bags to first flush single growth loose leaves. Like I mentioned earlier, when I was in Dharamshala, tea is not just about boiling and mixing. If you ever visit Assam, take some time out to walk through the estates, and drinking some tea amidst the bright green plants.

This was the last leg of my travel and walking through the gardens in Assam I reminisced about my journey and I realised that even though I have travelled all over the world, the beauty of India was unparalleled. Every state has a different feeling, a unique landscape and lots of love to offer.

DAY 96 AND 97

I was going back to Delhi, my home, and I just couldn't wait to get there.

Day 98
10 November / Delhi

After two days of a cross country train journey, I finally reached my destination and completed my journey. I had not yet reached home, but I was in my home town. Let me formally introduce you to my city, New Delhi.

Being the capital of the country, it is the heart of the nation. Extremely popular worldwide for its Punjabi weddings, street food, family culture, insane drivers and its new and shiny metro. Though what I love most about this city is how involved everyone is in cooking, eating and sharing of food. Discussions in Mumbai might be about business or lifestyle, but in Delhi, the topics of conversation are about meals, restaurants and cuisine. People here are very particular about what they eat and are very conscious of flavour profiles and taste.

Delhi's food culture really started to take form with the advent of the Mughal rule. Places like Chandni Chowk have been around since the seventeenth century. Mughlai food is one of the most popular types of Indian food, here and abroad. Now that I have travelled, I can say that India does not have one cuisine, even though in abroad Mughlai is synonymous with Indian food. What is more important in Delhi, than any cuisine or restaurant, is the street food and the *dhaba* culture. Some shops from the eighteenth century are still around rubbing shoulders with new-age eateries.

The people of Delhi are an interesting bunch. Over the years they have managed to set up some well-established culturally-crossed themes that separate them from other states in the country. For example, Delhi loves its Punjabi-Chinese food (call it *Chinjabi* if you must!). It is a spicy, saucy version of the subtle Oriental cuisine and the people of Delhi, no matter how rich, will always be in love with it. When Delhi-ites finish a night in the town, they will drive straight to the nearest *dhaba*. That neighbouring shop which serves up hot kebabs, rolls, *parantha*s and tandoori *roti*s, will never be too far. Each market, in every part of the city will have the standard *chaat* guy, who started his business on a makeshift cycle, and now owns a multistorey air conditioned *chaat* shop. Last but not the least; I must mention the love that Delhi has for its *dosa*s, *idli*s (south Indian steamed cake of rice), and *sambar*. A standard vegetarian meal for every class, this limited choice of menu is always available for the Delhi*wala*s as a light meal that reflects everything about south India in Delhi.

It had been many days since I ate the food of my hometown. I walked through those familiar streets to warm my stomach with the food of my city and show viewers what Delhi had to offer. I started my day with *chole bhature* (combination of chickpea curry and fried breads called *bhature*) at Om Di Hatti in Kamla Nagar. North Delhi is flooded with such shops, everyone has their own favourites, and everyone's willing to argue to prove who the best is. The *bhatura*s that you get here have the slight tang that correct fermentation lends to the dough. They are stuffed with *paneer* and smell of thick sour yoghurt. With that I got my *Pindi chole*, popular for its look and colour. It was semi-dry and was coloured black with tea bags. It was cooked in pure *ghee* and garnished with fried potato. This cost me only Rs. 50; not even one US dollar. After my meal, to wash it all down I went to a milkshake shop. The original one is in Connaught Place, but there was one close by in Kamla Nagar market, very popular among Delhi University students for milkshakes. These milkshakes are creamy and frothy and the favourites are butterscotch, pineapple and strawberry; and they are made with toned milk. I grabbed my butterscotch milkshake, a tiny 400 ml chilled bottle, and drank it all in one shot. That heroic deed was followed by the customary burps that are not considered rude in this part of the country! It only means you enjoyed your food.

I had planned a walk through Old Delhi for this evening but I forgot that it was Diwali, the biggest and the brightest festival in our country. Before I could go off on another food trail, I was going to buy some *phuljhari*s (sparkler firework), *anar* bombs, lamps, flowers and chocolates. Behind red fort there was an entire gully with all the items that needed to be bought for Diwali. After that I went to buy a box of *mithai*. At Chandni Chowk in Old Delhi I made my way towards Kanwarjeet's, a *namkeen* (savouries) and *mithai* shop, for the best *namkeen* in India. He is considered the Willy Wonka of the *namkeen* world. Like most of the establishments here, this store is over 100 years old. All *namkeen*s are made with pure *ghee* versus the trans-fat version, *Dalda*. They are extremely popular for *dal biji*, a mixture of *sev*, different melon seeds, cashew nuts and *moong dal* (skinned green gram). All these are fried and then tossed in Indian spices. I packed a kilogram of that and a box of the *pista barfi* (pistachio fudge) and *gulab jamun*s (ball of deep-fried cottage cheese, boiled in sugar syrup).

After all this walking, of course, I was hungry again. It was time to bring out the one and only, the famous, the filling, Delhi *ki chaat*. I went straight where everyone should go, Raju Chaat Bhandar, in Bharat Nagar. This guy got his fame from the nickname he got, '*gande naley wala*.' This nickname came about after he set up shops near a sewage pipeline! Nobody should get ideas from the nickname; it has nothing to do with the quality and hygiene maintained here. His widest selling dish is the *dahi bhalli papdi*. Being a big fan of this dish I had tried it at several shops all over the country, but nobody made it better than my guy, Raju. The yoghurt was thick, creamy and sweet. The roasted and powdered *jeera* was sprinkled generously on the top, with *garam masala* and *kala namak*, the aromas of which reached you much before the plate and the server. The *bhalla*s are as big as the palm of an average-sized hand. They are of ground *dal* that had been shaped into discs and fried. Then the *bhalla* was soaked in salt water to make it soft. Green chutney, tamarind chutney, *boondi* (savoury made of chickpea flour), and pomegranate kernels were sprinkled on the yoghurt. One plate of his *chaat* is quite expensive by the general standard; Rs. 100 is the price and every bite is worth it. I ate the other street favourites like the *pao bhaji* (spicy preparation of mixed vegetables had with a dollop of butter and warm bread, fried in butter), *gol gappa* (popular street snack consisting a round, hollow flatbread, fried crisp and filled with a mixture of flavoured water, tamarind chutney, chilli, boiled potatoes, onion and chickpeas), *kathi* kebab and *aloo tikki* (snack made of boiled potatoes, onions and various spices).

Later that evening, I went for a stroll to India Gate. If you are from Delhi you know for a fact that India Gate is the place to be in on an idle evening. The lawns in front were flooded with people lazing on the grass, eating ice cream, drinking whiskey on the sly from *chai* mugs, and buying little gimmicky toys and balloons from street vendors. I walked around the manicured lawns and bought myself *kala khatta*; the most popular form of *chuski*, a flavoured ice pop with lemon and salt.

Home is home, nothing can take away the feeling that you get when you are on home ground. I know how the air smells, I know where the roads lead, I know where to go. It feels good to be back, and tomorrow, I head home. WOW!

DAY 99
11 November / Delhi

Before anything else… Happy Diwali! My mother drew a parallel with the way Lord Ram returned to Ayodhya after his 14-year exile. I was only away for a 100 days, but I got a Lord's welcome anyway. Diwali is the festival of lights, gifts, crackers and lots of food. Gifts are circulated, *mithai* is eaten, and new clothes are tried on. My parents were shocked to see me; I looked like the backpackers that you see on the streets of hill stations, with my untidy beard, and my dark tan. We spent a long time just discussing my trip, sharing memories, and catching up on family gossip. My father, who generally is the wise one, was also astonished and pleased to learn about how hospitable the people of India had been to me. He told me that in his 53 years he had not been able to see even half the places I had been to. My grandmother was most excited to see me. I touched her feet and she blessed me; she was very relieved that I had come back in one piece. I won't blame her for being so worried; even I had the same concerns!

I had brought gifts from different corners of the country for all my family members. I had brought a *bandhni* sari for my mother from Gujarat, a T-shirt for my sister from Ladakh, *paan-daan* (a ornately carved box to keep betel leaves and other condiments) for my father, and a *shawl* for my grandmother from Kashmir. After I designed the *rangoli* (traditional Indian decoration and patterns made with ground rice, particularly during festivals), with my sister, which took us a good two hours, my mother came out to ask me what I wanted to eat; something I had been craving this whole trip and didn't have a chance to eat. At this point, I knew exactly what I wanted to eat, and now both you and I will get my mother's **Sindhi *Kadhi*** recipe.

It takes very long to make this dish; the process is tedious and you need a whole extra recipe for patience for this curry. Since my mother was by my side, the *kadhi* was going to have a strong taste of love and family. Sindhi *kadhi* is a soupy gram flour and tomato-based curry made with fried vegetables and tamarind water.

SINDHI *KADHI*
(Fried vegetables cooked in gram flour and tamarind curry.)

Ingredients

1½ tbsp refined oil
3 tbsp gram flour *(besan)*
1 tsp fenugreek *(methi)* seeds
1½ tsp turmeric *(haldi)* powder
3 lt water
2 potatoes
500 gm tomatoes
1 drum stick (optional)
1 long or 2 small pieces of lotus stem
1 big or 2 small cauliflower
200 gm colocasia *(arbi)*
200 gm okra *(bhindi)*
Salt to taste (4 tsp approximately)
3 lemon-sized balls of tamarind *(imli)*, soaked in 1 cup
  warm water for 2 hours

Oil for frying
1½ tsp mustard *(sarson)* seeds
20-25 curry leaves *(kari patta)*
1½ tsp cumin *(jeera)*
2 tsp red chilli powder
2 tbsp coriander leaves *(dhania patti)*, chopped

Method

1. Put refined oil in a deep vessel. Once hot, shallow fry gram flour until golden brown. Do this on a very low flame for about 15 minutes. Add the fenugreek seeds just as it starts to change colour.
2. Once it is golden brown, add turmeric powder and after a few seconds add all the water to it. With the water add cubed potatoes as they take longest to cook; let it all come to a boil. Then reduce the flame to medium.
3. Purée the tomatoes and add to the vessel. Let the *kadhi* simmer away on a low flame for an hour.
4. In the meanwhile, heat water in another small pot. Chop drum sticks into three-inch pieces and lotus stem into one-inch pieces. Parboil these and keep them aside.
5. Also heat the oil for frying after parboiling is done. Deep fry cauliflower florets, colocasia and okra till golden brown. While frying add some salt to the vegetables.
6. After the *kadhi* has simmered for an hour, add parboiled lotus stem and drum sticks to it.
7. After another 10 minutes add the fried cauliflower, colocasia and okra to it.

8. Now strain the thick tamarind water which was soaked two hours back. Add this to the *kadhi* and simmer for another 10 minutes.

9. For tempering, heat the oil in a tempering or small frying pan. To hot oil add mustard seeds, curry leaves, cumin seeds and red chilli powder and add this tempering to the *kadhi*. Garnish with coriander leaves and serve hot *kadhi* with peas *pulao* or steamed rice.

~

My mother always tells me that when you follow a recipe from a book, you must always leave room for instinct. Your tastes and habits should also influence the recipe you may be following, at least as far as the spices go.

The evening was about me being back home. We played a few rounds of cards and let off a few crackers. It still felt like I would have to wake up and leave for a new destination. It took about a week for me to realise that I was finally home, at least for now.

I spent Diwali with my family and friends, as everyone is supposed to.

DAY 100
12 November / Delhi

Today is officially the last day of my travels around India. Everything had fallen into place exactly as planned. I was thinking about the streets, the alleys, the farmlands, the rivers, and the mountains I crossed. I found myself drifting away every so often and replaying a memory. India is a big country when it comes to its people, its culture, its traditions and of course, its food. Even though 100 days was not enough to explore everything that India had to offer, I had only explored the tip of the iceberg and I had a long way to go on my journey, whenever I go back on one.

After travelling for 100 days by road and covering as many cities all over India, meeting different people and exploring local cuisines and recipes was not an easy job, but it definitely was a wonderful one. As I documented the diversity of Indian food and its regional cuisine, I had noticed that it changed every 200 km.

I still remember, on the ninth day of my programme, I had a huge fight with the crew complaining that they didn't have the right knife for me to chop the vegetables with: 'You are making me squeeze lemons with my hand,' I had said.

On the 11th day, I had to make spinach, which I had to chop as finely as I could using a blunt knife. After 15 days of shooting, my first episode went on air, and among the first messages I got from viewers was, 'It was so good to see you squeezing lemons with your hand.' It was enlightening! I never thought someone would want to see me use my hands for cooking on TV. I realised that at the end of the day we are all common people. We appreciate gestures that are human and basic. Food is not a luxury, it is still a necessity, but we just love it a little more now, is what my learning was.

There is so much the world doesn't know about India and its food, the whole idea of writing this book was a daunting thought, multiplying my dilemma by three-fold. One, I had to share my experiences and learning with viewers and readers. Two, I had to go back a step and use a book, in the actual physical form (instead of the online social platform) to document finer points of regional traditional Indian cooking. Three, I had to appeal to my viewers' and readers' patriotic side and urge them to choose Varanasi over Venice, or Gujarat over Geneva, the next time they plan their holidays!

As I drove through the valley and walked through the crowd,
I noticed that life in India is very loud.

I danced, I ate, I cried, I sang...
In my heart the temple bells rang.

I love my country, I love my life,
But my profession involves the use of a knife.

I cut, I chop, I bake, and I eat.
I used to be a vegetarian but I now love meat.

I want to tell you to get on the road,
Explore our country, in traveller mode.

Be proud, be happy, be inquisitive and nice,
You might want more rasam *with your* papad *and rice.*

Acknowledgements

Like all good authors, I too am supposed to acknowledge people who made this possible. But first, let me acknowledge you, my reader, for believing in me and picking this book up. If you love to travel and eat, we're friends forever.

Now to the following people…I am not only thankful but I owe you a five-course meal.

Chef Sanjeev Kapoor and the entire team of FoodFood Channel for believing in me and giving me a platform like *Roti Rasta aur India* that changed my life.

People who had to bear with me for 100 days on the road! Thanks to Small Screen Productions, especially Aakriti Arora, Anshul Kumar, Vishal Chib, Mohit Kundu and the brilliant driver, Narendra.

I was lost. Thank you Pallavi Mithika Menon and Megha Sundaresh for saving me, finding me the right words and making this book possible.

If you think the cover looks awesome or I look good in it, the credit goes to photographer Pallavi Gupta, and the director of Culinary Communications Pvt. Ltd, Kavneet Sahni, who had the vision.

Hugs to Ajay Mago and Dipa Chaudhuri for agreeing to publish this book, and the next one to come. (Though they don't know about the next one yet!)

When I received my first edit, it was soaked in red. It was like I was back in school. Let me bow down to my editor, Shoili Sarkar-Seth.

Thanks Rachel Tanzer for trusting and believing in me and getting this deal.

Index